POETIC ACTS & NEW MEDIA

POETIC ACTS & NEW MEDIA

Tom O'Connor

University Press of America,® Inc.
Lanham · Boulder · New York · Toronto · Plymouth, UK

Copyright © 2007 by
University Press of America,® Inc.
4501 Forbes Boulevard
Suite 200
Lanham, Maryland 20706
UPA Acquisitions Department (301) 459-3366

Estover Road
Plymouth PL6 7PY
United Kingdom

Library of Congress Control Number: 2006933349
ISBN-13: 978-0-7618-3630-8 (paperback : alk. paper)
ISBN-10: 0-7618-3630-6 (paperback : alk. paper)

To Thomas, Rae, and Carolyn O'Connor, who have supported me
unconditionally throughout my life

Contents

Contents

Preface

While reading Brian Greene's *The Elegant Universe,* I was struck by his observation concerning what often defines disciplines of thought and many peoples' world-views: *the tendency to perceive phenomena in absolute or ideal terms.* Greene's remark speaks volumes about literary theories and philosophies in the humanities as well. Many intellectual theories have traditionally separated different mediums and aesthetic styles into neatly-organized chronologies or modalities. Unfortunately, such categories may contain unchecked or pre-determined assumptions, such as the notion that different mediums are distinct to begin with.

Since histories of thought are often strictly separated in the humanities, it has become necessary to continually challenge such polarizing assumptions. According to the philosopher Nietzsche, there are no absolutes in any traditional field of study; hence, their apparent differences likely arise from their familiar or 'normal' separations. The impetus for this book arose from one such desire to re-think academic/aesthetic demarcations from a vantage point that allows different sensory mediums or modes of expression to interact.

In transposing the term *symmetry* from Greene's field of physics to new media studies, sensory/aesthetic mediums can be seen as *symmetrical* to each other (they're indirectly similar but not identical) because they operate by the same laws at their cores: as processes of simulation—not representation. All sensory/aesthetic mediums are space-times of possibility/Becoming, and they have *symmetries* (or *qualities*) that are intimately inter-related in a new, virtual-media environment, i.e., anything capable of expression can be reinterpreted in the linkable 'languages'/digital-convergences of alternative media forms. In the terminology of the philosopher Gilles Deleuze, the logic of simulation is a meta-poetic quasi-cause that is directly opposed to the logic of representation, which postures itself as the pre-determined meaning of a particular phenomenon. With simulation, there are no absolute properties of expressive mediums, contrary to what many politicians or cultural elites would want you to believe (i.e., no one should question their messages because they *appear* perfectly transparent or truthful, needing no further validation). Hence, the ability to create *critical discourses of illusions* is vital both in assessing artistic production as well as the navigation of everyday life.

Cultural illusions often create feelings of negativity or self-loathing because they can subordinate everything to unattainable norms/ideals. Whenever such illusions are coded as desirable/healthy, it heralds what Roberta Seid calls *the new religion*. In her article "Too 'Close to the Bone': the Historical Context for Women's Obsession with Slenderness," Seid critiques the social reasons why women are most susceptible to envisioning illusions (like pathological thinness) as gateways to *the ideal*. It is truly a sad state-of-affairs when people desire *the illusion* of health/beauty/wealth/status, etc. instead of the experience of happiness/accomplishment/self-awareness/fulfillment, etc. This *new religion*, which only lauds 'metaphysical' lies/deceptions, can even be seen as nihilistic since many of the contingencies that make up the here-and-now then become coded as worthless. Thus, nothing is more necessary than creating ever-evolving ways of perceiving and knowing that can combat such negativity in all aesthetic and critical modalities.

As physicists like Greene have often noted, nothing in the universe likes to be cornered and, according to *the uncertainty principle*, the more one tries to isolate/control a particular matter, the more it refuses to be isolated. The fact that I can refer to a theoretical physicist in the Preface to a book on the poetics of inter-relating media, and that the linking of separate disciplines does not do violence to either, exposes the reality that apparently discreet phenomena are, in fact, interrelated to their mutual benefit. New media studies can create such symmetries with digital or inter-media convergence. According to Ruskiewicz, Anderson, and Friend, in their Composition Reader *Beyond Words,* "the boundaries have largely disappeared between knowledge, art, news, and commerce;" however, this is not a serious critical problem because a single medium can also embody multi-media *possibilities* or *virtualities* (3). In the terminologies of new media critics, multi-modal descriptions of artistic productions have become commonplace. Take, for example, the following terms for mixed-media art that include but are not limited to: *free, indirect discourses; media links; hypertext art; intertextual art* or *interart;* as well as *media poetry*, which is the main focus of this book and which hopefully contributes to creating new possibilities for expression that can also transform mass culture.

I am indebted to many people. First, I'd like to thank McKenzie Wark (since the term *media poetry* first arose in one of our many and fruitful discussions), as well as Neil Christian Pages, John Matthias, Lennard Davis, and my father Thomas O'Connor for pointing me in the right direction a couple years ago. I'd also like to thank John Kinsella and David Trinidad for being supportive of this project, as well as the editors of the journals in which earlier versions of some chapters appeared, especially Stephen Tropiano of *The Journal of Film & Video*, Terry Threadgold of *Social Semiotics*, and Matteo Bittanti who edited the collection *Ready Made: The Film Remake in Postmodern Times*.

This book could not have been possible without the great counsel and support of Leslie Heywood and Michael Hames-García. In addition, I would like to thank Tom Rechtin and Margaux Fragoso for proofreading this manuscript as well as providing insightful editorial advice. In an earlier version of this project, Pamela Gay and Melissa Zinkin also offered useful advice and necessary encouragement. To all, I'm deeply grateful.

                                        T.O.
                                        Binghamton, N.Y.

Acknowledgements

A section of the Introduction was first published in *The Journal of Film & Video,* 1995.

Sections of Chapter 2 were first published in the edited collection *Ready Made: The Film Remake in Postmodern Times (Costa & Nolan)* 2006.

Chapter 3 was first published in *Social Semiotics,* 2004.

Excerpts from "Ancient History" and "Essay with Movable Parts" from PLASTICVILLE by David Trinidad. Copyright © 2000 by David Trinidad. Reprinted by permission of the author.

Excerpt from "Cliff Notes", from THE FIGURES, by Bob Perelman, copyright © 1986. Used by permission of the author.

Excerpt from "The Dream of Instant Total Representation", from PICK UP THE HOUSE by Anselm Hollo. Copyright © 1986 by Anselm Hollo. Reprinted with permission of Coffee House Press: Minneapolis, Minnesota.

Excerpts from "Hey Joe", from THE FALLING HOUR, by David Wojahn, copyright © 1997. Reprinted by permission of the University of Pittsburgh Press.

Excerpts from "Meet The Supremes" from HAND OVER HEART: Poems 1981-1988 by David Trinidad, Amethyst Press. Copyright © David Trinidad, 1991. Reprinted by permission of the author.

"Movies", from THE COLLECTED POEMS OF LANGSTON HUGHES by Langston Hughes, copyright © 1994 by The Estate of Langston Hughes. Used by permission of Alfred A. Knopf, a division of Random House, Inc.

Excerpts form "The Shower Scene in *Psycho*" from ANSWER SONG by David Trinidad, High Risk Books/Serpent's Tail. Copyright © 1994 by David Trinidad. Reprinted by permission of the author.

"Sympathetic" from SEARCH PARTY: Collected poems of William Matthews. Copyright © 2004 by Sebastian Matthews and Stanley Plumly. Reprinted by permission of Houghton Mifflin Company. All Rights Reserved.

"TV1", "TV2", and "TV-Epilogue" from TV by John Kinsella. Copyright © by Arc Publications, 2006. Used by permission of Arc Publications.

Introduction: Poetic Acts & New Media

> Appearance is for me the active and living itself, which goes so far in its self-mockery as to allow me to feel that there is nothing here but appearance and will-o'-the-wisp and a flickering dance of spirits—that among all these dreamers I, too, the 'man of knowledge', dance my dance, that the man of knowledge is a means of spinning out the earthly dance and to that extent one of the masters-of-ceremonies of existence, and that the sublime consistency and unity of all knowledge is and will be perhaps the supreme means of *preserving* the universality of dreaming and the mutual intelligibility of all these dreamers, and thereby *the continuance of the dream.*
> —Friedrich Nietzsche (*The Gay Science* 54)

****

> If we had not approved of the arts and invented this kind of cult of the untrue, the insight into universal untruth and mendaciousness now provided to us by science—the insight into illusion and error as a condition of knowing and feeling existence—could in no way be endured. *Honesty* would bring disgust and suicide in its train. But now our honesty has a countervailing power which helps us to avoid such consequences: art, as the *good* [will-to-appearance]. [. . .]. As an aesthetic phenomenon, existence is still *endurable* to us, and through art we are given eye and hand, and above all a good conscience, to *enable* us to make of ourselves such a phenomenon. (107)

David Lynch's *Mulholland Drive* (2001)—one of the many recent popular films to explore the phenomenal nature of reality-production in a mass-media culture—continually foregrounds how we the audience cannot verify a consistent representational-realism in the film. Although *Mulholland Drive* is too complex to give a full reading here (a fully-developed reading of the film occurs in chapter 2), Lynch's dream-esque narrative continually highlights, as in

Nietzsche's above quote, how appearances are always mediated, i.e., they can't be judged as purely 'real' or 'unreal' as any referential theory of representation assumes. As we shall see, to disown what's creatively 'unreal' in such appearances is a potentially deadly self-delusion. A key example of the dangers inherent in reading appearances as purely-'real' representations occurs when Rita (Laura Elena Harring) wakes up in the middle of the night and demands that she and Betty (Naomi Watts), the film's protagonist, go to an old Spanish theater, Club Silencio, whose emcee is revealingly a magician/Nietzschean-master-of-ceremonies (Richard Green). Throughout *Mulholland Dr.*, the 'real' and the 'unreal' are continually blurred to a point of indiscernability for both Betty and audiences alike. At Club Silencio, Betty is faced with the crushing realization that her relationship with Rita may only be a projected fantasy (i.e. a simulation). Moreover, we spectators must also confront *Mulholland Drive*'s undermining of the phenomenal 'ground' that our common-sense perceptions of contingent-reality supposedly 'rest upon'.

We watch as Club Silencio's magician gives a bizarre lecture/performance on the difference between the representation and simulation of reality-productions; Betty is shocked to see that appearances are called into being solely according to their simulation. The magician continually mentions serio-comic, poetic phrases about the background music in the scene like "no hay banda (there is no band) and yet, we hear a band," and, "if we want to hear a clarinet, listen . . ." Then we hear a clarinet as if the magician summoned it from nowhere. The simulated nature of the music, in the magician's act, offers Betty a significant poetic realization: she is, in effect, the primary simulator of *Mulholland Drive*'s dream-narrative; this realization is what forces Betty to 'wake up' and accept the fact that she is, in actuality, an out-of-work, struggling actress named Diane. To re-enforce the simulated-nature of this curious scene—when the magician 'magically' disappears in a puff of smoke—the singer Rebekah Del Rio steps on stage to lip-sync the song *Llorando* (Roy Orbison's *Crying* sung a capella in Spanish).

Del Rio's stunning performance of that torch song about lost love then ends according to the magician's prior message: the woman singer collapses but the tape recording continues, which implies that everything in the film to this point is not 'ideal' at all. Betty/Diane can only cry herself, watching the fact that the romantic melodrama she had authored with Rita, in the first half of *Mulholland Drive,* is exposed to be solely a simulation ("no hay banda"). Unfortunately for Betty/Diane, she cannot accept the constructed nature of her own story-poem. Throughout *Mulholland Drive*'s shifting levels of narrative, she tragically refuses to acknowledge how representation's supposed mimetic/transcendent capacities are artificial 'unities' or illusions a la the magician's mocking performance. Club Silencio, which also exposes the performative/simulated nature of identity, reveals how Betty/Diane is primarily an actor to herself. She, nonetheless, is willing to do *anything* at all—even destroy herself—in order to find an illusory, 'transcendent' gateway to an ideal form she desires to 'represent' (see below).

Because each of us, like Diane, exists in an environment saturated with simulation, poetic capacities for transforming/re-mediating those environments are becoming increasingly necessary. Since we understand ourselves *through how we portray ourselves* in different sensory mediums like language, gestures, signs, etc., we can also become acutely-conscious of the fact that there is no purely-'real', unmediated relation to experience in general. Poetic writing and perception can be life-saving skills in Western culture because a potentially deadly connection exists between mediated environments and one's body/identity—a la Betty/Diane's tragic fate. Pre-established ideals/norms (illusory representations), unfortunately, can become more powerful than one's own sense of critical/creative potential, which has the power to productively re-mediate any such 'representation'.

For Nietzsche, 'appearances' can never reference a world of metaphysical meanings; in other words, appearances are never capable of a *timelessly-true* representation: "the term 'appearance'—like 'phenomenon'—is intended to stress the partial, artificial, and fabricated aspects that belong to all relations with [what we term] reality" (Granier 194). The Nietzschean philosopher Eric Blondel fleshes out this concept:

> [woman and] man's relation to existence is fictional or poetic, inasmuch as it is a condensation, a kind of poetry about poetry. [. . .]. Thus, from the start, knowledge has no privileged position: on the contrary, "there is no intrinsic knowledge without metaphor." [. . .]. Nietzsche does not understand by this that everything is tantamount to the illusions of fantasy: rather, the real manipulation of appearances—lying appearances at that—has been preformed by science, morality, and religion—precisely what had formerly passed themselves off as "the truth." Only art, by virtue of its acknowledged metaphorical [or mediated] character, is true: "Art treats *appearance as appearance*, therefore it does *not* seek to deceive; it *is true*." The criterion of "truth" will thus be paradoxical: art is truthful because it enhances and increases metaphor—hence the illusion: precisely what, for science, morality, and religion, is blocked. What is false—indeed, morbid—is thus designated as the repetitive blockage of metaphor.   (171)

Whatever exposes the self-consciously-mediated nature of signification in the appearances of contingent life can also break open the illusions of 'representation' that threaten to homogenize/pre-determine any and all of our world-views.

In a similar vein, film critic Thomas Schatz—in his film-genre theory—describes all media art that seeks productive re-mediations of our ideologies/world-views as "social problem-solving operations [. . .]" (24). It should go without saying that how mass-media phenomena effect each of us is not just a subject for intellectuals in Academia, since all mass-media—i.e.

dominant forms like TV, film, the Internet, popular music, mass-print journalism, etc., as well as less-dominant ones like printed poetry—help to construct not only our identities but our desires as well (see below). Poetic perceptions that generate alternatives for personal/cultural significations are vital tools for halting the homogenization, sterility, and inertia that often plague many cultural constructions (not solely linguistic ones). *Mulholland Drive,* like the other media art I explore below, can be seen as a paradigmatic example of how poetic perception *can become a problem-solving force* that overcomes any static/codified 'representational-realism' (in any sensory medium).

Mulholland Drive is one of the most recent films to take up this questioning of what constitutes the phenomenal nature of reality-production in a mass-media culture. In the history of popular/Hollywood film, many past filmmakers—especially Alfred Hitchcock, Billy Wilder, and Orson Welles—have explored and undermined the illusions inherent in any regime of representational-realism (see chapter 2). Although *Mulholland Drive* is not alone when it comes to the artistic/poetic blurring of the supposedly 'real' and 'unreal', it is symptomatic of a new emphasis on how simulation creates all such reality-productions in a new-media environment. 'Realism', for artists like Lynch, is never grounded by a literal, common-sense view of either linguistic or perceptual reference. Rather, life itself generates multiple possibilities for experiencing virtual or previously-unknown alternatives that do not have to be empirically 'real' in order to have actual effects; hence, 'reality' can be understood as *the effect* of appearances/meanings that are *always* called into being according to their simulation, *not* their representation. For artists like Lynch and Welles, reality-production can contain both the manifest and un-manifest, the actual and virtual; without understanding things in the context of their potentiality or virtuality, one can miss the fact that life itself always exceeds all pre-determinations/totalizations. In other words: 'reality' must be creatively engaged to work most effectively.

In line with this Nietzschean realization, the philosopher Gilles Deleuze explains a theory of poetic or "minor" language-use that he first developed with Félix Guattari in *Kafka: Toward a Minor Literature*:

> as Proust says, ["minor" literature] opens a kind of foreign language within language, which is neither another language nor a rediscovered patois, but a becoming-other of language, a minorization of this major language, a delirium that carries it off, a witch's line that escapes the dominant system. Kafka makes the swimming champion say: I speak the same language as you, yet I don't understand a single word you're saying. Syntactic creation or style—this is the becoming of language. The creation of words or neologisms is worth nothing apart from the effects of syntax in which they are developed.   (*Essays Critical & Clinical* 5)

For Deleuze and Guattari, minor uses of language are self-consciously-authored experiments of life; they create simulated "intensities where contents free themselves from their forms as well as from their expressions, from the signifier that formalized them. There is no longer anything but movements, vibrations, thresholds in a deserted matter" (*Kafka: Toward a Minor Literature* 13). Such creative/poetic uses of language are inextricably linked to the multi-media potentials of sensation, i.e. *Sense-events, which are incorporeal & virtual powers of sensory transformation*: "the writer's specific materials are words and syntax, the created syntax that ascends irresistibly into his work and passes into sensation" (*What is Philosophy?* 167).

Daniel W. Smith further expounds on how minor language-use anticipates how language (syntactic creation and style) is re-coded as primarily Sense-event in virtual-media environments:

> [a] major treatment of language [is one] in which the linguistic system appears in principle as a system of equilibrium defined by its syntactical, semantic, or phonological constants; the second is the minor treatment, in which the system itself appears in a perpetual disequilibrium or bifurcation, defined by pragmatic use of these constants in relation to a continuous internal variation.   (xlix)

Any minor or poetic use of language—where language becomes a multi-modal, virtual sense—is inseparable from its context, which further implies that linguistic significations (as forces of sensation) can never be completely abstracted from the empirical/corporeal forces of contingent life.

Deleuze and Guattari, in the following, lay out the actual-world concerns at stake in simulated/minor poetic acts:

> how many people today live in a language that is not their own? Or no longer, or not yet, even know their own and know poorly the major language that they are forced to serve? This is the problem of immigrants, and especially of their children, the problem of minorities, the problem of a minor literature, but also a problem for all of us: how to tear a minor literature away from its own language, allowing it to challenge the language and making it follow a sober revolutionary path? How to become a nomad and an immigrant and a gypsy in relation to one's own language? (*Kafka: Toward a Minor Literature* 19)

Such virtual/minor potentials for generating sensible aggregates in language and reality-productions in general do not need to conform to any traditional, common-sense 'realism'; they are the necessary conditions for simulating/re-mediating new relations not only within language, but between all the actual and virtual forces possible. Deleuze has defined *the virtual* as both "the prior conditions of all actualisation [and] determination" as well as "the pure locus of the possible" (*Cinema 1* 109). For Deleuze, the virtual is a mediated space-time of event-possibilities: "mediators are fundamental. Creation's all about mediators. Without them nothing happens. [. . .]. Whether they're real or imaginary, animate or inanimate, you have to form your mediators" (*Negotiations* 125). Thus change/transformation only happens *through* mediation. Deleuze further explains this notion through criticizing Lacanian/psychoanalytic distinctions between the Real, the Symbolic, and the Imaginary: "the question of whether events are real or imaginary is poorly posed. The distinction is not between the imaginary and the real, but between the event as such and the corporeal state of affairs which incites it [. . .] or in which it is actualized" (*The Logic of Sense* 210). Furthermore, poetic acts that make good use of such event-possibilities in language-use (as well as in all other mediums of sensory expression) can productively 'falsify'/re-mediate any previous corporeally-created connection, which then generates the possibilities for multiple Becomings/transformations in the future. This perplexing and dramatic opening-up in what constitutes 'realism' demands further critical/creative exploration.

'Realism', at any particular moment, may be dependent on what different media render possible. Recent media debates have, in fact, isolated historical eras by the different media that became dominant in each: in Western culture, we have supposedly moved on from eras of orality and literacy to a 'secondary orality', which is comprised predominantly of virtual/electronic communication. These new media have created traditionally 'unreal' ways of interacting with and transforming the empirical world[1]. However, in light of new/digital media that can encode audio, visual, and textual phenomena in non-hierarchical ways, previous literary theories that always privilege verbal structure or code over audio and visual information need to be radically re-thought. In essence, any hierarchy that privileges one medium of sensory expression over others no longer holds sway in virtual-media environments.

All linguistic and artistic constructions are media/technological phenomena; printed poetry is no different. When one re-interprets printed language as primarily a virtual-media phenomenon, and not a purely textual one, a new, inter-disciplinary paradigm is needed beyond any "major" theory based primarily on linguistic structure/reference. Marshall McLuhan observed in the 1960s that "our cultural historians have been oblivious of the homogenizing power of typography" (*Understanding Media* 322). The homogenizing concept of language as static or fixed codes/forms has erected the monstrous illusion that language can generate a transparent, common-sense reference to a 'representable reality'. Any theory based solely on linguistic structure/reference is overly-limited in a new-media environment because it erects a "major" theory that envisions linguistic indeterminacy as purely structural, which reduces possibilities for meaning rather than envisioning it as always occurring in multiplicitous, "minor" ways. Such theories are deceptive because even though they can appear logical, they often harbor a violent desire to force the world into conformity with pre-determined norms and ideals.

Such 'representations' can even function to break up the empirical, contingent world into 'controllable', abstract terms: "the breaking up of every kind of experience into uniform units in order to produce faster action and change of form (applied knowledge) has been the secret of Western power over man and nature alike" (McLuhan 85). Representation, in philosophy, can be defined as "the notion that there exists, in a large sense, a "mimetic" link between first entities (or clear ideas) and their instantiations ([or] objects) [. . .]" (Rajchman 34-5). This Platonic conception of representation is dangerous in that it "subsumes (re-presents) [any] particularity under a transcendental idea or category [. . .]" (Flaxman 12). The possibility of a timelessly-ideal representation problematically implies that one could discover *the* a-temporal/metaphysical perspective on something or someone, which would then be its transcendental, essential *meaning* or *truth*. Luckily, the powerful illusion of a 'metaphysical' uniformity/homogeneity is productively re-written or re-mediated whenever we read phenomena in "minor"/poetic manners.

Sense-events: A Re-birth of the Poetic

What finds its reflection in language, language cannot represent.
—Ludwig Wittgenstein (*Tractatus Logico-Philosophicus*, 4.121)

Thoughts are the shadows of our sensations—always darker, emptier, simpler than these. —Nietzsche (*The Gay Science* 159)

Since the era of print or textuality is currently no longer the sole, dominant mode of information and communication, many theorists like Friedrich Kittler have sounded the "death bell" for printed-text poetry as a vital, social art form (*Gramophone, Film, Typewriter* 80). Surprisingly, if one peruses AWP's *Poets & Writers,* no one in poetry circles seems concerned about popular/virtual media at all. The fact that such literary magazines often assume poetry is a separate and isolated artistic medium is a serious critical problem. In the current world of American poetry, many poets and poetry critics are either defensively silent or completely disparaging about the cultural effects of new media. Marjorie Perloff explains:

the most cursory survey of contemporary poetics would show that, at least as far as what Charles Bernstein calls 'official verse culture' is concerned, technology, whether computer technology or the video, audio, and print media, remains, quite simply, the enemy, the locus of commodification and reification against which a 'genuine' poetic discourse must react. In part, as I shall suggest [. . .], the most interesting poetic and artistic compositions of our time do position themselves, consciously or unconsciously, against the languages of TV and advertising, but the dialectic between the two is highly mediated. It is by no means a case, as poets sometime complain, of 'competing' with television, of pitting the 'authentic' individual self against an impersonal, exploitative other that commodifies the consciousness of the duped masses.   (19)

Perloff's claim that there exists a dialectic between poetry and other media problematically implies that they are radically distinct; nevertheless, what is important to note here is that contemporary poetry often attempts to exist within a self-contained fold in mass-media culture. Such a position is both illusory and destructive to poetic production as a social process because it may then exile itself from the whole field of communication where culture is continually re-created.

However, there are many poets who overcome such isolationist attitudes and seek to create with the multi-media possibilities of language-use a relation to dominant media that isn't cynical (see below); in fact, how poetic signification relates to other media is a topic that has been explored by such diverse thinkers as Friedrich Kittler, Pier Paolo Pasolini, Gerald Bruns, Marshall McLuhan, Donald Theall, Gabriela Mistral, Laurence Goldstein, Marjorie Perloff, Robert Richardson, P. Adams Sitney, George Landow, Charles Bernstein, Roland Barthes, Gilles Deleuze, Julia Kristeva, and McKenzie Wark among many others; several literary magazines have even devoted recent issues to such debates[2]. In what follows, I will argue, contra Perloff, that acknowledging the productive potentials of mass media—especially virtual media—is beneficial to poetic productions at large.

In his introduction to *The Best American Poetry: 2001*, Robert Hass sums up the dominant trends in recent, printed poetry as if other media do not exist at all:

there are roughly three traditions in American poetry at this point: a metrical tradition that can be very nervy and that is basically classical in impulse; a strong central tradition of free verse made out of both romanticism and modernism, split between the impulses of an inward and psychological writing and an outward and realist one, at its best fusing the two; and an experimental tradition that is usually more passionate about form than content, perception than emotion, restless with the conventions of art, skeptical about the political underpinning of current practice, and intent on inventing a new one, or at least undermining what seems repressive in the current formed style.   (21)

Hass's remarks are very typical in their formal romanticism, i.e., they understand poetry as solely printed-code/text. It is not my contention that Hass is wrong about how most contemporary poets envision their craft, only that there are alternative ways to conceptualize what poetry is and does in a new-media environment. There exist other possible/emergent experimental-traditions in contemporary poetry beyond the formal ones that concentrate solely on the textual artifact. Poetic signification need not be confined to a codified, verbal-text 'representation' since we no longer live in solely a linguistic/textual universe. Poetic events can be both written as well as read as "minor," productive acts that simulate vectors of multi-sensory transmissions; in these simulated events, "it is no longer sensation that is realized in the material [or medium in question] *but the material that passes into sensation*" (Deleuze & Guattari, *What is Philosophy?* 193).

An inter-media art of pure Sense (i.e. virtual sensation) can generate a multi-media, poetic literacy that operates within the surfaces/appearances of all cultural (or mass-media) information. In other words: a significant, material relation can be constructed between the poetic imagination and the ontological potentials of virtual media; virtual signs (including linguistic ones) always exceed any pre-determining concept of enunciator/reference/structure/ equivalence/poetry-in-itself. Although different mediums do not possess a homogenous or essential similarity, they can be linked together through inter-media/artistic events, i.e., they're never completely separate from each other.

A poetry of virtual sensation, moreover, overcomes any abstract or intellectual separation; it "is a zone of indetermination, of indiscernibility, as if things, beasts, and persons (Ahab and Moby Dick, Penthesilea and the Bitch) endlessly reach that point that immediately precedes their natural differentiation" (*What is Philosophy?* 173). It is a new form of sensation (a multi-modal/virtual Sense-event) that exceeds empiricist definitions of sensory phenomena in a purely-actual, naturalized world; furthermore, it can replace the traditional/representational notions of timeless/ideal forms, meanings, or essences. The Sense-event is an immaterial/virtual simulacrum that can paradoxically re-write/mediate the corporeal world of Being/history, and that can become a transformative "quasi-cause" (i.e. "an unreal and ghostly causality") that operates within the Nietzschean domain of surface-effects/appearances (Deleuze, *The Logic of Sense* 33). For Nietzsche and Deleuze, "everything happens at [this incorporeal] border," which is, in effect, "like a fogged-up windowpane on which one can write with one's finger (9, 133).

Hence, artistic creativity (i.e. the re-assembly/re-mediation of appearances) is a virtual-ontological necessity that can create new personal or cultural significations in the here-and-now. Deleuze, therefore, defines the "extra-Being" of the Sense-event as paradoxically both "the thin [virtual] film at the limit of words and things" as well as "the effect of corporeal causes and their mixtures" (31, 94). Thus, the Sense-event is a Becoming that operates according to new lines-of-flight or future possibilities; it's never reducible to an actual event in a historical space-time. Every Sense-event unfolds in a virtual process of Becoming-other, i.e., it is a poetic simulation that has no grounding other than its own transformation. In addition, to read poetic production as existing not solely in printed or spoken language but within a multi-modal/media studies implies that poetic meaning, too, has a virtual *say* in our current era of "secondary orality."

Kittler's previous claim that printed poetry is becoming obsolete in the face of popular/virtual media demands that we re-theorize both language and poetry's relations to new media. Perloff, in *Radical Artifice: Writing Poetry in an Age of Media*, the one book of poetry criticism so far that directly confronts this dynamic issue, claims that the greatest influence on recent American poetry is the popular/electronic media. However, she further remarks: "we have not yet understood the interplay between lyric poetry, generally regarded as the most conservative, the most intransient of the 'high' arts, and the electronic media" (xii). The obstacle, for Perloff, appears to be that the two may be irreconcilable. It's unclear, however, as to exactly who constitutes Perloff's "we" because neither lyric poetry nor electronic media are completely separable from popular communication.

The current, institutionalized poetry scene as it exists in Academia, which too often sees strict divisions between different media, can fall into the same oppositional stance that always envisions language-arts as privileged. Gerald Bruns, aware of this critical problem, provides an alternative conception that challenges reductive assumptions about how poetry and electronic media are distinct phenomena: "poetry is internal to the discourse of everyday life; it is not the product of a logic of exclusion but is conceptually, and therefore aesthetically, nondifferentiated" (133). A potentially-destructive bias may be lurking in Perloff's above-claim that may render poetic productions mostly irrelevant to multi-media culture. Since Perloff's *Radical Artifice* does not offer any clear theoretical guidelines whereby the relations between printed poetry and electronic/virtual media can be mapped out, I propose to do exactly that in this book.

N. Katherine Hayles, in her article "The Condition of Virtuality," states that when a particular medium dominates a cultural moment, media environments can generate different assumptions or even biases. She describes the 'Oral subject' as "fluid, changing, situational, dispersed, conflicting;" the 'Written Subject', alternatively, is "fixed, coherent, stable, self-identical, normalized, decontextualized" (93). In our current, virtual media culture, the 'Written Subject' has been superceded by the multi-media orality of the 'Virtual Subject', which Hayles describes as "formed through dynamical interfaces with computers" (93). Virtual subjects, then, always create meaning within the context of a globally-networked system of immanent Sense-events; all subjects can transform not only themselves but the virtual network itself as well as its inter-connections. According to Hayles in *How We Became Posthuman*, electronic communication and information have also rendered commonsense understandings of linguistic reference virtually unstable and re-writable:

> the computer restores and heightens the sense of word as image—an image drawn in a medium as fluid and changeable as water. Interacting with

electronic images rather than a materially resistant text, I absorb through my
fingers a model of signification in which no simple one-to-one correspondence
exists between signifier and signified.   (26)

There exist an un-determined plethora of "minor" possibilities that language-use
(as a Nietzschean mnemotechnology of Sense-events) can generate for virtual
subjects.

Virtual subjects, furthermore, can be described as occupying the ontological
space-time that Hayles and Nicholas Gessler term "the slipstream of mixed
reality" (483). In fact, they explore *Mulholland Drive*—in "The Slipstream of
Mixed Reality: Unstable Ontologies and Semiotic Markers in *The Thirteenth
Floor, Dark City*, and *Mulholland Drive*"—as a paradigmatic example of a
mixed, inherently-*poetic* reality. Hayles and Gessler further explain: "when
reality is mixed, ontological and epistemological issues tend to be foregrounded,
because the represented worlds often cannot be assigned unambiguously to
science fiction or ordinary reality" (483). Hayles and Gessler mention other
films such as Christopher Nolan's *Memento* and Tom Tykwer's *Run Lola Run*,
as well as novels such as *Gravity's Rainbow* by Thomas Pynchon and Mark Z.
Danielewski's *House of Leaves*, which all foreground a fresh birth of the *poetic*,
i.e. the inter-mixing of the virtual with 'ordinary reality'. In addition, many of
Lynch's films, especially *Eraserhead, Blue Velvet, Lost Highway*, and *Twin
Peaks: Fire Walk with Me*, occupy this "mixed diegetic-reality" (see chapter 2).

However, as Hayles and Gessler state, this 'sci-fi' world-view no longer
needs to rely directly on futuristic technology:

> thinking of the mind as a virtual-reality machine (as Richard Dawkins, among
> others, has argued it is) implies that the notion of mixed reality has so
> permeated our contemporary context that it no longer needs to be linked with
> an actual technology to shake the ontological and epistemological ground on
> which consensus reality is built .   (497)

Any crisis in the verification of what is empirically 'real',—a la Betty/Diane's
disquieting moments at Club Silencio—becomes a potentially productive crisis
whenever one doesn't disown what's creatively constructed/'unreal'; such a
realization can then become a vital rite-of-passage into the poetic/virtual
possibilities inherent in Sense-events.

To re-iterate: any transparent representation that predetermines what is
'real' can act as a censor upon such virtual significations. According to Gregory
Flaxman, any common-sense regime of "realism is essentially based on a
distinction between the subject and the world" (31). In this sense, Deleuze
mockingly defines realism in cinematic theory as the narrow domain of the
already "represented or reproduced" (*Cinema II* 1). If representation sets up a
priori ideal-forms where all the forces and elements that constitute the 'real'
world are judged according to their fidelity to those pre-existing forms, then all

things that do not reflect them are in danger of being dismissed, banned, mocked, violently controlled, or eradicated. Such a 'transcendent' or 'common-sense' fixing of reference only levels our creative capacities for Sense-events.

Luckily, there is a way out of the totalizing, homogenous ideologies inherent in representation. Simulation, which generates virtual Sense-events, replaces the notion of the representation of a priori ideal-forms (or static, common-sense relations) with signs that are singular conglomerates of forces possessing no fixed referents. As Jean Baudrillard explains,

> representation starts from the principle that the sign and the real are equivalent (even if this equivalence is Utopian, it is a fundamental axiom). Conversely, simulation starts from the Utopia of this principle of equivalence, *from the radical negation of the sign as value,* from the sign as reversion and death sentence of every reference. Whereas representation tries to absorb simulation by interpreting it as false representation, simulation envelops the whole edifice of representation as itself a simulacrum. (*Simulacra and Simulations* 170)

Baudrillard conceives of simulation as a constructive "operation [that] is nuclear and genetic, and no longer specular and discursive" (167). Simulation, therefore, recreates *all* the conditions within which Sense-events unfold. The appearances that are re-created/simulated in a particular context are only directly valid within that particular event or staging. Therefore, any theory of linguistic 'equivalence' is a poor description of simulation's potentials for generating meaning and communication.

Baudrillard's notion of simulation, unfortunately, leaves signs dangerously cut-off from the actual forces/events that constitute the empirical world. If we understand simulation more in line with Deleuze's notion of singular/"minor" Sense-events, it can become a much more *beneficial* force in the here-and-now (see below). Mark Poster, even though he is describing virtual-reality systems, offers a practical way of conceptualizing how virtual simulation and media relate to the actual forces of the empirical world: they "continue the Western trend of duplicating the real by means of technology. They provide the participant with a second-order reality in which to play with or practice upon the first order" (117). The notion of duplication here is unfortunate because it conjures up the problematic history of mimetic representations. Rather, a more useful analogy for simulation is *Virtual-becoming* because it eradicates all concepts of signs as models or copies of 'idealized'/ 'naturalized' forms. Constructed signs are never generalizable as a transparent system of representational-realism.

According to McLuhan, new media only amplify the practical, everyday attributes of minor-language/media-use that naturally extend beyond any totalizing logic of 'representation': "language does for intelligence what the wheel does for the feet and the body. It enables them to move from thing to thing with greater ease and speed and ever less involvement" (79). Therefore, what must be stressed here is that anything expressed in language is never completely reliable as representational-reference because there exists no transparent connection or absolute, common-sense relation between its virtual instantiation in language and the actual object it describes (if one exists in the first place). In this sense, language is always highly provisional and dependent on its creation of experience-possibilities or Sense-events. As Derrida's philosophy explains this phenomenon, *the letter never arrives*. Perhaps Kittler's 'death bell' only tolls for the idea of poetry as a spatialized set of static, structural, or purely-abstract/equivalent forms, i.e. as safe havens of a permanent textuality. According to Hayles, language's relations to multi-media environments are better described by Derrida's theoretical program of deconstruction:

> in the transition from the written subject to the virtual subject, deconstruction played a significant theoretical role, for in reinterpreting writing (emphasizing its instabilities, lack of originary foundations, intertextualities and indeterminacies), [. . .] it made the written subject much closer to the virtual subject [. . .]. (*The Condition of Virtuality* 92)

Nonetheless, it must be noted that deconstruction, i.e. a "hermeneutics of suspicion," is radically incomplete if it doesn't re-enter the processes of writing or reality-production back into virtual-actual Becomings (Žižek, *Organs Without Bodies* 47). Deleuze and Guattari explain: "those who criticize without creating, those who are content to defend the vanished concept without being able to give it the forces it needs to return to life, are the plague of philosophy" (*What is Philosophy?* 28).

Deconstruction, therefore, borders on the potentially-nihilistic notion of absolute equivalence (i.e. everything that signifies must be distrusted because it is reducible to a specular or discursive abstraction/contradiction). Nietzsche explains the potential consequences of such ontological distrust: "an unspeakable amount of painfulness, arrogance, harshness, estrangement, [and] frigidity has entered into human feelings because we think we see opposites instead of transitions" (*A Nietzsche Reader* 86). Moreover, an ontologically-based theory of virtual or poetic signification, which bypasses any nihilistic intellectualism for *purely-temporal* contingencies/events, also touches upon Post-Colonial theories that stress the importance of oral traditions in generating singular capacities for Sense-events/Becomings.

Such minor/secondary oralities are not only aesthetic forces but socio-political ones that can introduce alternative perspectives into 'pre-established representations'. Dennis Kwek explains how postcolonial theory's enemy is also a totalizable regime of representation: "representationalism, or the ideology of representation, is the belief that theories are attempts to accurately describe and represent reality as it is in itself" (125). The danger in any such representational theory is that it is reductive and simplifying: "representation is an effort to essentialize, to reproduce objects of the world in a limited and miniaturized form so that they can be more easily engaged" (126). However, what renders such efforts to be deceptively dangerous is their "justification to use language as an object of desire and an instrument of colonial or national domination" (Walter D. Mignolo, *Local Histories/Global Designs* 255). In order to overcome 'representation', "historicist antiuniversalist multiculturalism" must possess dynamic powers of Virtual-becoming that can challenge any reductive/ normalizing world-view (Žižek, *Organs Without Bodies* 14). The current popularity of oral phenomena like rap and hip hop (what the group *Naughty by Nature* calls "poor man's poetry") speaks to how the written/oral hierarchy (which postcolonial theories often problematize) is, in fact, being toppled in our new-media era. Both oral and written *poetic acts* can create singular expressions that re-write any 'official rhetoric of domination'.

Lennard Davis further explains how recent intellectual fads have been mostly ineffectual in introducing actual difference into cultural life/discourses: "the by now outmoded postmodern subject is a ruse to disguise the hegemony of normalcy" and its 'representations' (30). In lieu of that awareness, *difference itself* (i.e. the infinite potentials of experience-possibilities/Sense-events) can be constructed as a virtual multiplicity that functions at both personal and collective levels (see below). Singular differences are vital not just for the identity politics of historically-oppressed groups like African Americans, Latinos, Native Americans, Gay people, the poor, etc., but for other under-represented groups like Intersexuals, People with Disabilities, etc. All politically-active groups/individuals must rely "on the electronic senses as well as the neoclassical five" to productively transform/re-write Western culture's often ineffectual world-views and politics (Davis 31). Therefore, the identities of *all* individuals must be conceived as incorporating not only the limitations/determinisms/inter-dependencies inherent in a historical space-time that each of us must inhabit, but the poetic multiplicities or virtualities that can re-mediate any socio-political failure.

Mckenzie Wark and Alan Sondheim's theory of codework is helpful as well in understanding how poetic acts of articulation can resist any representational reduction or simplification through their virtual-codings or experience-possibilities in new-media practice:

> codework draws attention to writing as media, where the art of writing is a matter of constructing an aesthetic, an ethics, even a politics, that approaches all of the elements together. Codework makes of writing a media art that breaks with the fetishism of the text and the abstraction of language. It brings writing into contact with the other branches of media art, such as music and cinema, all of which are converging in the emerging space of multimedia, and which often have a richer conception of the politics of media art as a collaborative practice than has been the case with writing conceived within the prison house of 'text'.
> (Wark, *American Book Review* 6)

It is important to emphasize how such codework re-situates any "major" theoretical or philosophical conception of language as static/fixed codes (or common-sense relations) onto infinitely-variable continuums of Sense-events. In an electronic-media environment, such codes are solely re-writable vectors for re-mediation/transformation. In codework, language-acts are singular manifestations of Virtual-becomings that always exist within the larger context of all mass media.

All language-events, when they're coded within the context of Virtual-becomings, become singular as well as metonymic phenomena. According to Walter Ong, language-use/Sense-events can best be thought of in the actual-world context of an "open-system paradigm;" all such globally-networked information-flows portray

> the individual in the way in which it must live, that is, in context, inextricably related to the other, the outside, the 'environment'. The environment acts on the living individual so that the individual responds and thereby changes the environment, which acts differently upon the individual so that the individual must then respond to it differently, too. The different responses thereby further change the environment, which thus evokes a new response—and so on. (325)

To envision the processes of simulation within a globally-networked, un-determined context is a productive/constructive notion that can break open thoughts, feelings, concepts, etc.; however, it comes with responsibility. If we all simulate (like Betty/Diane in *Mulholland Drive*) the signs/narratives that both affirm our Becomings as well as our relations to others, we must then accept the awesome responsibility *that we are the creative agents of our own perceptual processes*; however, as Deleuze explicates, this responsibility should not be tied to a burden:

> *to affirm is not to take responsibility for, [or] to take on the burden of what is, but to release, to set free what lives.* To affirm is to unburden: not to load life with the weight of higher values, but *to create* new values which are those of life, which make life light and active. There is creation, properly speaking, only insofar as we make use of excess in order to invent new forms of life rather than separating life from what it can do. (*Nietzsche & Philosophy* 185)

If we do not accept this pragmatic responsibility, i.e. how we use media—in actuality—creates the world we inhabit, then our only option is the pre-determined 'representations' that have been scripted for us by 'official rhetorics of domination'.

Poetic-expressionism: A Resistance to Hegemony

What is the seal of freedom attained?—No longer to be
ashamed of oneself. —Nietzsche (*The Gay Science* 275)

In order to fully grasp the ontological implications of virtual media as space-times of personal/communal Becoming, Deleuze's philosophy is useful; for Deleuze, ontology itself is continually re-created from a virtual plane of Sense-possibilities that subtend the historical/corporeal world of Being. This constant re-generation of what can constitute ontological experience allows ever-new transformations of Becoming and Being that are not reducible to a single historical-progression or a circumscribed unity/whole. Being, in effect, becomes the medium through which Virtual-becoming can create new forms of life (i.e. actual-virtual Sense-events). According to Deleuze, Becoming confounds all static systems of knowledge *because* it brings about *the new*:

> to become is not to attain a form (identification, imitation, Mimesis) but to find the zone of proximity, indiscernibility, or indifferentiation where one can no longer be distinguished from *a* woman, *an* animal, or *a* molecule—neither imprecise nor general, but unforeseen and nonpreexistent, singularized out of a population rather than determined in a form. (*Essays Critical and Clinical* 1)

According to Deleuze's philosophy, reality-in-itself is never closed or complete. Hence, the inability of human beings to solve/control the world of Being does not mean that we should mourn the impossibility of an absolute human knowledge, since such open-ended possibilities are the very contingencies of reality itself, i.e., they're the very conditions of human freedom—in a self-limited sense—because they all possess an infinite possibility/virtuality. In lieu of this realization, individuals only become free to invent new forms of life when they self-create that freedom as an actual-virtual *Sense-event*. This notion also sheds light on why Betty/Diane's plight is tragedy incarnate in *Mulholland Drive*; she places an absolute/ideal condition on her desires, which eradicates all productive possibilities for her own Becoming.

Since Deleuze's philosophy is primarily preoccupied with Virtual-becoming, it can be seen as arguing for a radical version of what Betty/Diane rejects about contingent life, i.e. the Nietzschean-Deleuzian notion of Becoming-art. According to Deleuze, Becoming-art doesn't separate artistic creativity/imagination from external fate/Being; in Deleuzian thought, one can paradoxically re-affirm 'fate' itself as one's own artistic will. Becoming-art implies that *everyone* can re-write/transpose the actual in order to re-mediate/overcome whatever threatens to block or limit it (Nietzsche & Deleuze call this imaginative power *amor fati*). Therefore, artistic re-mediation (and not a purely-historicist, corporeal-reality of Being or a common-sense, representational realism) ultimately decides what things can Become, since Becoming-art is a continuously-variable "repetition" or "staging" that can *transform* (either directly or indirectly) an always-unmoored/immanent world.

Deleuze and Guattari explain how virtual potentialities are inherent in any re-mediated surface-effect/appearance: "whether through words, colours, sounds, or stone, art is the language of sensations" (*What is Philosophy?* 176). Their terms for all such sensory aggregates are "percepts" (new ways of seeing & hearing) and "affects" (new ways of feeling & becoming), which must be differentiated from pure abstractions or an idealized representational-realism that grounds signification on a 'naturalized' common-sense:

> by means of the material, the aim of art is to wrest the percept from perceptions of objects and the states of a perceiving subject, to wrest the affect from affections as the transition from one state to another: to extract a bloc of sensations, a pure being of sensations.   (167)

Such Becomings, which can generate virtual powers of sensory transformation, are never completely reducible to the specific materiality/medium in question.

Deleuze and Guattari further address how re-writing/mediating the empirical world of Being is a creative *necessity*:

> *affects are precisely these nonhuman becomings of man*, just as percepts [. . .] are *nonhuman landscapes of nature*. Not a "minute of the world passes," says Cézanne, that we will preserve if we do not "become that minute." We are not in the world, we become with the world; we become by contemplating it. Everything is vision, becoming. We become universes. Becoming animal, plant, molecular, becoming zero.   (169)

Language acts—as well as signs in general—are never transparently-reducible to some 'essential' identity because they always exceed the personal; for Deleuze, echoing Nietzsche, a person only becomes when s/he dares to "make fiction, to "make up legends," and to "become another" (*Cinema II* 150). For Deleuze and Guattari, the multiple is never given or granted a priori but instead "*must be made*" (*A Thousand Plateaus* 6). Affects and percepts are always Sense-events that occur within the pre-individual processes of an un-determined multiplicity, i.e., they *are the potentials* for bifurcations and infinite variations in contingent states-of-affairs (either actual or virtual). Whenever "one undoes the individual and the person," one *becomes* the genesis of such incorporeal, "nomadic singularities," i.e. Sense-events (*The Logic of Sense* 141). However, to be productive, poetic acts (i.e. the Virtual-becoming inherent in Sense-events) must avoid two pitfalls: they must not create "incoherent dust" or "generalities which retain mere resemblances" (Deleuze, *Cinema II* 123).

A still-relevant example of a poetic act that is truly productive in a multi-media environment is Langston Hughes' poem *Movies* (1951); Hughes's poem is an instance of how multi-sensory, virtual simulation *is a new poetic expressionism* that seeks, in part, to make obsolete the formal/textual artifact of previous poetic scholarship. Because the sense of language is virtual, many poets are responding to how *all virtual-media phenomena* create new possibilities for language-use; such "media poets" create the quasi-causes that can generate Virtual-becomings, i.e. poetic acts (see chapter 1). Hughes's "media poem" appears as follows:

> The Roosevelt, Renaissance, Gem, Alhambra:
> Harlem laughing in all the wrong places
>   at the crocodile tears
>   of crocodile art
>   that you know
>   in your heart
>   is crocodile:
>
>   (Hollywood
>   laughs at me,
>   black—
>   so I laugh
>   back.)   (395)

Hughes' poem productively acknowledges his own interpretive ability to re-mediate how Hollywood 'represents' black people. His defiant tone both acknowledges the danger inherent in such constructions (their crocodile-esque, potentially-destructive effects) as well as how such mass-media forms are only as powerful as he re-interprets/authors them to be. Hence, Hughes' poem fits rather well with Deleuze's definition/description of poetry: "...the poem is evaluation and the art of evaluating; it articulates values" (*Nietzsche and Philosophy* 31). Such poetic re-mediations can generate new socio-political possibilities as well. Deleuze further remarks:

> [artistic] signs simply imply ways of living, possibilities of existence, they're the symptoms of life gushing forth or draining away. But a drained life or a personal life isn't enough for an artist. You don't write with your ego, your memory, and your illnesses. In the act of writing [or filming] there's an attempt to make life something more than personal, to free life from what imprisons it. [. . .]. Creating isn't communicating but resisting. There's a profound link between signs, events, life, and vitalism: the power of nonorganic life that can be found in a line that's drawn, a line of writing, a line of music. It's organisms that die, not life. Any work of art points a way through for life, finds a way through the cracks. (*Negotiations* 143)

Therefore, according to Deleuze, mass-media communication is often ineffectual unless it can become *resistance/a-poetic-expressionism* that can also re-write social codes in non-normative capacities. Media poems like *Movies* are always oriented towards what Aristotle had in mind when he stated a rather long time ago: "it is not the function of the poet to relate what has happened, but what may happen,—what is possible [. . .]" (*Poetics* 35). Nietzsche further echoes this multi-temporality of the poet and his/her Becomings: "I am of today and of the has-been [. . .]; but there is something in me that is of tomorrow and of the day-after-tomorrow and of the shall-be" (*Thus Spoke Zarathustra* (150).

In line with Hughes' poem, the most effective way to explore the personal/cultural construction of ideology is through continually re-mediating sensory experiences to see the actual-world effects of such ideologies. Such "media poets" chart the potential effects of particular world-views and modes of perception on our personal/communal Becomings. Blondel warns that resistance to such un-determined Becomings can easily generate resentment against the contingent world: "the resentful man [. . .] is incapable of metaphor," i.e., artistic transformation (172).

All virtual media—which have no stable structures to ground 'representation'—create a more nomadic, unstable cultural milieu, i.e., they create a version of McLuhan's global village that's potentially replete with all the conflict imaginable. Hence, poetic transformations/Becomings are impossible without the virtual, which furthermore implies that Sense-events can be easily generated anywhere in a new-media environment. The virtual, however, *is never equivalent to pure illusion*, since illusion (in a virtual-actual paradigm) arises from the mis-perception that something can be timelessly itself or have a timeless ideological significance.

Virtual percepts and affects always possess the power to re-mediate the contingent world of Being for more productive possibilities; unfortunately, people often disavow how everything is constructed/mediated and, instead, treat most phenomena as transparently 'ideal' or 'real', which is a profound philosophical/cultural problem in the sense that *everything can then be taken for granted*; a la Nietzsche and Blondel's prior insights, Slavoj Žižek comments:

> "Truth" as opposed to "mere rhetoric" is nothing but rhetoric brought to its extreme, to the point of its self-negation; literal sense is nothing but metaphor brought to self-negation; *logos* nothing but myth brought to self-negation, and so forth. In other words, the difference between rhetoric and truth *falls within the very field of rhetoric*; the difference mythos/logos is inherent to the very field of myth; the difference metaphor/literal sense depends upon [the] self-differentiation of metaphoricity. (*For They Know Not What They Do* 32)

Even for the predominantly-psychoanalytic critic Žižek, we always-already exist within a virtual/poetic relation to the actual. This realization therefore acknowledges that we're each the author/creative-agent of our own perceptual processes; furthermore, contingent-life-at-large can be affirmed in non-negating/representational capacities. Below, Žižek even affirms a Deleuzian way of conceptualizing realism itself so the traditional/philosophical distinction between epistemology and ontology can be erased:

that which seems to *separate* us from the way reality really is out there, is already the innermost constituent of reality itself. [. . .]. Our process of approaching constituted "objective" reality repeats the virtual process of Becoming of this reality itself. The fact that we cannot ever "fully know" reality is thus not a sign of the limitation of our knowledge but the sign that reality itself is "incomplete," open, an actualization of the underlying virtual process of Becoming.   (*Organs Without Bodies* 56)

Virtual-becomings always incorporate the paradoxical "action[s] by which something or someone is ceaselessly becoming-other (while continuing to be what they are) [. . .]" (Deleuze & Guattari, *What is Philosophy?* 177). Since technological creations are materially-embodied ideas, virtual media offer one of the most tactile and palpable ways of interacting with the virtual-actual potentialities that always exceed any codified perspective on a wholly-contingent world. Moreover, this book will endeavor to show how Deleuze's philosophy can be used to elucidate not solely 'high art' forms (as many elitist critics have tried to claim) but popular ones as well.[3]

Since our current cultural era is dominated by virtual and electronic communication, it is vital to engage how poetic productions/Becomings are shaping that mass-media environment; our newly-virtual era of "secondary orality" can continually re-create how we use and interpret both signification as well as our Virtual-subjectivities. Hans Magnus Enzensberger articulates this notion as follows: "the contradiction between producers and consumers is not inherent in the electronic media" (76). All mass-media phenomena, even film and TV, are active interfaces that allow us to participate in the constructive nature of perception if we choose (see chapters 2, 3, & 4).

McLuhan has prophetically claimed that artistic creativity/Becoming will stay front and center in a mass-media culture: "the artist is indispensable in the shaping and analysis and understanding of the life of forms [...] created by electronic technology" *(Understanding Media* 65). Deleuze and Guattari further edify this notion: "no art and no sensation have ever been representational" (*What is Philosophy?* 193). Artistic or poetic perception is culturally vital precisely because:

people are constantly putting up an umbrella that shelters them and on the underside of which they draw a firmament and write their conventions and opinions. But poets, artists, make a slit in the umbrella, they tear open the firmament itself, to let in a bit of free and windy chaos and to frame in a sudden light a vision that appears through the rent—Wordsworth's spring or Cézanne's apple—the silhouettes of Macbeth or Ahab. Then come the crowd of imitators who repair the umbrella with something vaguely resembling the vision, and the crowd of commentators who patch over the rent with opinions: communication. Other artists are always needed to make other slits, to carry out necessary and perhaps ever-greater destructions, thereby restoring to their predecessors the incommunicable novelty that we could no longer see. [. . .]. The painter does not paint on an empty canvas, and neither does the writer write on a blank page; but the page or canvas is already covered with preexisting, preestablished clichés that it is first necessary to erase, to clean, to flatten, even to shred, so as to let in a breath of air from the chaos that brings us the vision.   (*What is Philosophy?* 203-4)

If McLuhan, Deleuze & Guattari, etc., are right, then we especially need to read all popular-media productions as occurring within the context of simulation as well—especially mainstream outlets like CNN, FOX News, the CBS News, etc.—since many viewers often dangerously assume they only 'represent' actual events in neutral, naturalized, or common-sense manners.

It's important here to re-stress how *virtual/popular media are never enough solely by themselves to render the illusions of homogenous/common-sense representations obsolete*, and to 'magically' return us to the heterogeneous nature of McLuhan's "global village." Electronic media only become virtual space-times of undetermined possibility when their capacities for signification and communication are engaged poetically, i.e. as self-consciously-constructed simulations. Deleuze, in *Negotiations*, directly addresses this often-overlooked issue:

people who haven't properly read or understood McLuhan may think it's only natural for audiovisual media to replace books, since they actually contain all the creative possibilities of the literature or other modes of expression they supercede. It's not true. For if audiovisual media ever replace literature, it won't be as competing means of expression, but as a monopoly of structures that also stifle the creative possibilities in those media themselves. [. . .]. It's not a matter of comparing different sorts of medium. The choice isn't between written literature and audiovisual media. It's between creative forces (in audiovisual media as well as literature) and domesticating forces. It's highly unlikely that audiovisual media will find the conditions for creation once they've been lost in literature. Different modes of expression may have different creative possibilities, but they're all related insofar as they must counter the introduction of a cultural space of markets and conformity—that is, a space of "producing for the market"—together.   (131)

Hence, the key conflicts dramatized in mass culture are not based on elitist conceptions of competing aesthetic mediums, but on domesticating/normalizing forces as opposed to the more radical ones of Becoming/transformation, which all mass-media practice can generate. Virtual media need poetic utterances as much as poetry needs multi-sensory capacities. What follows is a pragmatic map that charts how these two phenomena can be theorized anew within a productive inter-relation and interaction.

Notes:

1 Timothy Allen Jackson offers a useful catalogue of what constitutes new media: it includes "all types of computers and other communication devices using microprocessors, digital audio and visual, local and global networks (such as the Internet, internets, and the World Wide Web). New media content can also be found in toys which communicate, CD-ROM and DVD disks for interactive educational and entertainment use, virtual reality environments, interactive kiosks and other multimedia environments, high-tech surveillance equipment, telemetry devices, artworks incorporating or produced by digital means, bionic communication devices, and various input, output and storage devices for electronic content" (352).

2 See *Electronic Book Review #5: (electro)poetics*, Spring 1997, or, *Conjunctions* 42, *Cinema Lingua: Writers Respond to Film*, Spring 2004.

3 According to Clare Colebrook in *Gilles Deleuze*, there is no specific "Deleuzian movement" in literary criticism (150). One aim of this book is to put forth *media poetry* as a non-elitist "Deleuzian" movement. Needless to say, media poetry is more than just a literary movement since it's simultaneously open to all media art.

POETIC ACTS & NEW MEDIA

1.
Media Poetry Vs.
L=A=N=G=U=A=G=E Poetry

> The poet's spirit wants spectators, even if they are only buffaloes!
> —Nietzsche (*Thus Spoke Zarathustra* 151)

> Flow on, river! Flow with the flood-tide, and ebb with the ebb-tide!
> —Walt Whitman, "Crossing Brooklyn Ferry"

Since poetic or artistic production in a new-media environment can generate the potentials for Sense-events at any particular moment, supposedly-transparent or common-sense 'representations' should become more and more obsolete; alternatively, a productive *media poetry* of virtual simulation can create Becomings or fabulations (Bergson's term) that seek to transform the assumptions and expectations inherent in mass culture. The key term I'm putting forth here—media poetry—demands a clear definition, one that will be explored below from multiple perspectives. Media poetry can be defined by revisiting how simulation is differentiated from representation. Since no representation can fully capture the entirety of an actual event in a historical space-time, we can only simulate or describe such phenomena as Sense-events, i.e. as virtual percepts & affects that can furthermore overcome the 'false hope' inherent in Platonic copies/imitations of supposedly 'timeless' forms;

> [through] introducing time into Elizabeth Anscombe's principle that all action is action "under a description": [even] the past would then be intrinsically "indeterminate" (or "virtual") since it is always capable of falling under new sorts of description in the present [. . .]. (Rajchman 165)

Any event, regardless of whether it appears to be actual or fictional, past or present, can generate alternative, virtual possibilities for articulation when it is described or perceived. In an unmoored/virtual-media environment that operates most effectively by the logic of productive simulations, it is important to stress: "information is immaterial but never exists without a material support. Information may be transferred from one material support to another, but cannot be dematerialized—[. . .]" (Wark, *A Hacker Manifesto* 127). Hence, poetic information does not need to be limited solely to printed/spoken language in a new-media environment. Poetic acts can become hybrids of multiple mediums; as McLuhan has observed: "the content of a particular medium is always another medium" (23). In this sense, the virtual-content of language in media poetry is primarily multi-sensory perceptions. In Deleuzian terms, all examples of printed/spoken media poetry "reach a region in which language no longer has any [absolute] relation to that which it denotes, but only to that which it expresses, that is, to sense" (*The Logic of Sense* 25).

Media poetry, therefore, is a multiplicitous mode of expression that blends conventional, mass-media codes with poetic simulations. This audio/visual and/or textual poetry forces one to re-think bourgeois mythologies that constitute mass culture, i.e., it presents alternative forms of making meaning, but in an entertaining, pleasurable way that makes it no less serious. Media poems thus stand in opposition to the formal and purely-theoretical bases of such poetry movements as L=A=N=G=U=A=G=E poetry, which seek to separate and abstract printed text from Sense-events (i.e. incorporeal and virtual powers of sensory transformation). Audio, visual, and textual meanings are not simply arbitrary (a la Structural Linguistics) but rather mediated through a multitude of practices and ideologies (see below).

This mediation of linguistic/audio/visual phenomena is precisely what is responsible for the multiplicity of signification and the multi-sensory potential of media poetry. This generative potential is an aspect of all media use, but media poetry specifically highlights and exploits the capacity of new multimedia to exponentially enhance *the possible*. This may also occur through either the actual use of virtual media, through a critical ambiguity with regard to official ideologies and formal/generic constraints, or through thematic content that destabilizes fixed meanings/representations and entertains possibilities for new meanings that can re-write/mediate any transcendent 'realism'. Since virtual/digital media are hybrid space-time continuums in which textual, audio, and visual information are re-write-able, converging codes, we need an aesthetic criticism that engages—either directly or indirectly—this logic of virtual media and that doesn't examine predetermined genres or artifacts, but the cultural effects and world-views of all media/artistic productions.

In a contemporary context, the possibility for a multi-modal media poetry implies that literary theory itself can no longer exist in a separate fold from mass media except to the detriment of that theory: *media poetry belongs to new-media studies more than to any traditional literary theory*. Media poetry re-mediates any linguistic/visual binary that privileges either term in sensory significations. A relevant example of how that phenomenon happens is found in Hughes' previously-mentioned *Movies.* Media poetry, a la Hughes' poem, is also a self-consciously-created process (i.e. a Becoming-as-overcoming). In this process, the reader/user can become a virtual participant in the hybrid space-time of Becoming, i.e. personal & social problem-solving, which media poetry generates.

In Foucault and Deleuze's terminology, media poetry always exceeds the personal because it envisions language (and all other media production) as *Pure Utterance* and *Sense-event*; such utterances are

> pure language events: not elements of a structure, not attributes of subjects who utter them, but events that emerge, function within a field, and disappear. [. . .]. The paradox is thus that transcendental [i.e. virtual] becoming inscribes itself into the positive order of being, of constituted reality, *in the guise of its opposite*, of a static superimposition, of a crystallized freeze of historical development. [. . .]. In short, one should oppose here development *within time* to the explosion of *time itself:* time itself (the infinite virtuality of the transcendental field of Becoming) appears *within* the intra-temporal evolution in the guise of *eternity.* The moments of the emergence of the New are precisely the moments of Eternity in time. The emergence of the new occurs when a work overcomes its historical context.   (Žižek, *Organs Without Bodies* 10-11)

This is precisely why artistic production is vital for Deleuze, since he sees productive change/transformation happening only when media-art engages not "things happening in [historical] time, but new forms of coexistence, ordering, transformation. . . ." (*Negotiations* 123). Hence, Deleuze's philosophy *is anti-communication* in a globally-networked media-environment in the sense that communication itself is often uncritically passed-off as a wholly-transparent and self-evident opinion.

Therefore, I do not mean by the term 'media' the mainstream-ideologies inherent in the institutions and corporations that control the flows of information and communication in Western culture but, rather, the multi-media capacities for simulating new meanings in sensory mediums that are never codified by pre-determined/naturalized forms. Signification does not have to exist on a computer screen or on the Internet to create virtual/poetic potentialities. Poetic expression is not inherent in the abstract forms or structures of printed language either; instead, they exist "in the concrete poetic construction. These characteristics do not belong to language in its linguistic capacity, but to the construction, whatever its form may be" (Medvedev & Bakhtin 84).

A precursor for media poetry is poet, filmmaker, and theorist Pier Paolo Pasolini's notion of *free, indirect discourses,* which are never limited to abstract and 'timeless' linguistic structures. V. N. Vološinov, from whom Pasolini borrows the term indirect discourse, explains that critical "analysis is the heart and soul of indirect discourse" (129). Free, indirect discourses treat language according to what Pasolini called the "translinguistic" (198). Such a trans-media discourse becomes "an action 'placed' in a system of symbols, as in a vehicle, which becomes action once again in the addressee, while the symbols are nothing more than Pavlovian bells" (Pasolini 198). For Pasolini, this re-mediation/re-writing of Sense-events—a virtual/actual hybrid—*is* poetry:

> it seems to me that the first language of men [sic] is their actions. The written-spoken language is nothing more than an integration and means of such action. Even the moment of greatest detachment of language from such human action—that is, the purely expressive aspect of language, poetry—is in turn nothing more than another form of action: if, in the instant in which the reader listens to it or reads it, in other words, perceives it, he frees it again from linguistic conventions and re-creates it as the dynamic of feelings, of affections, of passions, of ideas, he reduces it to an audiovisual entity, that is, the reproduction of reality, of action [. . .].   (204)

Such "action" reverberates with the quasi-causes that are also generated by virtual-media. Media poetry, since it is a productive mnemotechnology of virtual simulation, re-creates/transforms *all* the material and social processes that constitute both the individual's perceptual processes and (potentially) his/her environment as well. As stated previously, the actual can always be re-written/mediated by extra-personal perceptions. A la Wittgenstein, meaning in such a paradigm *depends wholly on articulation, not representation.*

Another precursor for media poetry is Deleuze's terminology for a poetic speaker or a singular individual's generation of pretextual percepts and affects, i.e. "crystalline description," which can be defined against "organic description" (*Cinema II* 126). For Deleuze, a cinematographic or linguistic description is organic when it "assumes the independence of its object," and "the setting described is presented as independent of the description which the camera [or speaker] gives of it [. . .]" (126). Organic descriptions occur in the context of a "supposedly pre-existing [and 'representable'] reality" (126). Crystalline description, on the other hand, "stands for its object, replaces it, both creates and erases it [. . .] and constantly gives way to other descriptions which contradict, displace, or modify the preceding ones" (126). Crystalline description itself "constitutes the sole decomposed and multiplied object" (126). In our virtually-mediated environments, crystalline descriptions offer the greatest poetic capacities for meaning and articulation because they generate quasi-causes/Becomings with perception, not representational similarities or abstractions. According to Deleuze, only crystalline descriptions generate Sense-events: "events are like crystals, they become and grow only out of the edges, or on the edge" (*The Logic of Sense* 9).

N. Katherine Hayles sums up why poetic utterances that transcend static definitions of language and linguistic code are culturally vital: "words never make things happen by themselves" (*How We Became Posthuman* 83). The ontological contexts (both actual and virtual) within which Sense-events occur are of central importance in a new-media environment. The possibility for a multi-modal media poetry has also arisen from the shift in the cultural place of literature as isolated 'high' art to one inter-related with many other cultural and popular forms.

The dissolution of the elitist place of *literature* as high culture and privileged knowledge, according to Antony Easthope, is a direct result of "1960 popular culture—music, film, television, advertising—[that] came to permeate everyday experience" (19). No longer could literature be thought to exist in an atemporal relation to everyday experience: "if the text could no longer be treated as a complete, self-sufficient *object*, then the implied *empiricism* presuming the text was simply there outside any theory and practice for its construction had to go" (19). In fact, how the term 'text' is being re-conceptualized in literary theories brings it much closer to a virtual-media phenomenon: "if the text cannot be seen as unified, if it consists of a plurality of meaning which is potentially infinite," then there exists no stable ground for an absolutely or purely 'real' representation (20). This notion implies that literary production is no longer an intransient 'high' art, but everyday media: "the text exists inside as a system of movement, its meanings changing as others do; the lonely hour of the final reading never comes" (33). The traditionally Modernist study of literature as the quest for a single, unifying meaning or representation is dangerous precisely because of the ideological assumptions it perpetuates: "pursuing this wished-for hierarchisation of differences within the text into a unified metareading, literary study has been in quest of a moment of presence, time as a point, a totalizing now" (35).

Easthope further argues that understanding literature as primarily a mass-media phenomenon wreaks havoc upon any transcendently-ideal aims for art: "as speaking subjects we only experience the world from within discourse, from inside, so that for us everything is 'mediated;' in relation to Being (one might say) our being is always *there*, materially situated—how could it be any different" (50)? That notion harkens to William Burroughs' description of all media-production as *the reality studio*, which re-enforces how we always-already exist within the contingent world of simulation, not a universal one of representation. Wittgenstein had this anti-Platonic notion in mind as well when he stated: "we are unable clearly to circumscribe the concepts we use; not because we don't know their real definition, but because there is no real 'definition' of them" (*Blue and Brown Books* 25). The media theorist Raymond Williams further explains that language's materiality has to be re-thought in a new media environment: literary texts are not "objects but *notations*," i.e. multi-modal quasi-causes that are never strictly dependent on a medium's materiality (47). More precisely, all notations are vectors that simulate virtual/immaterial Sense-events. Conceiving of language or poetic acts as Sense-events also means that studying literature must "break from the notion of isolating an object," and "discover the nature of a practice and then its conditions" (Williams 47). Within the processes of Virtual-becoming, language-use can create its own plurality and socio-political possibilities (see below).

Theoretical claims in recent, experimental poetry movements like L=A=N=G=U=A=G=E Poetry, which foreground abstract code and printed text as the primary mediums of poetry, must be, in a virtual-media environment, radically "erased/cleared-away." Language Poetry is often off the mark in its attempts to break up romantic conceptualizations of poet and poem because it frequently romanticizes language (a la Hass's previous summary that conceives of poetry as an isolated field of study) as permanent form/structure. Language Poetry is often radically incomplete in the sense that it seeks a purely theoretical/"major" understanding of language-use, as if it's possible to conceptualize language outside of other mass-media phenomena. Language Poetry's foregrounding of language as solely concept, instead of percept and affect, can block poetic utterances from entering into virtual-actual Becomings. Printed language, as a medium of knowledge, can be utterly inadequate by itself because it can 'appear' to break up the empirical world into conceptual terms and illusory 'representations'. This purely abstract or arbitrary nature of language is nothing but a romanticized illusion.

L=A=N=G=U=A=G=E Poetry & Its Discontents

Theorizations of L=A=N=G=U=A=G=E Poetry often problematically privilege language-use as wholly-abstract, structural code, which then becomes the sole, 'legitimate' alternative to all other forms of mass-media rhetoric (see below). The Language poet and critic Lyn Hejinian expresses a common ideology in Language poetry that envisions all popular/virtual-media discourse as homogenous and dismissible: "language writing is indeed in opposition to the mainstream [. . .]" (Hejinian 171). It is not my contention, however, that Language poetry is also a homogenous, easily definable movement, since many different poets are lumped under that umbrella term; I specifically want to examine anew the common, theoretical assumptions in Language poetry rhetoric that rest on an outmoded, "major" understanding of language-use/popular-media-at-large. Linda Reinfeld's description crystallizes this hierarchical view that gives linguistic expression primacy over any other media expression:

> the focus of this new American writing has been not simply the word as such but on the structures and code—the language—through which both word and world come into meaning; thus, it is frequently referred to as language-oriented or language-centered writing, or formally active writing, or Language poetry. (2)

Peter Schakel and Jack Ridl, in their anthology *250 Poems*, offer a more rigorous and succinct description of Language poetry, which "evince[es] skepticism about the ability of written language to record, represent, communicate, or express anything other than its own linguistic apparatus" (388). However, contrary to many Language poets' claims, neither written language nor speech-acts are reducible to a pure set of abstract, structural relations when one takes into account language-use as Pure Utterance or Sense-event.

According to Bruns, Language poetry's most noteworthy attributes arise not from reducing language to arbitrary or equivalent codes, but from acknowledging that language-use is always embodied in some im/material or temporal relation. For him, exploring the sense-making potentials of language is

> [the] attempt to write in such a way as to situate us at the limits of knowing or, even more radically, outside the site of the knowing subject, outside our concepts, no longer in a position to say that the text at hand is authentic, faithful to criteria.   (143)

However, Language poetry runs into trouble whenever its poets render their concepts solely in abstract and overly-intellectualized terms. Language poetry has often succumbed to the dangerous tendency to take language for granted in the sense that language is assumed to arise from a homogenous space, i.e., it can be effectively 'trapped' in purely conceptual terms or codes prior to its actual, temporal manifestations in speech-acts/language-events. The movement's semiotic symbol, L=A=N=G=U=A=G=E, is misleading in the sense that it narrowly privileges only one aspect of language, i.e. its 'constant' structures/codes.

Many Language poets have already theorized the 'avant-garde' movement in terms that bring its processes of writing more in line with media poetry than a purely-abstract, Language poetry. This contradiction in Language poetry rhetoric deserves further comment. Language poet and critic Charles Bernstein has written at length about how Language poetry re-conceptualizes language not as a medium of representation but one of simulation. For Bernstein, language cannot perfectly represent a 'real' essence inherent in empirical objects or experience, but is instead "a simulacrum" that unfolds amidst a myriad of other empirical forces (*Blood on the Cutting Room Floor* 354). Bernstein further comments: "I use the term 'language' for all forms of socially exchangeable meaning—visual, verbal, gestural, or tactile" (*Words and Pictures* 119). Even the model Bernstein chooses for a Language poem is revealingly a multi-media hybrid or dominant-media metaphor—"Dr. Frankenstein's creation"—which implies that Language writing is not solely an abstract structure, but a virtual/temporal/mass-media phenomenon as well (*Blood on the Cutting Room Floor* 352).

However, Bernstein's own poetry can codify such theorizations in pure abstractions (as if they were automatically profound). Take for example *Whose Language* from the book *Rough Trades* (1991):

> Who's on first? The dust descends as
> the skylight caves in. The door

closes on a dream of default and
denunciation (go get those piazzas),
hankering after frozen (prose) ambiance
(ambivalence). Doors to fall in, bells
to dust, nuances to circumscribe.
Only the real is real: the little
girl who cries out "Baby! Baby!"
but forgets to look in the mirror
—of a ... It doesn't really
matter whose, only the appointment
of a skewed and derelict parade.
My face turns to glass, at last.   (25)

Although Bernstein's command of language is striking, this poem is problematic in the sense that language itself is completely detachable from the forces of the empirical world—the speaker revealingly claims that only the young girl is 'real'—which implies that even the speaker is pessimistically condemned to a "skewed" and "derelict" relation to her because there exists no possibility for constructing in language-use any meaningful *virtual-content/Becoming-art* in a foreclosed, 'real' world. In the context of the poem's language-use, all things become sadly reified in the poem's last line, even the 'static' speaker himself. Bernstein's pessimistic/detached poem assumes that language arises solely from an abstract "apparatus," which generates only an infinite-regress/"incoherent dust." Such a skewed perspective is even encoded into the formal language of the poem, rendering it utterly separated from an immanent world of *Virtual-becoming* in a potentially-nihilistic relation. Deleuze explains why any such duality is dangerous: "...the true and the real are the avatars of nihilism. [They are] ways of mutilating life, of denying it, of making it reactive by submitting it to the labor of the negative, *by loading it with the heaviest burdens*" (*Nietzsche & Philosophy* 184).

An "unburdened" poetry, which can directly engage the social and material construction of meaning, can also confront how popular media (i.e. TV, radio, the Internet, popular film, mass-printed journalism, etc.) influence all mass-media possibilities, including less dominant ones like printed poetry. The space-times of artistic productions are not pure abstractions as language-use parades them to be in Bernstein's poem. What Bernstein does not acknowledge, then, is the fact that his own image of poetic production—Frankenstein's creation—is a better model for electronic/virtual media. All virtual media phenomena are self-consciously authored processes that unfold in a multiplicitous space-time. John Rajchman edifies what's at stake in such a productive realization: "the best world is the one with the greatest virtuality" (*The Deleuze Connections* 74).

The end result of viewing language as solely abstract code is nihilistic and anti-contingent-life. Bob Perelman's *Cliff Notes* (1986) exemplifies this situation perhaps better than any other language poem because it actually celebrates the nihilistic shortcomings of its own narrow, purely-abstract view of language-use. The poem begins:

> because the languages are enclosed and heated
> each one private a separate way
> of undressing in front of the word window
> faces squashing up against it
> city trees and personal rituals of sanitation
> washing the body free of any monetary transaction
>
> The parts of the machine take off their words and die away
> in a description read to the senses
> by the leftovers on TV that no one would think of eating
> even in the very act of swallowing.
>
> It's these "very acts" that we must
> Pay attention to the flatness of the screen now!
> For it's this very flatness
> that the frailly projected containment of the humanized body
> is designed to be pinned to
> by, naturally, forces outside our control. [. . .].   (498)

Perelman's speaker's satirical take on language's interrelations to larger social forces, a.k.a. popular media, is problematically pessimistic and cynical. In the vein of Bernstein's poem, language-use—for Perelman—becomes separated/ abstracted from the contingent world by another glass-barrier, i.e. the "word window" in the poem. There is a hierarchy in operation of different media: language is equated wholly with potential health, whereas television and other visual mediums are solely forces of alienation and contamination. What is presented on TV has no nourishing attributes whatsoever: "the leftovers on TV that no one would even think of eating / even in the very act of swallowing." The poem's satirical perspective on the difficulty of a singular approach to language-use ("the languages are enclosed and heated / each one private a separate way") or to popular-media phenomena is a critical problem because the speaker is totally pessimistic about the sense-making possibilities of all media, even his own use of printed language.

In effect, Perelman's speaker doubles the pre-existing problem that the poem diagnoses by foregrounding his own doubts as to whether language can ever generate positive cultural-significations. Discussing the history of the Greeks and the Romans, he states: "We can still see traces / of the tracts where they lived / and can still understand their language / which consisted entirely of dirty jokes about money" (499). Such an abstract position, regardless of how satirical it is, is homogenizing and leveling. The speaker makes that abstract-stance even more extreme by equating all language-use with commodification. It is tragically pessimistic that the speaker negates the potentials for productive, singular speech acts in Western history. In fact, for him, the 'cliff notes' for

Western culture have already been written, and we're all doomed to be puppets of commodification. However, Perelman's poem is revealing precisely because it foregrounds the impossibility of a Language Poetry—which concentrates solely on the abstract nature of linguistic code—to productively transform our relations to popular/dominant media as well as to the sense-making potentials of a contingent world. The poem doesn't put a final nail in the coffin of Western history; rather, it places one in its own misguided theory of language's relation to sensory experience and the empirical world at large.

The Language-poetry theorist Bruce Andrews, who edited with Bernstein the famous $L=A=N=G=U=A=G=E$ *Book* (1984), also overtly acknowledges that language-acts are not purely a linguistic practice, but a multi-sensory, simulated one. Andrews explains, in *Poetry as Explanation, Poetry as Praxis*, that Language poetry is primarily a

> desire for a social, political dimension in writing—embracing concern for a public, for community goods, an overall concern for language as a medium: for the conditions of its makings of meaning, significance or value, & sense. Technicians of the Social—the need to see society as whole. That has meant, in recent years with this work, a conception of writing *as* politics, not writing *about* politics. Asking: what is the *politics* inside the work, inside *its* work? (669)

Language Poetry, as stated previously, runs into conceptual trouble whenever it re-situates the "building blocks & limits of meaning and sense back inside the writing, giving you greater distance by putting them within the internal circuitry" of language (669). Such a distance levels all sensory experience because it creates a hierarchy in which linguistic code *is the primary alienating agent/factor* in a purely-abstract world.

Even though Bruce Andrews attempts to theorize Language Poetry within the wider sphere of a social—and not purely abstract—literacy, it is still commonplace for poets and poetry critics to conceptualize popular media as derogatory cultural forces, and as domains of shallow, totalized, and clichéd images that threaten to turn everyone into anonymous, alienated beings. To totalize the virtual-worlds of media to be solely havens of destructive illusions is derogatory not only to those media, but to all of us who exist within their spheres of influence. Such a homogenized stance also problematically assumes that no one reads mass-media phenomena critically. If poets are always-already living inside a cultural milieu saturated by mass media, it is a troubling fact that they often ignore or belittle those media's effects on how we interact with the world around us and each other. Many poets already embrace the more-dominant digital/virtual media phenomena and receive information daily through the Internet, but they are still mostly dismissive of the impact those media are having on everything from social interaction to human subjectivity itself. Poets, in a new-media environment, are also wittingly or unwittingly in the *business* of re-writing/mediating communication and subjectivity at-large.

It is important, therefore, to differentiate the virtual possibilities generated by electronic/virtual media from the stereotypes that threaten to codify the forces they generate as well as propagate. Electronic media's multiplicities of space-times (especially popular television and film) are often vehicles for corporate bottom-lines: an undemocratic spirit is lurking within popular media's dominant position in Western culture. Phillip Jenkins, although he discusses in his book how dominant media portray religious scholarship, addresses a larger, mass-media concern:

> for many reasons, news media and popular culture outlets have a powerful prejudice in favor of scholarly theories that are weird or extreme, and tend to succumb easily to poorly substantiated fads, if their proponents have the skill to present their ideas appropriately. (197)

Many important theories, either because their proponents do not perform well on television or they are not sensational enough, are never heard in popular media. Gone are legitimate debates in favor of an illusory sensationalism. However, there are dangers lurking in any social medium; a major danger lurking in printed poetry is the attempt to turn its space of orality into either a Romanticized celebration of a purely-abstract language or the individual ego's ability to 'be above' social forces. Charles Olson mockingly calls this particular phenomenon *"the private-soul-at-any-pubic-wall"* (613).

Another similar danger is the 'weird, extreme' notion that poetry can disregard popular media in exploring the social contexts of Western culture. Poetry has always engaged in current events and social criticism, but often to demean mass-media's cultural influences. For example, the following passage from Anselm Hollo's *The Dream of Instant Total Representation* clearly takes such an anti-electronic-media perspective:

> to paraphrase Blaise Pascal, I'd rather be
> a confused, blundering, warm-blooded
> hairy creature with language
> to complain in, to praise with, no matter what,
> than nature's prototype for the microchip.   (289)

Even though Hollo is not a 'card-carrying' Language poet, his stance does reveal a common mis-perception in much oppositional, contemporary poetry. Hollo's speaker's stance is absurdly extreme, and it reveals the intense anxiety people often feel surrounding how technology transforms and extends what constitutes the human. The choice is not between being a warm-blooded human or a technological automaton; technology and the human subject are irretrievably inter-connected in Western culture, and it is a Romantic fantasy to assume that one can avoid being affected by electronic media. Poetry will become even more socially irrelevant if it keeps up this oppositional stance.

Nevertheless, it must be acknowledged that there will always be a place for the Romantic lyric in culture at large; however, such spaces are becoming increasingly interactive in virtual-media environments. All media phenomena, especially contemporary poetry, need poetic simulations that can re-write/overcome the illusion of a timeless/abstract 'private-soul'.

In a new-media environment, contemporary poetry—in order to become more socially relevant—cannot keep reducing language to an abstract set of timeless, structural relations. Instead, it must take a cue from how linguistic signs operate within electronic media. A more practical way to conceptualize language as code *is to envision it as capable of digital convergence.* Poets can digitize (not neutralize) printed language into Sense-events, i.e. virtual space-times in which words (morphemes and phonemes) become forces of convergence that are, in effect, doctorable. Digital/virtual media makes all means of information digitally converge in a globally-networked system. In digital cyberspace

> convergence is the coming together of all forms of mediated communications in an electronic, digital form, driven by computers and enabled by network technology. Convergence presents profound challenges for the existing media order, and has paved the way for the development of multimedia products blending text, data, graphics, full-motion video, and sound and their universal accessibility and interactivity in the online world. (Pavlik 134)

Convergence makes audio, visual, and textual information 'equivalent' to one another in digital codes of 1s and 0s. Digital space-times, which allow different mediums of sensory expression to converge, have huge implications for the inter-connections between language use, communication, and all personal/social identity construction.

In his essay *Digital Identities—Patterns in Information Flows,* Felix Stadler explains:

> identity is, in large part, dependent on communication. What one can be—and what can be one—is determined in interaction. If this interaction takes place through communication media, it consists primarily of exchanges of information. The shapes of such identity-building exchanges are molded by the media in which they take place. If these media change, then the possible and actual shapes of identity change with them. (9)

Enter the virtual subjects that Hayles describe above. If language-acts are always a multiplicitous interface with other mass-media phenomena, poets and poetry critics are wise to keep such inter-media spaces open and interconnected with all mass-media communication. Electronic media shape the multi-modal potentials through which we virtual-subjects generate future possibilities (*amor fati*). Therefore, the most relevant contemporary poetry will necessarily generate a multi-media space-time of "secondary orality," i.e. the multi-modal consciousness inherent in Sense-events. Stadler extrapolates:

> identity is dynamic and unstable; it is the result of negotiations between claims and counter-claims; it reflects and defines the relationships between individuals and their environment; and, the way identity is built or deconstructed is deeply dependent on the communication technologies available. Identity, then, is not an intrinsic property of the person or thing identified, but a social characteristic emerging from interaction. The media that shape this interaction are shaping the possible forms of what can emerge. (9)

The mediated environments that surround individuals are saturated with virtual/poetic possibilities. Take Hejinian's descriptions of printed poetry that sound uncannily similar to virtual-media space-times: "language is nothing but meanings, and meanings are nothing but a flow of contexts [. . .]. It is transitions, transmutations, the endless radiating of denotation into relation" (1); it manifests as "radiating structures and as behavior in sentences" (109); it appears "in multitudes of context, it is multitudes of context" (162). Such statements reveal that printed poetry and virtual media can, and do, converge, because both arise from contingent Sense-events.

Language poetry's printed words on white pages can be better conceptualized in terms of digital convergence than 'major', static codes. Words invoke unlimited potentials for re-coding/mediating textual, audio, and visual phenomena—enter Frankenstein's monster. However, linguistic simulation is both similar and dissimilar to digital codes of 1s and 0s, since its potential for creating multiple shades of meaning can be characterized as both digital and analog. While a poem is structured by constant morphemes and phonemes that can be described as digital, the typography and form of a poem on a printed page varies in an analog dimension. The sounds and rhythms of language vary in infinite, analog capacities as well. Both mass media and printed poetry are interdisciplinary sites of convergence, which means that if 1s and 0s can accomplish such feats on computer screens, surely letters (Pasolini's *Pavlovian bells*) on a white page can as well. This hybrid-logic of media poetry, moreover, doesn't homogenize different mediums in terms of a secret essence or similarity, since all poetic relations are constructed solely in terms of their externality, i.e. in terms of their capacities for simulating new links/relations between perceptual phenomena (percepts, affects, and concepts). Regardless of whether mass-media info is audio, textual, and/or visual, the interactivity between poetry and social contexts can transform the synchronous databases of all mass-media phenomena.

Language poems (a la Perelman's *Cliff Notes*) often envision all popular media as *the* villains that commodify meaning, which levels readers/users' capacities for a productive, social awareness. For Marjorie Perloff, in *Radical Artifice: Writing Poetry in an Age of Media*, a commodified consciousness is incapable of critical thinking. Perloff only situates 'legitimate' avant-garde movements against popular-media forms. Perloff appears to be playing into a totalizing logic: all communicative acts in dominant media are perfectly co-extensive with the ideology of commodification, which denies the fact that popular media are already potential fields of differences or multiplicities of information—even within the often poorly democratic mediums of TV and mass-print journalism. As noted previously: *we viewers/perceivers can re-mediate/write any and all media productions through how we interpret them.*

Perloff's logic that makes popular-media phenomena an 'other' that is the enemy to social progress contradicts her own claim that we cannot live outside media: our contact with cultural forces "tends to be always already mediated by a third voice, the voice of the media" (47). Perloff's invocation of a 'homogenous' third voice inherent in mass media reveals her misreading of mass-media space-times. It's problematic for her to hold up Language poetry's attempts to exist in a fold separate from popular-media productions as a plausible artistic goal. Language poetry's "making strange," according to Perloff, "occurs at the level of phrasal and sentence structure so that poetic language cannot be absorbed into the discourse of the media" (78). One must ask whether this is the sole option. It is dangerous to assume that popular-media discourse is never self-aware, never dripping with irony, and that viewers/users don't resist the mainstream 'commodification of meaning' with already satirical attitudes towards it. Enter the pop performers who *satirize or mock the repression inherent in social codes* like Madonna, Rob Zombie, and The Wu Tang Clan, among a myriad of others.

Gerald Bruns takes a step toward creating *media links* between contemporary poetry and virtual media through envisioning poetry as the productive interfacing of forces that are not determined by commodification, even when commodification is internal to the poem: "the whole of the everyday is, in effect, drawn into the poem. Our contemporary form of life, in all its gritty, commercial debris is internal to the poem's horizon" (Bruns 147). One of poetry's jobs in a new-media environment can be the de-stabilization of the stereotypes/codifications that create the illusions of transparency in our whole cultural field of communication, not just in 'private' poetry. Both poetry as well as all mass media's enemy is not solely the commodification of art, but the *illusion* of transparency that threatens to normalize the ever-shifting information flows as well as the ever-new possibilities inherent in self-consciously-authored Sense-events.

Perhaps many Language poets feel that, if popular-media phenomena were allowed into their poems, they would nullify its avant-garde legitimacy as inherently oppositional. As Paul Hoover states, "avant-garde poetry endures in its resistance to mainstream ideology" (*xxv*). However, not all popular media consign themselves to mainstream ideologies, and many offer striking critiques of them (see chapter 2 on popular film as well chapters 3 & 4 on TV shows that do exactly that). Hoover, in his introduction to the *Norton Anthology of*

Postmodern Poetry that discusses Language poetry's social value, makes a revealing analogy to electronic/virtual media:

> in language poetry, as in Marshall McLuhan's theory of television, the medium
> is the message. Words are not transparent vessels for containing and conveying
> higher truth; they are instead the material of which it is shaped. *(xxxvi-xxxvii)*

According to McLuhan, *how communication happens is more significant than the meanings it carries.* What escapes Hoover is that electronic/virtual media also do not carry any 'higher truths' in converging-diverging flows of virtual information. Hoover refuses to openly acknowledge that new media have forced a re-conceptualization of what constitutes language's materiality. Language is more notation (or Sense-event) than object, a la Raymond Williams's afore-mentioned claim, and it simulates perceptual events, not pre-determined representations. If we users understand mass media in transparent terms, then we are limiting our own potentials as virtual-subjects. We users cannot make Betty/Diane's mistake in *Mulholland Drive* of reading media/sensory phenomena solely in idealistic terms. All differentiating users can refuse the illusory 'totalizations' and 'transparency' in mass-media phenomena that appear to create 'major' truths/illusions. Because there is no outside to media, any oppositional gesture is currently regressive and reactionary. Politics, too, can only occur within the virtual worlds of multi-media.

Reinfeld, like Hoover, revealingly invokes popular-media in an attempt to explain why she is fascinated with Language poetry: "what I found in Language poetry was consistently—in William Carlos Williams' sense of the word—news" (8). However, such theorists often mention new media solely as analogies for the more 'legitimate' language-arts. Like Hoover and Reinfeld, Perloff does not go far enough in theorizing how poetic production relates to a new-media environment:

> we must avoid the impasse of the Englit or Creative Writing classroom, where
> the literary text too often continues to be treated as an object detachable from
> its context, as if a 'poem' could exist in the United States today that has not
> been shaped by the electronic culture that has produced it. There is today no
> landscape uncontaminated by sound bytes or computer blips, no mountain peak
> or lonely valley beyond the reach of the cellular phone and the microcassette
> player. *(xiii)*

However, Perloff's judgmental approach to "contaminating" media, alongside the vagueness of her claim that media in fact shape our culture, undercuts any possibility for the generation of poetic/productive uses of mass-media phenomena. Perloff even quotes Richard Lanham, who theorizes that the personal computer and its electronic display are changing communication itself: such "'digital equivalency' [. . .] means that we can no longer pursue literary study by itself: the other arts will form part of literary study in an essential way" (quoted in Perloff 17). It appears that the opposite is more accurate: virtual media are dissolving literature as a separate, privileged space of knowledge. Digital convergence, which is inherent in all electronic media, breaks down not only the distinction between author and audience, but "'verse' and 'prose'," and "'creator' and 'critic'." (Perloff 17). What is of crucial significance here is what I stated previously: literary theory cannot exist in a separate fold from the media, except to the detriment of theory.

Several theorists of Language poetry have already begun to lay the virtual vectors that can create *media links* between popular media and any 'Language' poetry. What is also necessary for creating multi-modal vectors between virtual media and printed poetry is redefining the poetry critic's role to acknowledge how poetry already exists within mass media. The images and spectacles of mass media are fundamentally surface phenomena, without depth; Deleuze and Guattari explain that "the ideal for a book would be to lay everything out on a plane of exteriority [. . .], on a single page, the same sheet: lived events, historical determinations, concepts, individuals, groups, social formations" (*A Thousand Plateaus* 9). Bruns even sees in these externalized/simulated surfaces of sensory information a potential/virtual interface with Walt Whitman and the entire history of American poetry:

> Whitman taught us to make poetry out of lists of places, on the principle that the list is our only recourse in a world where space is more surface than container, where master narratives and deep structures have no application—a world that resists the analytic frame of mind, as if made for traveling rather than penetrating. (156)

The illusion of depth in this passage is similar to the illusory discourse of transparency: both reveal the falsity of a 'transcendental nature' inherent in language itself. No such 'depth' is possible on either a printed page or digitally-equivalent space-time. For the media poet, language and information have no 'ideal structures', which means we readers can only experience them through re-mediating them.

And Now Back to Media Poetry

Media poetry, unlike L=A=N=G=U=A=G=E poetry, fulfils the *multi-sensory* goals of the William Carlos Williams/avant-garde Modernist tradition that heralded anything could be poetry, including "newspaper clippings" (*Kora in Hell* 70). Williams had hoped to make poetry an inter-media art of lived time and sensory experience sans transcendent capacities for idealized/purely-naturalized forms. His famous rallying-cry for poetry, "no ideas but in things," can now, in a new-media environment, expand to incorporate virtual events/significations. Furthermore, media poetry renovates a critical problem inherent in poetic Modernism. Shari Benstock explains:

> the determined emphasis on the Word or Logos overshadowed all other divergences among Modernist practitioners. The one scared belief common to all was what seemed to be the indestructibility of the bond between the Word and its meanings, between symbol and substance, signifier and signified. (158)

In Benstock's summary, regardless of whether one is a High Modernist, Imagist, Confessionalist, Objectivist, Deep Image poet, etc., 'all' shared the common assumptions that the word was sacred as Logos and that the poet's main function was to represent a homogenous, 'organizing truth' of the empirical world and human experience. The Williams tradition undermines both Benstock's totalizing claim as well as that common logocentric strain in Modern poetry by constructing a colloquial poetry that is always local and provisional, and that must *simulate* perceptual events in a contingent world.

Williams's "no ideas but in things," therefore, acknowledges "the limitations in one's mind and in language that restrict how much of the larger world one can honestly grasp" (Lowney 127). Williams conceives of the poem as possessing no special, intrinsic privilege or unity. In fact, Gertrude Stein's famous line from *Tender Buttons*, "the difference is spreading," serves as an excellent summation of what was productively *new* in Anglo-American, poetic Modernism (1). Williams's desire to write from locality and discrete perception completely re-mediated High Modernist fragmentation, which is famously and strikingly portrayed in T.S. Eliot's *The Waste Land* (1922), and which "would misleadingly assume a reconstitutable logic of propositions" (Nicholls 250). For Benstock, the debate over whether language is stabilized by a universal Logos registers the break between Modern and Postmodern modes in poetry. As Joseph Conte explains: "we cannot trust literary history to provide us with an accurate gauge of Postmodern poetics," since not every contemporary poet writing after WWII (the supposed historical period of Postmodernism) has a postmodern poetics; postmodern poetry, therefore, needs a non-historical theorization (9).

Media poetry also varies from theoretical conceptualizations of postmodern poetry. In formal terms, Donald Davie states that Joseph Conte's description of the "breaking free" from "Coleridgean 'organic form'" is a "distinctively postmodern" phenomenon, and a practical and useful description of postmodern poetry (365). Postmodern poetry is 'a new form', one that is open-ended and multi-linear, and which has no organic links to any Logos or organic logic that organizes either its language or themes. Postmodern poetry is often thought of, in Roland Barthes' terminology, as a "'writerly text'," which "encourages the reader to become a 'producer of the text' and by [taking] an active role in its composition, to gain 'access to the magic of the signifier, the pleasure of writing'" (qtd. in Conte 57). All the above-quoted Language poems are manifestations of postmodern poetry in this theoretical sense. The reader, as undetermined other, is granted freedom to engage such an abstract text in any manner whatsoever, since it offers no absolute, organizing message or authorial direction. Because many modern poems argue for and articulate a representational link with 'organic' forms, they do not possess the radically incomplete form of a postmodern 'open text'.

However, debates about postmodern poetics are filled with evaluative controversy. Critics like Lynn Keller believe that claiming postmodern poetry is a project where 'anything goes' is "a narrow evaluative label" that does not tell us enough about the poetry itself (8). What is dangerous about such generalizations, according to Charles Alteiri, is that they become a petty "absolutizing of sheer mobility as our basic orientation toward the world," which levels/negates the actual limitations inherent in the historical space-time we inhabit at any particular moment (312). In addition, as Stanley Rosen explains, such a position is similar to nihilism, which can take root "when everything is permitted. If 'everything is permitted', then it makes no difference what we do, and so nothing is worth anything" (*xiii*). One cannot absolutely discard the actual effects of specific ideologies/world-views if one desires to be socially relevant. Furthermore, if postmodern poetry requires a worldly ethics, its philosophical and poetic projects must be limited (as historically and socially determined) as much as they are undetermined by any absolute.

Gerald Bruns confronts this problem in an imaginary dialogue with the philosopher Stanley Cavell, who characterizes postmodern poetry in the following manner:

> it does not follow that anything goes, or that everything collapses into aporia. If we cannot distinguish between poetry and talk, poetry and prose, poetry and philosophy, this does not mean that they are indiscriminate or identical. What you say about criteria is true: they float and drift and fail to settle things once and for all, but all this means is that they do not decide for us independently of where we stand or where our history places us.   (158)

Bruns explains that the "self [is] embodied in another's words," which further implies that language is not the domain of an essential identity, but of percepts, affects, and concepts, which always operate in non-personal or virtual manners (162). Words can then open up inter-subjective domains of provisional contact with actual-virtual forces/events; they are not reductive forces that reveal some absolute aporia. Whenever postmodern poetry becomes a purely abstract or intellectual enterprise like in Language Poetry, it does not fulfill the multi-sensory, ontological goals of Williams's "indigenous Modernism" (Hirsch 72). Postmodern poetry, like Language poetry, often falls into the trap of taking the abstraction of language to an extreme, whereby the empirical world becomes reducible to a structural textuality. Media poetry is different than the modernist quest for the unifying representation and the postmodern leveling of all empirical forces to the equivalent (and dangerously homogenous) codes of textual, abstract 'equivalence'. Žižek explains how abstract equivalence is solely an illusion: "equivalence only emerges because no system of differences can ever complete itself, it "is" only the structural effect of this incompleteness" (*Organs Without Bodies* 65).

Media poetry, which incorporates an aesthetic logic of inter-media convergence—not a nihilistic one of absolute equivalence, is currently identifiable in a multiplicity of forms in our current era of secondary-orality. Media poetry generates aesthetic forces that can productively re-write/mediate the postmodern, theoretical 'equivalence' of Language poetry and, alternatively, re-inscribe any abstraction into immanent/virtual Sense-events. For example, Tony Medina's poem, *The Way We Move*, from *Bum Rush the Page* (2001), can be interpreted as a rally cry for overcoming any abstract, safe-haven for language-use in a new-media environment. The poem begins:

> the way we move, funk groove
> beat the rhythm out some pavement,
> our elegant violent attitude, quick
> slow motion movement in quicksand
> in somebody else's shit house shanty town
> shingly jingly chains clamped on our neck,
> hang to the floor scrape spark and clink
> and we made music out of this cool behind dark
> shades, taught to fear the sun, hiding in
> beauty parlors and bars draggy face with
> hatred and ugliness,
>   and it only comes when you don't
> accept the natural gifts, the fingerprints of a
> higher order of peace and simple logic, what makes us
> phenomenal is that we can sleep walk in
> harmony, never breaking a sweat 'cept in factories
> or bars, prisons we even build systems for, our
> own street logic and survival, but this is not where
> we're meant to be, not on the operating table of
> extinction or at the broken doorstep of finality
> stumbling drunk confused scagged out on whiteness
> and greed and stupidity into the bleeding face of our
> dead father, and we are not supposed to move
> this way, slow mumbling suicide in quicksand and defeat
> we must refocus, we must see again   (1)

Medina's poem fills out the socially-aware rhetoric of Language poetry in a much more effective manner than any of the aforementioned Language poetry. All of the abstractions and metaphors in Medina's poem unfold in the context of a worldly "street logic and [fight for] survival." The quicksand in the poem is an overt metaphor for the complacency and inertia that underpin the naturalized status quo, which many people uncritically believe in solely because it promises mythic solutions to their fears/anxieties; Medina's poem is utterly ironic about any such mystification. The fact that many people are rendered alienated and unhappy 'sleepwalkers' by those myths is *the social problem* that must be re-written/mediated in the poem's last line. This desire to re-mediate experience, i.e. to get it productively moving again in a poetic manner, is the multi-modal "music" that can transform the social stagnation inherent in culture-at-large.

The content of Medina's rallying-cry poem succeeds where much Language poetry fails because it overtly foregrounds the abstract nature of alienating social myths like normalcy and complacency, all the while calling attention to the actual, ontological miseries and violence they create in a historical space-time. The solution to social alienation here is not an abstract exploration of language's apparatus and code; over-intellectualizations of social problems have no capacities for Virtual-becomings that can potentially transform actual-world suffering/violence.

Media poetry, therefore, is never confined to a particular genre or poetic style, and it does not have to be radically unconventional to invoke the transformative logic of virtual-media phenomena. The examples that follow below illustrate the multi-sensory possibilities of media poetry at the level of both form and content, which exposes how mainstream- and popular-media phenomena are vital preoccupations for many contemporary poets. Many poets from many different backgrounds write media poetry.

William Matthews' *Sympathetic* (1984), from *A Happy Childhood*, is a fascinating exploration of how Shakespeare's plays can comment on and illuminate key themes across literary/media genres (in this case, film), as well as across cultural and historical periods. The poem, which uses pre-existing media/art like a virtual database, appears as follows:

> In *Throne of Blood*, when they come to kill
> Macbeth, the screen goes white. No sound.
> It could be that the film has broken,
> so some of us look back at the booth,
>
> but it's fog on the screen, and from it,
> first in one corner and then in another,
> sprigs bristle. The killers close in further—
> we're already fogged in by the story—
>
> using pine boughs for camouflage,
> and Birnam Forsest comes to Dunsinane.
> Even in Japanese, tragedy works:
> he seems to extrude the arrows
>
> that kill him—he's like a pincushion—,
> as if we grew our failures and topples,

as if there were no larger force than will,
as if his life seemed strange to us

until he gave it up, half-king, half-
porcupine. We understand. We too were fooled
by the fog and the pines, and didn't
recognize ourselves, until too late, as killers.   (139)

This poem's speaker finds an ontological self-realization here in Akira Kurosawa's cinematic rendition of *Macbeth*. For Matthews' speaker, the audience has as much to learn from identifying/sympathizing with the killers of Macbeth as Macbeth the tragic hero. The white fog in Kurosawa's scene stands for how we can often lose any 'objectivity' in comprehending our own reactions to startling sensory phenomena like our own capacities for violence. In effect, the poem foregrounds how we often like to see terrible things happen to great characters/people. This blood-lust inherent in the audience, however, is not rendered in moralistic terms.

Matthews' speaker implies that in acknowledging such blood-lust, one can generate a more self-aware, productive relation to one's own creative potentials, which can then transform such unconscious propensities. The way to avert violence in actual-world contexts, therefore, is to become self-aware of such desires and how they operate in all of us. The greatest danger is to live in the 'leveling' white fog (an empty percept and affect) that the poem describes. What is being exposed here in Matthews' poem is not a cynical picture of humanity, but how artistic productions can explore the actuality of human desires without moralizing or abstracting them into safe, conventionalized, and mythic modes that are potentially even more dangerous/violent because of how shrouded/mystified they've become. The poem implies that the most dangerous fog is the one in which self-deceptions can effectively cover over actual desires and motivations in a repressive common-sense (*i.e. only actual killers are violent towards the world*).

If we take a look at how different media appear in other hybrid constructions of media poetry, we can become acutely conscious of the fact that artistic and media productions continually transform our relations to the contingent-world-at-large. David Wojahn's *Hey Joe* (1997) explores how many different media phenomena interrelate and inform each other. His poem surveys such diverse mass-media phenomena as Dante's *Inferno,* the CNN coverage of the O.J. Simpson trial, as well as the Jimi Hendrix version of *Hey Joe*—a song about a man who shoots and murders his unfaithful female lover; the poem begins:

For Hendrix it's a sweet slow blues, Stratocaster
pummeling leisurely the opening bars,
a gracile firestorm that Mitchell's drums

and Redding's bass must fan and chisel, 4/4 stabs,
    the conflagration firewalling, as Jimi
        asks where he's *going with that money*

in his hand, that *cold blue steel .44,*
    the questions almost querulous. The Leaves
        and the Byrds do it faster, lyrics slurred with shock,

and Willy de Ville implores it to strings,
    a Mariachi band, accordion-slathered to his
        lounge-lizard croon. But Hendrix knows

the song is gallows tree and killing floor,
    that death angels turn his will incarnadine,
        definitive. The ceremonious blood.

He must take both parts—killer and chorus, strophe
    and antistrophe forged from feedback of an amp
        hiked up to ten. *Where you goin' with*

that blood…your hands…I heard you shot
    your woman down. Fadeout and the jukebox lights
        have dimmed. And Bill shambles back toward

our table, balancing a foamy pitcher. The no-time
    of early afternoon, and Nick's is empty,
        the drinkers Dantescan, the barkeep channel surfing

until he crests on Court TV, pre-trial motions
    with the sound turned low, the nattering lawyers
        resplendent with their clipboards and Armanis,

the aging football star expressionless, jotting notes
    while a rumpled coroner aims a magic marker
        at a drawing of a face, of a woman's slit throat,

x's and arrows to mark trajectories.
    And even photos of the murdered woman's *dog.*
        "They're saving the hi-tech stuff for later," says Bill,

and I answer that the pot we smoked
    sneaks up on you. [. . .]   (7-8)

Wojahn's poem recounts how media productions create and inform our world; it also fleshes out how the illusion of 'representation' can harbor potentially destructive forces a la Hughes' aforementioned *Movies* (i.e. how destructive 'representations' possess a "crocodile" nature). In addition, the Dante-esque scene in the above passage reveals how many people are not only fascinated by media portrayals of murder and violence, but that they often disown (a la Matthews' aforementioned poem) their own blood-lust in such matters. For example, one common reason why violence is so often romanticized in American culture is that many erroneously believe it is a vehicle for forcing/manipulating the world into conformity with idealized forms/meanings, i.e., violence often harbors the illusion that it is *the* vehicle for possessing an absolute control over life itself.

The fact that the O.J. trial became fascinating entertainment for many people implies that the white fog in Matthews' poem operates in peoples' psychological lives in manners often dangerously and critically unchecked. Wojahn's speaker does not disown his own fascination with mass media, since the poem productively acknowledges other media phenomena that have influenced his life and desires. Mimi Marinucci, in her essay *Feminism and the Ethics of Violence*, which explores how the TV show *Buffy the Vampire Slayer* portrays violence, explains how self-awareness of one's propensities can serve as a productively-poetic deterrence to violence:

> rejecting the false dichotomy between passivity and hostility, I propose that the empowerment that comes with the ability to do violence can be tempered by the awareness of that ability. There may be some truth to the old stereotype that physically intimidating men, whose strength is not in question, are confident enough to walk away from challenges issued by men whose strength is less obvious. When threatened, a woman with intimate knowledge of her ability to cause harm is more likely to respond with appropriate violence than a woman who lacks such self-knowledge. At the same time, however, she is also less likely to respond with inappropriate violence, say, by attacking her sleeping husband's genitals with a butcher knife. A morally viable alternative to unwarranted passivity and unwarranted aggression alike is the readiness to use appropriate violence in response to inappropriate violence. (74)

In addition, Marinucci's passage alludes to conceptual forms of violence, in the sense that many people seek to control or manipulate the forces of the empirical world by forcing them to reflect idealized forms or ideas, which can also lead to inappropriate violence. Lorena Bobbit's media fame speaks to our cultural fascination with such inappropriate violence.

Any 'foggy' or inappropriate connection to violence helps to explain the media-sensationalism inherent in high-profile cases of famous people charged with violent crimes. In fact, in Wojahn's poem, the abstracted "white-fog" of inappropriate violence becomes exaggerated way out of appropriate proportion. Such violence takes on a dangerous, other-worldly air when conceptualized as a 'representation' more than a tragic event; the poem's fevered end happens as follows:

> [. . .]. The leaps, the choke chain loose
> against the reddened slick cement,

> falling back each time until his flank
>   is lathered and drenched, circle and wail, his slippery
>   paw prints to be mapped and measured, circles
>
> in circles, tightening, his howl against ensanguined cries,
>   until it seems he turns to us, his muzzle
>   pulsing huge from every screen, the click
>
> of his nails as he paws at the nether world's gates.   (9)

Nicole Simpson's dog, in the above passage, 'represents' the unchecked aggression and violence of a world that often disowns/mystifies its capacities for actual violence. Nicole Simpson's dog is not a fantastical or mythic hellhound but, if people cannot re-mediate or "see again" their own relations to such potentials for violence, *the dog can symbolize such tendencies toward destructive mis-perceptions.*

Wojahn's speaker, who is both drunk and high in the above scene, 'prophetically' realizes that the sensationalism inherent in mystified-representations is not culturally productive. The family-dog-turned-hellhound 'appears' to want to release that destructive 'power' onto everyone watching the Court TV saga. Needless to say, some people would not interpret the violent scene on Court TV in such a productively-poetic manner as Wojahn's speaker. However, this is not cause for hopelessness. If anything, Wojahn's poem is a cultural warning that reveals how media can reflect and inform not only our conscious desires, but our dangerously disowned ones as well. *Hey Joe* implies that mass-media forms have the power to create a 'hell on earth' only if people choose to live in an uncritical or unconscious relation to such media/actual-life desires. Poetic production, in Wojahn's poem, can foreground this dangerous repression or self-denial in Western, mass-media culture that treats violence like a spectacle that possesses an illusory, 'representational power' over life itself.

In this sense, many people's desire for vicarious experiences of violence exposes a more fundamental problem that Medina's poem also foregrounds, i.e., our current culture is often dangerously nihilistic and violent towards our own productive/poetic potentials in everyday life. It's much easier for people to live vicariously through myths of idealized power and control than to explore their own actual/creative potentials. Medina's poem, as well as Matthews' and Wojahn's, all reveal the fear and anxiety at the root of many peoples' inability to achieve their own poetic potentials in the world. It's sadly easier to live in a 'white fog' that levels/destroys everybody's potentials, i.e. so no one has to take responsibility for their actual-world desires. It's a sad fact that many people, as Medina's poem implies, choose to sleepwalk through not only their own lives, but everyone else's as well.

The Media Poetry of David Trinidad: "I Didn't Know Why I Was So Fascinated by Murder"

The above quote is taken from David Trinidad's poem *The Shower Scene in Psycho,* which explores (like the media poems above) the motivations for violence in order to come to productive terms with such impulses. However, Trinidad's poem is also a complex exploration of how creative processes (simulations) of perception can virtually re-mediate the objects they describe for different and productive effects. In fact, I want to explore Trinidad's entire career, since he is one of the few contemporary poets to have consistently written media poetry. His poetry reveals how, a la Deleuze's insight, "if literature dies, it will be murder" (*Negotiations* 131).

The speaker in Trinidad's *The Shower Scene in Psycho,* from *Answer Song* (1994), generates a collaborative/inter-media art that takes visual media as its primary focus. The poem begins:

> *She closes the bathroom door to secure her privacy, slips off her robe, drapes it over the toilet bowl, steps into the bath, and closes the shower curtain behind her, filling the frame with a flash of white (5.89).*

> Shortly before midnight on Friday, August 8, 1969, Manson called together Family members Tex Watson, Susan Atkins, Patricia Krenwinkel, and Linda Kasabian to give them their instructions.

> *From Marion viewed through the translucent shower curtain, Hitchcock cuts to (5.90), framed from within the space bounded by the curtain. At the top center of this frame is the shower head.*

> Fortified with drugs and armed with a gun, knives, rope, and wire cutters, they were to take one of the Family cars and go to 10050 Cielo Drive in Beverly Hills.

> *Marion rises into the frame. Water begins to stream from the shower head. She looks up into the stream of water and begins to wash her neck and arms. Her expression is ecstatic as the water brings her body to life (5.91).*   (87)

The first comment that needs mentioning is a formal one. Trinidad's poem has dropped any strict formal or lyrical properties. The textual artifact is not what is sought here; rather, the poem sets up interactive relations between multiple, unfolding events. With such a potentially sensational topic as murder, it is perhaps obvious why Trinidad's speaker does not seek to overlay the poem with lyrical/aesthetic flourishes. The blocks of text that make up the poem do not fetishize the poem as abstract language or structure. Trinidad's poem becomes a media event through the inter-cutting between multiple, simultaneous contexts and simulated re-enactments, which generate a mixture of organic and crystalline descriptions. Trinidad's speaker, in effect, becomes the multi-media reporter or narrator of the poem's events.

Trinidad's speaker re-mediates, without attempting to alter what has actually happened, several horrific events: the poem juxtaposes the roughly 50 edited shots that make up the shower scene in Alfred Hitchcock's *Psycho* (1960), the Manson Family murder of Sharon Tate and her friends in 1969, as well as the speaker's memories of his life at that time when he was 16 years old and "fascinated by murder." What the speaker virtually transforms in the poem are his own relations to those events in order to understand *exactly why they're fascinating.*

The poem's speaker overtly implicates himself in the desire to witness these events so as not to see them from a separate, detached, or purely-intellectual stance:

> (The first time I saw *Psycho,* I was baby-sitting for a couple
> who lived at the end of a dark cul-de-sac.)
>
> *This shot frames part of Marion's body along with the intruder's
> arm, still shadowy in the frame (5.109).*
>
> (I prayed they'd stay out late. I wouldn't have been allowed
> to watch it at home.)
>
> *Viewed from overhead, the shower-curtain bar cuts across the
> screen. As Marion tries to fend it off, the knife strikes three times
> (5.110).*
>
> (There was a storm that night: rain and branches beat
> against the windows. I waited anxiously for "The Late
> Show" to come on.)
>
> *Marion's face fills the screen, expressing bewilderment and pain
> (5.111).*
>
> (They'd cut most of the shower scene for TV).
>
> *Marion holds onto the shadowy arm as it weaves three times in a
> spiraling movement (5.112).*
>
> (I felt cheated.)

Reprise of (5.111).

(I wanted to be scared.)

Reprise of (5.112).   (91-2)

What makes up the speaker's curiosity concerning murder is, in part, the fact that it has been censored from him not only by cultural 'standards', but by his own mother who, early in the poem, threw out his collection of newspaper clippings of famous murders. The speaker does not want to deny or hide from the fact that such violence is an alluring phenomenon. The speaker also does not blame the media for creating violence. Rather, he strives to understand the implications of the fact that he, like everyone else, always-already exists within a mediated world (William Burroughs' *reality* studio) wherein virtual simulations have actual effects.

Throughout the poem, the speaker constantly refers to his mediated environment that includes newspaper clippings, TV shows, books like *Valley of the Dolls*, and popular films like *Psycho* and the film version of *Valley of the Dolls*, which starred Sharon Tate. The speaker wants to experience everything his mediated culture has to offer: *he wants to be truly scared by Psycho; it does not matter to him whether intense experiences are actual or virtual.* In the context of the poem, the simulated instructions for the filming of the shower scene become that much more terrifying when juxtaposed with the actual stabbing of Sharon Tate. They become a very intimate form of "action" for each reader since s/he becomes, in effect, the simulator of the violence within the poem. For the speaker, there never exists a separation from which to view them safely.

Within Trinidad's poem, anything is capable of being poetry (even *actual* mass murders); a virtual murder, in sensory terms, can be just as 'real' in its effects upon the speaker. The most unsettling moments in the poem happen as follows:

The hand and knife come into clear focus. Water bounces off the glinting metal of the blade (5.116).

Then they turned on the heavily pregnant Miss Tate.

Juxtaposition of blade and flesh (5.117).

(In secret, I read *Valley of the Dolls* several times.)

Marion recoils, but still looks dazed, entranced (5.118).

(My mother found my hiding place and made me throw the book away.)

A low-angle view facing the door. The knife slashes through the
frame (5.119).

(I bicycled to Thrifty Drug, bought another copy, and
snuck it into the house.)

Marion's back and arms. The intruder's arm again enters the
frame (5.120).

Watson told Atkins to stab her.

Closeup of Marion's face. She is now clearly in agony (5.121).

When the actress begged to be spared for the sake of her
unborn child, Atkins sneered, "Look, bitch, I don't care..."

Blood drips down Marion's writhing legs (5.122).

"I have no mercy for you."

Marion turns her face from the camera. The knife enters the
frame (5.123).   (93-4)

Since violence began as something the speaker didn't understand clearly, the
fact it is so common in his cultural milieu makes it especially vital that he
confront it on his own terms; he refuses to exist in denial of it like his mother
demands. In effect, his desire to confront the personal/cultural myths that can
lead to murder also brings on a productive crisis in his relation to his mediated
environment. The speaker's unspoken question for the events in the poem
becomes: what kind of world is this that so often witnesses such violent
fantasies/events?
    The speaker, below, addresses this implied question:

This eye, which fixes the camera in its gaze, displaces the drain in
the frame, and appears to peer out from within it (5.136).

(We lived a few miles from the Spahn Movie Ranch.)

The camera spirals out clockwise as though unscrewing itself, dis-
closing the eye, Marion's, dead (5.137).

(There was a newspaper machine in front of the Chats-
worth Cinema. I always chained my bicycle to it.)

The camera keeps spiraling out until we have a full view of
Marion's face (5.138).

(When I left the theater that afternoon, I saw the face of
Sharon Tate.)

*Death has frozen it in inexpressiveness, although there is a tear
welled in the corner of her eye (5.139).*

(Then I read the headline as my eyes adjusted to the sun.)   (97-8)

The poem's ending brings up several curious issues. It would be a mistake to
read the last line as a romanticized vision of the empirical world in which, with
the return of the sun, violent acts can be completely eradicated. The ending is
much more ironic since it simulates the sensation after exiting a theater when
one's eyes must re-adjust to bright sunlight, i.e. to a world transformed anew.
The key question then becomes for the speaker: will the 'actual' world in which
he was a child ever be the same again? The answer to this question is *no*,
because what the poem itself enacts is the speaker's coming to terms with how
the world in which he lives allows such atrocities because each of us always-
already simulates our perceptions/actions within that world (violent or
otherwise), i.e., the world allows whatever we create it to be (sans Platonic
ideals). The speaker steps into a very different world at the poem's end, one in
which there exists no strict barrier between media and empirical 'reality'.

The potential dangers generated by such a radical freedom in which we all
help to create what is actual becomes at this moment very 'real' to the speaker.
However, those relations do not have to be solely about power and control over
the world and the people who inhabit it, as both the 'intruder' in *Psycho* and the
Manson Family horrifically embody. For Manson, Sharon Tate's murder
'represented' his own right to judge life itself, and how he was justified in
eradicating 'bourgeois' values and people. Such violent actions are doubly
unsettling because such murderers are acting out a representational view of the
actual world, i.e., the ideology of representation is predicated on a
transcendental judgment; thus, some murderers take pleasure in 'playing' the
judge who can make god-like decisions over what deserves to live and not live.
Blocking a person from entering into a multiplicity with other forces of the
virtual and actual worlds we inhabit is equivalent to the desire to halt life itself,
to fantasize that one is its atemporal God or judge. Trinidad's poem, then, is the
critical performance of the speaker's own transformation from a child, who
might have potentially seen the world in 'representational' terms, to an adult
who sees in the more productive terms of simulation. Trinidad's media poem
ends with multiple events pointing to a key realization: the adult speaker must
take full responsibility (i.e. *a more empathic one*) for his relation to that world
and how he simulates both his own actions as well as how his "eye" sees not just
everything that happens in that world, but all that might happen as well. What

the speaker disposes of through his "fascination with murder" is any desire to embrace the world in the fantasy terms of ideal representations.

In addition, there are many other examples of media poetry in Trinidad's career that point to the productive possibilities that mass-media forms can generate. In fact, one of Trinidad's strongest achievements to date is exposing how mass media help to create what we desire/perceive at the same time that it also de-mystifies/"de-fogs" the idealistic illusions inherent in those media. For Trinidad, media forms should never occupy the domain of 'transcendent ideals'. Trinidad's poetry is often very playful, but it never loses a critical perspective on the actual limitations that also inhabit such powerful/awe-inspiring media-simulations.

For example, his poem *Ancient History,* from *Plasticville* (2000), comically describes Hollywood treatments of historical and mythic stories solely from the perspectives of the actual Hollywood productions that simulated them:

1949	Hedy Lamarr snips Victor Mature's hair while he sleeps, but he regains his strength in time to heave the pillars apart. George Sanders, an urbane leader of Philistines, raises his glass with rueful approval as the temple collapses about him.
1955	Condemned to wander the Mediterranean after the fall of Troy, Kirk Douglas is bewitched by Silvana Mangano, while his crew are transformed into swine.
1956	Charlton Heston turns his staff into a snake, refuses Anne Baxter's advances, frees the Jews from Pharaoh Yul Brynner, majestically leads the Exodus and parts the Red Sea, and witnesses a rather jet-propelled inscription of the Ten Commandments.
1959	Gina Lollobrigida smoulders and heaves in a series of plunging gowns, drives a chariot with abandon, dances in a curious balletic orgy, and seduces Solomon (Yul Brynner) for political purposes.
	Charlton Heston wins a chariot race and an Academy Award.
1960	Kirk Douglas excels in gladiatorial school, falls in love with Jean Simmons, and rebels after a private games staged for Roman general Laurence Olivier. Olivier makes a casual (but unmissable) come-on to slave-boy Tony Curtis. (4)

The poem goes on from there until 1966. While some might dismiss this poem as hokey, comic fancy, it does foreground several interesting observations about Hollywood's production of meaning. It's utterly impossible to read any of the above films as representations (since the actual actor's names are used) and this calls overt attention to their simulated natures. It also ironically comments on the cult-of-personalities surrounding such larger-than-life media figures as Charlton Heston and Kirk Douglas. Since they are given the chance to play such great figures from history and myth, it is absurdly funny to think of the actors (not their characters) as accomplishing the feats described above. No one in their right mind would literally equate such power with the actual actors. The poem foregrounds the often fanciful and absurd natures of media productions; Trinidad's Hollywood poem does not despair as it confronts the lack of representational merit characteristic of such big budget films. Rather, there is much pleasure and humor to be found in transforming such events into simulations. The films above are not demeaned/mocked as poor or failed 'representations', for that would be to misinterpret the actual natures of virtual media.

A richer, more complex look at media culture in Trinidad's work takes place in *Essay with Movable Parts* from *Plasticville* (2000). As its title suggests, the poem is a multi-linear conglomeration of many different media and commodity-culture phenomena. The poem generates its meaning, and its questioning of common assumptions, through dynamic juxtapositions. It begins:

From Broadway to Hollywood, this is the fastest-selling, most whispered-about novel of the year. *And no wonder!* Jacqueline Susann's VALLEY OF THE DOLLS reveals more about the secret, drug-filled, love-starved, sex-satiated night-mare world of show business than any book ever published.

*

These tiny, whimsical characters were manufactured by Mattel from 1966-1971. Their name came from the combination of Little and Kid; thus the name Liddle Kiddles was born.

A wide variety of dolls was marketed, ranging in size from ¾" to 4" tall. The larger of these dolls are marked at the base of their neck "© Mattel Inc." Their bodies are made of a soft vinyl material and have wires in them that enable them to bend.

Kiddles came in just about everything

> imaginable—jewelry, perfume bottles,
> lollipops, ice cream cones, soda bottles,
> and tea cups.

                              *

> Show business—a world where sex is a success weapon, where
> love is a smiling mask for hate and envy, where the past is
> obscured and the future is oblivion. In this sick world where
> slipping youth and fading beauty are twin specters, the magic
> tickets to peace are "dolls"—the insider's word for pills—pep
> pills, sleeping pills, red pills, blue pills, "up" pills, "down"
> pills—pills to chase the truth away.   (13-14)

Hard-boiled descriptions of Hollywood from Susann's famous novel are serio-comically juxtaposed in the poem with young kids' playthings. What is uncanny about relating two such disparate phenomena is the fact that they may not be as distinct as first appears. What is missing from the often reified Hollywood-world of idealized images and appearances is the playful/malleable nature of toys like Liddle Kiddles. However, the toys' supposedly-innocent natures take on an air of sinister possibility since, for adults, *dolls* become the impossible cure-alls for fantasy-based play—like the desire for timeless youth or beauty. Trinidad's poem uses such juxtapositions to 'toy' with the apparent meanings of many taken-for-granted cultural 'appearances'. The poem further juxtaposes scenes from popular television shows (like *Gilligan's Island, The Addams Family, The Brady Bunch,* and *The Patty Duke Show*) alongside monologues from four female speakers, one of whom had a bitter, epic rivalry with her not so "well-off" cousin who was always jealous of her "clothes, games, books, [and] dolls" (22).

Another section of the poem relates these children's rivalry to the rivalries of the three main female characters in *Valley of the Dolls*:

> Each of them was bred in the
> Babylons of Broadway and
> Hollywood. Each of them
> learned about making love,
> making money, and *making*
> *believe*. Each of them rode the
> crest of the wave. And each of
> them came finally to the Valley
> of the Dolls.

                              *

> My cousin's interest in Kiddles seemed to grow in
> proportion to my collection. The more Kiddles I got,

> the more she begged to play with them every time they
> visited.   (22)

Thus, the adult obsession with fame and fortune may not be radically different from children's desires to possess highly-prized toys. In addition, the above-mentioned sinister tone returns when one of the speakers refuses to let her cousin play with her dolls since "she played too rough" (22). Even the games young kids play are never innocent, since there are obvious privileges some possess that give rise to all the feelings and problems the poet associates with the non-artistic/darker sides of Hollywood (i.e. resentment, envy, and the coveting of supposedly-ideal appearances).

Trinidad's poem blatantly juxtaposes the inevitable and disappointing ends of many games both adults and children play. Another section of the poem makes this fact glaringly obvious:

> VALLEY OF THE DOLLS is
> the story of three of the most
> exciting women you'll   ever
> meet; women who were too
> tough or too talented not to
> reach the top . . . and unable to
> enjoy it once they were there!

*

> My parents divorced when I was little. I lived with my
> mother. As time went on, she grew really angry with   my
> father   and wouldn't let me visit him.   I think   she
> thought I saw him anyway. One day, when I came   home
> from   school, she said that she'd thrown away all my
> dolls. I raced outside, but the garbage men had already
> taken them away. All she said   was: "I needed the clos-
> et space."   (20)

In this sad and unfortunate passage, one of the speaker's childhoods gets a similarly rude awakening to the snares of possessive passions a la the protagonists of Susann's novel. Throughout the poem, the poet observes how mass-media phenomena and his speakers' desires/troubles interrelate to a surprising degree. In fact, the poet's observations trigger associational memories with the mass media shows and commodities the speakers grew up around. Since the desire for vicarious experience is a common theme exposed and treated by TV narratives, the poet describes many such comparable events in popular culture.

One such example from TV is an episode of *Gilligan's Island* in which Mary Ann becomes jealous of Ginger who sings the same song as the icon of feminine sexuality in mass media (Marilyn Monroe):

> After watching Ginger sing "I Wanna Be Loved By You" to entertain the casta-
> ways, Mary Ann, wishing she could be like Ginger Grant, falls and hits her head,
> causing her to believe she is Ginger. After examining Mary Ann, the Professor
> suggests the castaways go along with her fantasy until he can come up with a
> cure, advising Ginger to dress like Mary Ann.   (18)

Mary Ann's desire to vicariously become Ginger is comically made into a
reality after an accident, which thematically reveals the potentially-alienating
effects of such covetous desires. In one speaker's rivalry with her jealous cousin,
such vicarious desires can harbor similar tendencies toward aggression:

> One time my aunt and my cousin came over when I
> wasn't home. My mother let my cousin into my room.
> When I got back, I found my Kiddles collection—com-
> pletely trashed! She'd cut off all their hair, written with
> magic markers on their little bodies, ripped off some of
> their heads. And she didn't get in trouble for it! "She's
> just expressing herself," said my aunt. "She's artistic."   (23)

For this speaker, no one could possibly know the personal significance she
placed on those dolls. The fact that her aunt downplays her cousin's trespass
implies that adults can often be purposefully ignorant as to the problematic
motivations that underlie many adult and child behaviors. This is yet another
disappointing rite-of-passage into the problems inherent in human nature and
social interaction; in addition, this passage foregrounds how many people do not
see artistic creation as a transformative re-writing of actual-life issues/concerns.
     Nevertheless, the poem continues to juxtapose many comical and satirical
perspectives on such human faults/mis-perceptions. One example is from an
episode of *The Addams Family*, in which normalcy is precisely what Gomez and
Morticia are protecting their child from: "When Pugsley abandons his pet
octopus to befriend a puppy, wear a Boy Scout uniform, and play baseball,
Gomez and Morticia fear their child is becoming normal" (14). Such
transversals of social assumptions are more common in mass media than cultural
critics often admit. In fact, this passage alludes to another of Trinidad's poems,
Playing with Dolls from *Answer Song*, in which a male speaker is the one who
loves dolls; in this particular poem, the male speaker is keenly aware that
normalcy would demand an end to his own, actual desires. However, this is not
the case, since mass media is not solely a medium for transparently reinforcing
normalcy. For Trinidad, popular culture also has transformative effects in the
sense that it allows him to craft an identity for himself (as a gay man) which is a
productive alternative to any traditional or repressive notion of masculinity.
Mass media shows and commodities have marked him profoundly, and he is
aware of how media forms can also be re-created/mediated for more productive

effects. Mass media, for Trinidad, does not always unconsciously edify the normalized and bourgeois attitudes of social control mechanisms.

Essay with Movable Parts ends with another transversal of social values. The poet refuses to moralistically condemn commodity culture. In fact, he sees something vital in how it can aid in re-constructing one's desires and identity. One of the speakers confronts these issues as follows:

> During the last two years, I've been on a virtual treasure hunt. Combing every nook and cranny, box, case, and container I can find to see what Barbie items I might have tucked away during my hiatus from collecting. Things have turned up in the unlikeliest of places. Maybe there was some logic in putting Casey's earrings in my j ewelry box. But what were a pair of silver glitter open-toe shoes doing in a 45 rpm record case with some amusement park novelties?

*

This is the doll,
JACQUELINE SUSANN,
who wrote

VALLEY
OF THE
DOLLS

which has been Number One on *The New York Times*
bestseller list for 28 consecutive
weeks—8 weeks longer than *The Group* or
Exodus—10 weeks more than *Peyton Place* or
Hawaii—15 weeks longer than *Marjorie Morningstar*!
Everything you've heard about it is true!

*

The moral of this story is don't give up the search. If your parents are still in your childhood home, comb the place. You never know what might turn up in a hard-to-vacuum corner of the carpet or that antique candy dish on the top shelf or in the dark caverns of a basement or attic. The key to success is familiarizing yourself with Barbie's accessories. Would you recognize Miss Barbie's planter without its plant? If Casey's earring lost its triangle, could you pick it out of a pin cushion? How many "Floating Gardens" bracelets have been tossed because they look like broken bits of plastic? Here's another hint. Be sure and check behind the drawers in all your cases. They're great hiding places.

*

Big, brilliant, savage, and sensational—Jacqueline Susann's
shocking, true story behind the
headlines of a glittering generation.

Jacqueline Susann's
VALLEY OF THE DOLLS

Don't miss it. And don't lend it
to a friend. You'll never get it
back.   (29-31)

The poet associates joy and pleasure with mass media/commodity culture. In
fact, Trinidad continually uses the language of advertising when he addresses
Valley of the Dolls. In this respect, the poem is not much different from a
commercial, since it is openly asking the reader to buy it. What is perhaps most
astonishing about one of the speakers in the poem is that she does not look back
on her past with resentment and anger. Rather, she has a renewed and edifying
desire to collect the same toys as when she was a girl. Despite the terrible things
that can happen to a child, the poet continually foregrounds the pleasure children
can also experience, which is often a missing element in adult behavior.

Trinidad's poem, therefore, is diametrically opposed to the narcissistic
desire to regress to childhood that Jean Baudrillard claims (in *The System of
Objects*) is evident in the obsessive/neurotic desire to collect commodities. In
Trinidad's poem, such collections actually signify the poet's overcoming of the
problematic desires associated with fantasies of possession, i.e. resentment and
envy. The poet's love of *Valley of the Dolls* also serves as a self-conscious
disclaimer for the destructive aspects of Hollywood fantasies. In fact, the de-
mystification of Hollywood and mass-media ideals is a pleasure in itself, since a
more playful approach to Hollywood appearances can then take its place. Poetic
production is the perfect site for re-assembling/re-creating not only such
'appearances', but the desires attached to them. Nowhere in Trinidad's poem is
the poet or the poem's speakers unconsciously victimized by such desires, as
Baudrillard's theory claims. Baudrillard's claim would only hold sway if one
treats collecting as an absolute desire for an impossible collection. It seems that
the solutions to the neurotic trappings of personal and cultural fantasies are
poetic perception/production, i.e., poetic simulations can de-mystify all such
fantasies outright, which then creates the possibility for actual joy and pleasure.
Such poetic play, therefore, can potentially overcome any dangerous cycle of
idealization and disillusionment.

Another Trinidad poem makes the constructive aspects of popular culture
glaringly obvious. Media signification, in his work, depends wholly on how one

re-mediates such Sense-events. In *Meet The Supremes*, collected in Trinidad's book *Hand Over Heart* (1991), the speaker explores the lessons to be learned in both the 'magic' world of popular music as well as its cut-throat business side. It begins:

> When Petula Clark sang "Downtown," I wished I
> could go there with her. I wanted to be free
> to have fun and fall in love, but from suburbia
> the city appeared more distant and dangerous
> than it actually was. I withdrew and stayed
> in my room, listened to Jackie DeShannon sing
> "What The World Needs Now Is Love." I agreed,
> but being somewhat morose considered the song
> a hopeless plea. I listened to Skeeter Davis'
> "The End Of The World" and decided that was
> what it would be when I broke up with my first
> boyfriend. My head spun as fast as the singles
> I saved pennies to buy: "It's My Party," "Give
> Him A Great Big Kiss," "(I Want to Be) Bobby's
> Girl," "My Guy"—the list goes on.   (47)

The pleasures inherent in these songs reach an ineffable dimension for the introverted speaker, who basically makes little distinction between his emotional-life and the lyrics of such popular hits. In fact, he uses them as the soundtrack to his own life experiences. However, he also acknowledges the dangerous, actual-world aspects of popular culture as a cut-throat business. It's a sad fact that fame and stardom seldom stick with the performers of hit songs. Another section of the poem addresses that unfortunate fact as follows:

> On my transistor, I listened to the Top Twenty
> countdown as, week after week, more girl singers
>   and groups
> came and went than I could keep track of:
>
>> Darlene Love,
>> Brenda Lee,
>> Dee Dee Sharp,
>> Martha Reeves
>> & The Vandellas,
>> The Chantels,
>> The Shirelles,
>> The Marvelettes,
>> The Ronettes,
>> The Girlfriends,
>> The Rag Dolls,
>> The Cinderellas,
>> Alice Wonderland,

Annette, The
Beach-Nuts, Nancy
Sinatra, Little
Eva, Veronica,
The Pandoras,
Bonnie & The
Treasures,
The Murmaids,
Evie Sands,
The Pussycats,
The Patty Cakes,
The Trans-Sisters,
The Pixies Three,
The Toys, The
Juliettes and
The Pirouettes,
The Charmettes,
The Powder Puffs,
Patti Lace &
The Petticoats,
The Rev-Lons,
The Ribbons,
The Fashions,
The Petites,
The Pin-Ups,
Cupcakes,
Chic-Lets,
Jelly Beans,
Cookies, Goodies,
Sherrys, Crystals,
Butterflys,
Bouquets,
Blue-Belles,
Honey Bees,
Dusty Springfield,
The Raindrops,
The Blossoms,
The Petals,
The Angels,
The Halos,
The Hearts,
The Flamettes,
The Goodnight
Kisses, The
Strangeloves,
and The Bitter
Sweets.   (47-49)

In this ecstatic litany of mostly forgotten girl groups from the 1960s, what is most striking is not only the similarity of many of the saccharine-esque names, but how endless such a list may actually be in the history of popular music. Popular culture, especially popular music, generates an infinite capacity for recycling themes like the power of romantic love.

While the pop culture recycling of romantic love is not itself seen as a critical problem for the speaker, he does provide the flip-side to such glossy and slick band names, i.e. the disillusionment that can occur when one falls out of love or from the public's often fickle favor:

> I preferred Marianne Faithfull to The Beatles and
> The Rolling Stones, was fascinated by the stories
> about her heroin addiction and suicide attempt.
> She's still around. So is Diana Ross. She made
> it to superstardom alone, maintaining the success
> she'd previously achieved as the lead singer of
> The Supremes, one of the most popular girl groups
> of all time. Their debut album was the first LP
> I owned. Most of the songs on it were hits—
> one would reach the top of the charts as another
> hit the bottom. Little did I know, as I listened
> to "Nothing But Heartaches" and "Where Did Our Love
> Go," that nearly twenty years later I would hit
> bottom in an unfurnished Hollywood single, drunk
> and stoned and fed up, still spinning those same
> old tunes. The friction that already existed
> within The Supremes escalated in 1967 as Diana
> Ross made plans for her solo career. The impending
> split hit Florence the hardest. Rebelliously,
> she gained weight and missed several performances,
> and was finally told to leave the group. The pain
> she experienced in the years that followed was
> a far cry from the kind of anguish expressed
> in The Supremes' greatest hits. Florence lost
> the lawsuit she filed against Motown, failed at
> a solo career of her own, went through a bitter
> divorce, and ended up on welfare. In this classic
> photograph of the group, however, Florence is
> smiling. Against a black backdrop, she and Mary
> look up at and frame Diana, who stands in profile
> and raises her right hand, as if toward the future.
> The girls' sequined and tasseled gowns sparkle
> as they strike dramatic poses among some Grecian
> columns. Thus, The Supremes are captured forever
> like this, in an unreal, silvery light. That
> moment, they're in heaven. Then, at least for Flo,
> begins the long and painful process of letting go.   (50)

In this passage, the speaker looks beyond the glossy appearances that are obviously manipulated and idealized to an absurd degree in popular culture. Such appearances often belie stories of actual-life heartache and tragedy, because many either willfully forget or ignore the fact that (in a wholly contingent world) the "painful process of letting go" is a necessity, and not what only happens to the unfortunate.

If one views such popular culture phenomena as de-mystified and incapable of any timeless ideal, then alternative perspectives can clarify the idealized-desires/unreal-expectations that are often attached to them. For the speaker, part of the pleasure of being a collector of such popular music is discovering the actual stories behind the glamour and the glitz. In fact, this awareness makes the music inter-relate to a more profound degree with his own experiences—especially when he himself "hit bottom." The speaker productively identifies with the unfortunate circumstances that surrounded Florence's life. No amount of fame and fortune can guarantee that such an idealized stature will last. In the vein of Nietzsche's philosophy, *nothing can stay identical to itself over time.* Trinidad's rock 'n' roll poem deserves to be noted alongside the many famous ones written by the likes of Paul Muldoon, Catie Rosemurgy, David McGimpsey, Kevin Stein, and David Wojahn.

To sum up what can be gained from taking a critical look at Trinidad's career-spanning media poetry, I want to re-emphasize his tendency to de-mystify the idealized and glamorized appearances of popular media without morally condemning popular arts as social contagions (which many cultural critics continue to do). *How media are used* must be critiqued without absolutely condemning all mass media forms and the possibilities they create—*the baby, so to speak, must not be thrown out with the bath water.* There is much to be gained from Trinidad's approach, especially the playfully-productive, critical re-mediations of popular media phenomena. Trinidad's poetry is also honest and accepting of the roles such mass media phenomena have in shaping peoples' identities and desires. Hopefully, more poets will follow his lead and keep forging poetries that stay in vital touch with other popular-media phenomena. Luckily, other recent poets have overtly explored the intersections between poetry and new media; they include but are not limited to: Jerome Sala, Stacy Doris, Ted Berrigan, Anne Carson, John Kinsella, Bob Kaufman, Mark Doty, Daniel Donaghy, Terri Witek, Brandon Downing, John Matthias, Geoffrey O'Brien, Allyssa Wolf, Debora Greger, Mary Ann Samyn, Claudia Rankine, R. Zamora Linmark, and Amy Gerstler, among others.

Reality Studios: From Text to Contexts

Flow on, river! Flow with the flood-tide, and ebb with the ebb-tide! Walt Whitman's aforementioned quote can be read anew as a rally cry for an ever-evolving, ontological understanding of poetic production. Media poetry can be seen as a hybrid heir of the Whitman tradition, which has sought a uniquely democratic function for artistic production. According to Deleuze, in his essay *Whitman*, Whitman hoped to generate multi-sensory Virtual-becomings in both language and art's relations to ontological experience. For Deleuze, Whitman's poetry created fabulations/re-productions of nature and culture that are better understood in the open terms of simulations—not fixed representations. For Whitman, poetry must have concrete political dimensions in the here-and-now. Since he was a peoples' poet who sought an anti-elitist poetry of the contingent world, which potentially includes everyone and everything, his poetry is diametrically opposed to the intellectualism of Language poetry or Structuralism, which both consciously attempt to stay mired in abstractions. Deleuze explains how Whitman's fabulations, in opposition to such abstractions, re-invent the generative forces inherent in nature and culture:

> Whitman's poetry offers as many meanings as there are relations with its various interlocutors: the masses, the reader, States, the Ocean. . . . The object of American literature is to establish relations between the most diverse aspects of the United States' geography—the Mississippi, the Rockies, the Prairies—as well as its history, struggles, loves, and evolution. Relations in ever greater numbers and of increasingly subtle quality: this is, as it were, the motor that drives both Nature and History.   (*Essays Critical & Clinical* 58-9)

It is, moreover, the job of everyone (and not solely artists) to generate the differences necessary for ever-new relations between all the elements that constitute life itself; such differences can catalyze the inertias that too often territorialize cultural productions. Contingent nature is, therefore, the model for generating the infinite potentialities inherent in human consciousness, i.e. the multi-modal possibilities of percepts, affects, and concepts:

> nature is not a form, but rather the process of establishing relations. It invents a polyphony: it is not a totality but an assembly, a 'conclave, a 'plenary session'. Nature is inseparable from   processes of companionship and conviviality, which are not preexistent givens but are elaborated between heterogeneous living beings in such a way that they create a tissue of shifting relations, in which the melody of one part intervenes as a motif in the melody of another (the bee and the flower). Relations are not internal to a Whole; rather, the Whole is derived from the external relations of a given moment, and varies with them. Relations of counterpoint must be invented everywhere, and are the very condition of evolution. (59)

For both Whitman and Deleuze, nature has no static capacity for the representation of ideal forms. Media poems are always direct outcomes of a simulationist/Whitmanesque view of nature and culture, regardless of whether it is specifically American or not. All interconnected "networks" wreak havoc on any normalized/idealized interpretation of cultural & natural phenomena.

Poetic signification also undermines the cultural ideal of information in Western culture that continually threatens to turn the relation between information and matter into one of domination. Virtual simulation subverts such hierarchies of information over matter because there never exists a strict separation between *the virtual* and *the actual* to begin with; we each, alternatively, can re-conceive all such phenomena in terms of virtual relations—not transcendent or timeless values/codifications. In media poetry, both the authorial and receiver's points of view can interact in potentially non-hierarchical ways. Words, in virtual simulation, have no literal capacity to determine what things mean in the empirical world since they always generate a virtual power that can possess "nuclear and genetic" capacities to re-create it. As Kittler states, awareness of our creative connections to the virtual is crucial for not only artists but for human innovation outright: "there is nothing finished in the brain, no real images; instead, we see only virtual, potential images waiting for a sign to be transformed into actuality" (*Gramophone, Film, Typewriter* 30). What we transform into actuality, in effect, becomes the world we inhabit. *Human consciousness, therefore, should not needlessly limit itself but extend its capabilities to all sensory/media possibilities.* Each of us can generate our own poetic critiques of the cultural myths and illusions which foster homogeneity, and which continually threaten to stymie the creative process at both personal and collective levels. *We each bear the responsibility of both processes in a mass-media culture.*

Re-conceiving both language and poetry as *virtual modes of expression* subverts the illusory notion that there is ever a safe haven/form (i.e. a transparent mediation) for identity, language, or perception in any sensory medium. Printed language, as well as any other sensory medium, simulates/re-mediates whatever it expresses. Printed poetry, then, is not dead a la Kittler's previous claim: *there is an emergent media poetry that operates in a dynamic interplay with our virtual-media environment.* Poetry slams and performance poetry, workshops, festivals, *Russell Simmons Presents Def Poetry* on HBO, poetry blogs, as well as all the poetry on the Internet, expose how poetic signification is not just a 'high', academic phenomenon. Printed language and other media must be re-conceptualized as multiplicities full of virtual potentialities that can give rise to a poetic, second nature—Deleuze's *Virtual-becoming* or *Becoming-art.*

Acknowledging the fact that we can virtually alter all perceptions/sensations is a transformative consciousness. We can then become poetic agents in both the actual and virtual worlds we inhabit. However, the magician's previously-mentioned message at Club Silencio in *Mulholland Drive*—"no hay banda"—is significant beyond Lynch's film, because artistic simulation never has transcendent capacities to codify idealized or naturalized forms (plus, a la Nietzsche's philosophy, creativity is not limited solely to the creation of art). Media poetry exposes how we must become content with the singular natures of sensory experiences. If we disown our own poetic capacities to generate singular Becomings, we'll be left with the cycles of idealization & disillusionment that can only offer death.

2.
A Hollywood of Poetry

"Sundance is weird. The movies are weird—
you actually have to think about them when you watch them."
—Britney Spears, at the Sundance Film Festival, 2003

Britney Spears' above quote at the 2003 Sundance film festival, which dismisses any *poetic* art-form requiring interpretation, *can also be read* as a desperate cry for the cultural necessity of a poetic—not a purely-real or ideal— popular cinema. Ms. Spears' statement exposes how the desire to *not think* is a major cultural temptation in contemporary American culture. Luckily there are many cinematic thinkers who have mapped out why such "thinking" is vital for social mediums like narrative cinema; a la Deleuze's philosophy, thinking can become a force of *"discovering, inventing, [and authoring] new forms of life"* (*Nietzsche & Philosophy* 101). Pier Paolo Pasolini (as discussed in Chapter 1) was one of the first multi-media thinkers to lay out a systematic theory of a Cinematic Poetry in the 60s and 70s; he hoped such a cinema could re-write/mediate the illusions inherent in idealized appearances. I would like to supplement his "Cinema of Poetry" with explorations of certain popular films that have been made predominantly after the 70s: a "Hollywood of Poetry."

Since the Sundance Film Festival is one of the premier independent film festivals in America that selects non-mainstream films, the types of movies that Ms. Spears calls "weird" would likely fit a descriptive label like a "cinema of poetry" that can "make one think." In the following, I will argue for the socio-political importance of a cinematic *media poetry*, which replaces any 'representational-realism' with crystalline descriptions that can self-consciously and productively transform mass culture. Popular film is a vital site for such poetic/disruptive re-mediations of mainstream ideologies, since it is perhaps our most influential medium of artistic expression.

Poetic utterances and images, in a Hollywood of Poetry, generate simulated perceptions (percepts & affects) that can transform the possibilities of a new-media environment. According to Deleuze, this fictive perception is "a power, not a model" (*Cinema II* 152). All such simulated Sense-events occur in singular contexts and cannot be read as copies/models of 'timeless' or abstract ideals. In a Hollywood of Poetry, singular speakers or perceivers create wholly-temporal simulations/Becomings that can continually transform the relations between one's perceptions, memories, actions, as well as the world itself. This *poetic* view of artistic production re-creates the whole notion of artistic mediums as such; the American philosopher Stanley Cavell explains how to conceptualize this process:

> one might say that the task is no longer to produce another instance of an art but a new medium within it. [. . .]. It follows that in such a predicament, media are not given *a priori*. The failure to establish a medium is a new depth, an absoluteness, of artistic failure.   (103)

Each artwork that has relevance or resonance in some vital fashion, in Cavell's paradigm, is a medium of undetermined possibilities; a "cinema of poetry," therefore, allows one to transform film's social medium through subjective perspectives. According to Pasolini:

> the use of the "free, indirect [discourse]" in the cinema of poetry [. . .] is pretextual. It serves to speak indirectly—through any narrative alibi—in the first person singular. Therefore, the language used for the interior monologues of pretextual characters is the language of a "first person" who sees the world according to an inspiration which is essentially irrational. Therefore, to express themselves they must make recourse to the most sensational expressive devices of the "language of poetry."   (185)

For Pasolini, there is no abstract or ideal 'medium' that can determine how words and images come to meaning: "the Code of Reality and the Code of Cinema (of the cinematographic 'langue', which does not exist because only films/'paroles' exist) are the same Code" (277).

David Lynch's previously-mentioned "cine-parole" *Mulholland Drive* centers its entirely-subjective narrative on one woman named, at different parts of the narrative, both Betty and Diane (played by Naomi Watts). Throughout the film, we viewers experience her singular, simulated perceptions of the *reality-studio* surrounding her as she strives to become a Hollywood actress. Betty/Diane's perceptions, therefore, are always pretextual; they generate poetic descriptions/simulations that operate within and transform the appearances of the actual world/reality-studio around her. The film's first scene (a bizarre, fantastic, and multi-dimensional image of a jitterbug contest that Betty/Diane wins by having her image superimposed over it at the end of the sequence) makes this fact glaringly obvious. However, it may take viewers a while to realize that the images and events that make up Lynch's film are never a purely 'rational' 'representation' of this woman's life; its images are all poetically or virtually distorted according to how this one woman *perceives* both herself and Hollywood. Deleuze describes the exact dynamic whereby cinematographic images become productively poetic:

> a character acts on the screen, and is assumed to see the world in a certain way. But simultaneously the camera sees him [or her], and sees his [or her] world, from another point of view which thinks, reflects and transforms the viewpoint of the character. [. . .]. We are no longer faced with subjective or objective images; we are caught in a correlation between a perception-image and a camera-consciousness which transforms it. [. . .]. In short, the perception-image finds its status, as free indirect subjective, from the moment that it reflects its content in a camera-consciousness which has become autonomous ('cinema of poetry').   (*Cinema I* 74)

In line with Pasolini and Deleuze's theories of a cinema of poetry, Lynch, as writer and director of *Mulholland Drive*, "enter[s] into a relation of simulation [. . .] with the character's [i.e. Betty/Diane's] way of seeing" (*Cinema II* 148). What we audiences then witness is a "pseudo-story, a poem, a story which simulates or rather a simulation of the story" (*Cinema II* 149).

Hence, one way to read *Mulholland Drive*'s shifting levels of dream-esque narrative is to interpret the entire film as a virtual or poetic exploration of how Betty/Diane simulates her own life or story-poem in a new-media environment (especially since she understands life itself through film). Lynch's cinematic media poetry, in the guise of Betty/Diane's perceptual consciousness specifically, explores how mass-mediated reality (which often fetishizes idealized appearances) can become destructive to a person's body and identity. Lynch, throughout *Mulholland Drive*, pulls us into Betty/Diane's perceptual processes that cannot generate enough productive conditions to re-mediate either those idealized 'appearances' or her own insecurities about herself. Betty/Diane's simulated story becomes an object lesson for the pitfalls inherent in 'the representation of ideal forms' when one desperately clings to those ideals' illusory natures.

The socio-political critique Lynch generates through this would-be-Hollywood-actress's story-poem is productive for audience members that are actively "thinking;" however, what happens to Betty/Diane (as author/simulator) is a different matter altogether, i.e., as we shall see, her fate becomes a tragic one because she can only simulate an impossibly-idealized view of it. Thus, *Mulholland Drive,* through Betty/Diane's counterexample, can be seen as a paradigmatic example of how poetic perception is a vital force in overcoming the illusions that can dominate a person's relations to other people as well as the contingent world at large.

Cruising Mulholland Dr.: Media Culture as Metaphor

Mike Clark, in his review of *Mulholland Drive,* alleges: "no movie has ever done a better job of showing how the industry chews up and spits out screening hopefuls, and on that level alone, *Drive* is an important and compassionate work." Lynch's film critically observes the violence and nihilism inherent in any mythical position of power/control over life itself. A la many of the previously mentioned media poems—Hughes' *Movies,* Medina's *The Way We Move,* Matthews' *Sympathetic,* Wojahn's *Hey Joe,* and Trinidad's *The Shower Scene in Psycho—Mulholland Drive* re-mediates the personal/cultural myths that can lead to violence. For the past five decades, Lynch's film-art has stayed hyper-self-conscious of the fact that all cultural meaning inherently relies on aesthetic phenomena—a la Nietzsche's philosophy, and, as I will show below, it attempts to overcome violent/repressive ideologies through re-mediating them in productive capacities: "culture is neither questioned nor revealed as such except when it is transposed or altered" (Blondel 167).

Deleuze also remarks on the cultural effects of aesthetic/ideological constructions: "the events which bring about the unhappiness of humanity are inseparable from the myths which render them possible" (*The Logic of Sense* 278). In an interview with Scott Macaulay of *Filmmaker* magazine, Lynch describes the road atop mythic/actual Hollywood Ca. that gave his film its title:

> [Mulholland Dr. is] a mysterious road. It's rural in many places. It's curvy, it's two lanes, it feels old. It was built long ago, and it hasn't changed too much. And at night, you ride on top of the world. In the daytime you ride on top of the world too, but it's mysterious, and there's an air of fear because it goes into remote areas. You feel the history of Hollywood in that road.

For Diane, 'riding on top of the world' brings all kinds of perils to the fore. Her desire to become a Hollywood star foregrounds a dangerously-mystified idealism that audiences often assume is essential to the cinematic medium itself.

The philosopher Stanley Cavell has elaborated at length why the Hollywood Star System continues to have such a powerful and lasting effect on audiences. For Cavell, the primary subject of film is the power of the singular and the ineffable in human experience: a common Hollywood manifestation of such phenomena is its production of "*individualities*" or types (33). Cavell notes that "what makes someone a type is not his similarity with other members of that type but his striking separateness from other people" (33). A type is unique and repeatable, similar to Hollywood genres themselves. Audiences react to such types as expressions of performative/virtual potentials: "the individuality captured on film naturally takes precedence over the social role in which that individuality gets expressed" (Cavell 34-5). According to Cavell, the Star System also provides audiences a vital emotional and sensory experience, which "establish[es] conviction in our presentness [and connectedness] to the world" (60). However, Hollywood types, when they 'naturally' imitate representational categories of idealized appearances and/or meanings, risk losing their capacities for singular expressions. Fortunately, such stars can be perceived sans any illusory, representational totalities that threaten to codify such star power. The Star System, for Cavell, must keep in vital touch with the individualities/particularities that give rise to it or it may drift into abstraction and irrelevance (a la the ideology of representation). Cavell, even though he refers to the singular as more mythic than actual, explains:

> [stars] realized the myth of singularity—that we can still be found, behind our guises of bravado and cowardice, by someone, perhaps a god, capable of defeating our self-defeats. This was always more important than their distinction by beauty. [. . .]. But then that made them even more glamorous. That they should be able to stand upon their singularity!   (35-6)

Hence, acknowledging one's own singularity is a challenging but worthy enterprise. Audiences, in a Hollywood of Poetry, can witness the dynamic enactment of singular expressive possibilities whenever they are in the presence of such 'mythic' stars who actually dare to "resolve" personal and cultural conflicts on their own terms. Whether audience members also apply such poetic potentials to their own experiences is another matter altogether; nevertheless, *Mulholland Drive* offers them the possibility of this constructive/critical perspective unlike idealized/solely-'representational' films (see below).

The media theorist Marshall McLuhan even prophesied in the 1960s that electronic media would replace a representational/'logocentric' textual literacy—our once dominant mode of information—with multi-media/poetic configurations that do not have to 'speak an absolute truth' about actual objects or events in either lineal or sequential manners:

> the movie, by sheer speeding up the mechanical, carried us from the world of sequence and connection into the world of creative configuration and structure. The message of the movie medium is that of transition from lineal connections to configurations.   (27)

The aim of both artistic and media production, for McLuhan, is "bringing about new perceptual habits" (vii). Therefore, media poetry like *Mulholland Drive* reveals that all such perceptual habits (within art and media) are configurations/Sense-events that possess no transcendent capacities. To speak of different media in the same context is to acknowledge the productive, poetic notion that "no medium has its meaning or existence alone, but only in constant interplay with other media" (McLuhan 38). Poetic or virtual configurations have relations which can continually be re-formed again and again, and which can be authored to confront our most pressing socio-political concerns. One does not have to be a Hollywood star to author such transformative powers, i.e., viewers/perceivers can accomplish such transformations of cultural/aesthetic ideologies on their own terms if they choose.

As if harkening to the cultural need for poetically-discerning viewers/perceivers, *Mulholland Drive* is in many ways a critical reformulation of Billy Wilder's *Sunset Boulevard* (1950), a film that also poetically exposes the dangerous pitfalls inherent in glamorized, idealized Hollywood fantasies. In fact, Rita in *Mulholland Drive* makes this allusion overtly obvious when she crosses Sunset Blvd. at the film's beginning and the camera pans up and pauses on one of its street signs. Betty's elderly Aunt Ruth (Maya Bond), who lets Betty stay in her apartment in the first part of the film, owns an apartment in a complex that invokes a similar old-Hollywood time period as Norma Desmond's (Gloria Swanson) mansion in *Sunset Boulevard*. Norma Desmond in Wilder's film becomes tragically trapped in an alienating, idealized fantasy similar to Betty/Diane's in *Mulholland Drive*. Betty/Diane, like Norma Desmond, is a noteworthy Hollywood example of someone who idealizes such singular, poetic potentials only in those people who appear to 'represent' an idealized recognition like Hollywood stardom. As we shall see, Betty/Diane feels she cannot live up to that potential herself, so she tragically projects that idealized/illusory power onto her love object in the film, Camilla Rhodes (also Laura Elena Harring), who then revealingly becomes the major Hollywood star of *Mulholland Drive* by film's end.

In order to continue discussing Lynch's multi-linear film, a summary of its twisting, hallucinogenic events is necessary. Betty/Diane is at least two characters in the film: she is an unhappy out-of-work actress as well as her own idealized self-image in the character of Betty—the woman who arrives in Hollywood at the beginning of *Mulholland Drive* to also become a Hollywood star. The fact that Betty is warned to "be careful" by an old couple that traveled with her to L.A. reveals how Lynch's film truly is a cautionary tale about the pitfalls inherent in resentful or unhappy idealizations. On Betty's first day in L.A. she discovers a woman hiding in her aunt's apartment's shower; this mystery woman has somehow survived both an attempt on her life by hit-men as well as a serious car accident. The two women then set out to learn the actual identity of this beautiful woman with no memories.

As Betty and this mystery woman become friends and even romantically involved for a fleeting moment, we also witness many behind-the-scenes business dealings in Hollywood. *Mulholland Drive* continually simulates how these business workings of Hollywood are distorted through the lens of how Betty/Diane re-mediates/interprets them, which exposes how the two otherwise independent narrative strains in the film's beginning are, in fact, intimately inter-related. The director Adam Kesher (Justin Theroux) of one film that is in production, *The Sylvia North Story*, has his creative input yanked from the project when two mafia-esque businessmen tell him that they are picking Camilla Rhodes for his lead actress—Adam has no choice at all in the matter.

Not surprisingly, Betty is picked by a casting agent to later try out for this particular lead actress job, but has no chance at all because those shadow conspirators have already chosen Camilla. At this point in the story, Betty/Diane's idealized fantasy to become an actual Hollywood star begins to collapse. The fact that Betty/Diane is also a lesbian who desires Camilla/Rita, an unattainable female star, further registers the fact that Betty/Diane feels her desires have been foreclosed from the repressively normalized/idealized Hollywood surrounding her. Nevertheless, Betty/Diane's lesbianism in the film is not a comment on lesbian relationships in general: Betty/Diane's world-view becomes so repressively-idealized that it can't help but wreak havoc on her romantic aspirations as well.

Since the first part of *Mulholland Drive* (Betty's story) is entirely a projected fantasy, Betty/Diane has to invent a reason for why she does not get what she wants most (Hollywood stardom), so she simulates, a la a Hollywood of Poetry, a conspiracy involving the mafioso businessmen who control casting decisions for key Hollywood parts. Adam, who is Betty/Diane's supposed big break, fails her because he must sell out to those who control the money side of Hollywood. He is a sympathetic character in Betty/Diane's story-poem at the film's beginning and her enemy by the film's end, i.e., in her nightmare world of the film's final act, Adam becomes a famous director who even gets engaged to Camilla—the "it girl" of Hollywood. Both Adam and Camilla's startling transformations into Hollywood successes at film's end expose how Betty/Diane is torturing herself with the impossibility of what she desires, i.e., she solely wants to escape herself by either *becoming Camilla or killing her out of spite*. Adam and Camilla's over-the-top success, therefore, must be understood as primarily a function of Betty/Diane's self-loathing. Their success also highlights the often over-the-top notion that many individuals like Betty/Diane have of Hollywood stardom when they dismiss or disown its constructed, i.e. mediated, nature.

In *Mulholland Drive*, only the Hollywood businessmen have the power to choose which 'Camilla' will occupy the mythic position of Hollywood stardom; there are, in fact, multiple actresses named Camilla Rhodes in the film. Nevertheless, the businessmen's key phrase, "this is the girl," which is repeated throughout the movie, exposes how talent plays little or even no role ultimately in such choices. Since Diane is the one who hires the hit man at the film's end to kill Camilla/Rita, this explains why, in the first part of the film that's wholly Betty/Diane's fantasy, Betty can magically protect Rita (her ideal love object) from the hit men who are trying to kill her. Betty can mold any identity for Rita/Camilla she wants, which is too ideal to be the 'actual' story, and which also 'magically' erases Diane's guilt for ordering the murder of her ideal love-object. However, Betty/Diane's too-perfect plan fails, since her anger at her 'ideal lover' culminates in the violent destruction of that ideal/illusion; however, her subconscious forces (i.e. several virtual characters in the film narrative) refuse to let her off the hook completely (see below). It is, nevertheless, a positive thing that Diane creates a fiction that forces her to let go of her idealized self-delusion/dream. However, her disillusionment becomes so strong in the last act of the film that she cannot author for herself any semblance of a positive self-image/identity.

Betty/Diane's fantasy attempts to 'ride on top of the world' in the first half of *Mulholland Drive* fail for two significant reasons: her fantasy is too ideal to be married to the actual world around her, and her insecurities become so strong that they take on a life of their own: they pull her into a psychotic self-immolation. The over-the-top idealism of Betty at the film's beginning is actually compensation for how Diane truly feels about herself. Betty/Diane's imagination has tragically been appropriated by Hollywood idealizations. Thus, since her 'Hollywood' world must conform to ideal representations, it becomes an all-powerful super-ego censor over her life, which tortures her because she feels that the 'actual' Hollywood would never embrace her as Betty implausibly embraces the possibility of success in the first half of *Mulholland Drive*. Lynch poetically demonstrates how the sum total of Hollywood's illusory powers becomes tragically equivalent to Diane's own insecurities about herself (i.e., Diane's 'representative' mode of looking at the world has utterly alienated her from even her own positive possibilities as the film's simulator).

The final act of *Mulholland Drive* showcases Diane's self-torment in jolting juxtapositions and, as she punishes herself for failing to garner the love of the successful star Camilla Rhodes (a.k.a. Hollywood-culture at large), everything in the first part of the film transforms horrifically for the worse. However, despite the unsettling subject matter, Lynch's film is not pessimistic or nihilistic. It is also not an absolute condemnation of Hollywood's cultural influence, since *idealized myths* are the phenomena that threaten to codify its nature as a medium of poetic Sense-events. The most striking socio-political critique of the film is that this reification of creative potential is precisely what creates the alienation and resentment many (like Betty/Diane) feel towards the world and themselves. *Mulholland Drive* is, therefore, a poetic call for empathy. We spectators are challenged to feel Betty/Diane's incapacity to exorcize the illusions that control her and to learn why *she* sees them as insurmountable.

In line with a transformative/simulated perspective on the world itself (i.e. a "cinema of poetry"), Lynch overtly foregrounds the simulated nature of *Mulholland Drive*'s narrative, which further implies that any Hollywood production (including *Mulholland Drive*) cannot represent ideal forms and meanings. The blue box and key that 'magically' appear to Rita and Betty in Club Silencio after Rebekah del Rio sings "Llorando," and that make both characters disappear from the narrative, expose how Hollywood's 'bread and butter' is often ideal representations that are 'empty promises'. The previously-mentioned lip-synching performance of *Llorando* also reveals that there are no purely real, transcendent, or ideal forms behind Hollywood appearances. They are solely Nietzschean-esque simulations, or "tape recordings," which never possess ideal capacities. Betty/Diane's story reveals how Hollywood ideals are often completely incongruent with the poetic/shifting natures of *the actual* and *the virtual*. There is no transcendent gateway to an ideal life in a contingent world. Betty/Diane's problem is that she believes one exists, and this illusion is what perhaps leads to her suicide at film's end or, if interpreted differently, to the cathartic 'death' of her own illusory self-projections a la the simulated performances at Club Silencio (see below).

In order to flesh out how Lynch poetically uses a tragic story as a productively cathartic one, we must look more closely at the productive elements of Betty/Diane's simulations. There are a host of simulated/virtual characters who attempt to aid Betty/Diane and to stop her self-destruction. She, in effect, *projects the truth about her actual place in life* onto 'disturbed' characters like the man (Patrick Fischler) who has the nightmare that implausibly comes true behind Winkie's diner and the 'eccentric' neighbor (Lee Grant) who lives in Betty's apartment complex. Both characters perceive that there is something very wrong with Betty/Diane's fantasy. Betty/Diane projects onto such marginal characters precisely because they cannot openly threaten her Hollywood story-poem. Those disturbed characters are not directly invested in a mythically-ideal system of reality-production, and can therefore more accurately perceive Betty/Diane's actual situation. Lynch uses these 'abnormal' characters to *reveal the truth* about Hollywood's often problematically-inflated system of cultural ideals that can possess a destructive, super-ego authority over a person's imaginative capacities (i.e., whenever one allows such capacities to give way to the illusions of idealized 'representations', one is in immanent danger of self-alienation or even destruction).

Betty/Diane's story-poem simulates other virtual characters that offer vital messages that can challenge such self-alienation in her narrative: key ones include the Cowboy (Monty Montgomery), the Creature Behind the Dumpster (Bonnie Aarons), and the elderly woman (Cori Glazer) who inhabits Club Silencio's balcony. The Cowboy can best be characterized as a serio-comic Hollywood-Buddha. He 'secretly' aids Betty/Diane by verbally bullying Adam into selling out and choosing Camilla for *The Sylvia North Story*; the Cowboy, in effect, prevents Betty (Diane's idealized self-representation) from working out perfectly. He also attempts to stop Diane's disillusionment and have her "wake-up" after Betty and Rita disappear from the film—he even tells her sleeping body at one point: "hey pretty girl, time to wake up"—but Diane cannot at this point. He is a comic portrayal of the lone hero/protagonist in Hollywood mythology who can transform the narrative; however, he does not possess that power absolutely because only Betty/Diane (as author or poet) can actually 'rescue' herself. His statement to Adam—"a man's attitude goes some ways, the way his life will be"—reveals to the audience that each of us, like Betty/Diane, has a *poetic say* in the story-poems of our actual and virtual lives.

The elderly woman in Club Silencio's audience also offers a key message about Hollywood's reality-production at film's end. She says one mysterious, poetic phrase that echoes the ending of Godard's *Contempt* (1963): "silencio" (however, Lynch uses this phrase to transcend the disillusionment inherent in Godard's film for a more empathetic world-view in line with a cinema of poetry/media poetry). The elderly woman's phrase is directed at *Mulholland Drive*'s audience first and foremost. Since we are all, to some degree, the cultural subjects and products of Hollywood-ideologies, only we can "silence" the power and misery inherent in Hollywood ideals that are unattainable in actual life. From the balcony, she has a productively-detached perspective on Betty/Diane's story-poem. The elderly woman, in effect, by having the final word, is an audience member who sees beyond the idealized appearances and illusions that torment Betty/Diane. This wise Crone-figure embodies the poetic potentials that can cathartically transform the misery inherent in the Betty/Diane's story-poem. By harkening back to an older woman a la the character Norma Desmond in *Sunset Boulevard*, the woman's poetic message in Club Silencio has significance beyond *Mulholland Drive* itself. We are also implicated in *the cultural problem* Lynch's film exposes whenever we buy into any idealized/normalized fantasy too much. "Silence," potentially, can become the poetic medium that allows one to re-write/re-think such misery and alienation. The elderly woman at film's end re-inscribes the production of personal and cultural meaning as a poetic and limited enterprise—not a totalized or transcendent one.

The Creature Behind the Dumpster at Winkie's also productively reveals just how 'degraded' Betty/Diane's self-image becomes as *Mulholland Drive* unfolds. The 'disturbed' character in Winkie's, who has a dream that comes true about that Creature, describes it as a "god-awful feeling." Since Diane relegates her *production of meaning* to an imaginary, fantastical place, this Creature is similar to The Man Behind the Curtain (Frank Morgan) in *The Wizard of Oz* (1939). The Wizard constructs figurative or poetic descriptions of power and authority over reality itself; *The Wizard of Oz,* like *Mulholland Drive,* ends by dispelling the 'transcendent' appearances of such simulations. The illusory Creature in *Mulholland Drive* exposes just how alienating such fantasies can become: he is the lie that exposes Hollywood illusions to be solely that. The creature is the epitome (i.e. a problematic 'representation') of both personal and Hollywood failure: our cultural ideals are often not married to the actual world at all. He performs the fact that Hollywood does not necessarily make dreams come true; often, it creates nightmares. Since that Creature is holding Betty/Diane's 'magical' blue box at the film's end, he is, in effect, a gatekeeper to Betty/Diane's *production of meaning* or *reality studio.* However, because he is so degraded, he only produces a terrifying outcome for Betty/Diane: the psychotic, miniature image of the old couple who said they would be 'looking' for Betty to show up on the silver screen at the film's beginning. However,

Betty/Diane is, in actuality, her own 'gatekeeper', and she has disowned her own "god-awful feeling" about herself.

In *Mulholland Drive*'s ending montage—for an instant—we watch blue curtains superimposed over the Creature-behind-the-dumpster that then dissolve into Club Silencio, which implies that the elderly woman who inhabits that Club has the virtual power to "silence" Betty/Diane's degraded self-image in a poetic act. The ending scene, therefore, brings up multiple ways of reading the entire film as well: if it is all a simulated dream, is the elderly woman Betty/Diane herself in a later time? Does Diane die only in the dream (since at the film's beginning the camera/Diane falls asleep into her pillow)? Is Diane actually the waitress (Missy Crider) at Winkie's whose nametag changes from Diane to Betty by the film's end? Is she also the prostitute (Rena Riffel) who aids the hit man 'on the street' and who looks strikingly similar to Betty/Diane? Does Betty/Diane have a *singular* identity at all? The film's possibilities are open-ended since they are presented as poetic/virtual Sense-events.

Hollywood ideals are problematic precisely because they threaten to erase such Sense-events, and as Betty/Diane learns to perceive them, they're often not in the business to empower people at all. In effect, Lynch's film can be seen as critiquing how people can create Hollywood itself to be an evil scapegoat that they can blame all their problems on, since Betty/Diane herself feels worthless for not being embraced by Hollywood. In *Mulholland Drive*, Betty/Diane's Hollywood has become a blatant Patriarchal conspiracy that "chews up" and "spits out" women especially. Betty's first movie audition makes this fact glaringly obvious: she has to do a sexual/romantic scene with a lecherous old actor; however, this scene ironically reveals that Betty/Diane has striking talent/poetic-power as an actress. In addition, the fact that the 'mystery woman' with amnesia chooses "Rita" as her makeshift name from a movie poster of Charles Vidor's *Gilda* (1946) is also significant: Rita Hayworth ironically performs/mocks her entrapment as a patriarchal pawn throughout that unsettling film noir.

Through viewing Hollywood as Betty/Diane sees it, we watch Hollywood's culture industry made comical and absurd in its supposed ability to 'represent' idealized forms: Lynch mocks and carnivalizes all the business decisions as absurdly arbitrary outright. A key image of Hollywood's influence over reality-production is the comically 'inflated' dwarf, Mr. Roque (Michael J. Anderson), who wears a gigantic business suit and sits in a wheelchair behind bullet-proof glass. Mr. Roque's bodily-distortions thematically imply that his 'authority' is also absurdly distorted, problematically inflated, and purposefully divorced from the actual world. Betty/Diane, unfortunately, uses her own familiarity with Hollywood's pulp narratives (the mafia conspiracies, romantic melodramas, and guns-for-hire, etc. that become *the conspiracies* of *Mulholland Drive*) to *author* her story-poem's tragic end. Therefore, Lynch's key critique of any and all

Hollywood norms is that they can dominate and effectively erase singular potentials, as Betty/Diane's lack of any positive identity attests.

   Mulholland Drive has an urgent message for audiences: we too must acknowledge the actual limits inherent in idealized personal and cultural signs. Lynch's film does similar critical work as many other Hollywood films in the past like *Sunset Boulevard* and Orson Welles' *Citizen Kane* (1941), as well as many of Hitchcock's Hollywood films. For example, according to Cavell, Hitchcock's *North by Northwest* (1959) behooves us to re-evaluate our "fetishistic, scopophilic [. . .] or narcissistic 'mode of attachment' toward experience" (quoted in Freedman & Millington 154). Cavell's assessment can serve as an accurate description of *Mulholland Drive* as well. The fatal flaw in Betty/Diane's own story-poem is that she wants her desires to have representational/ideal meanings. Such ideals, however, can only offer a death-wish, and this is made glaringly obvious in the scene when Betty and Rita prophetically discover a woman's dead body in Diane's apartment. Fortunately, *the movie we audiences see never portrays Betty/Diane's story in ideal terms.* Lynch, as writer/director, is arguing that cinematic constructions can become *poetic productions* that possess the virtual power to "silence" whatever threatens to block one's creative capacities. As the cowboy states: a *man [and woman]'s attitude goes some ways.*

   Thus, Lynch's critique of media powers can be delineated as follows: the only way to live congruently with the "slipstream of mixed reality" is to acknowledge that our primary relations to the world are based on simulation, not representation; the only way to productively overcome the illusions inherent in supposedly-ideal representations is to author simulations that are congruent with a contingent world. Popular, narrative cinema like *Mulholland Drive* can, therefore, fight such a battle for socially-productive outcomes.

Vanilla Skies & Body Portals: Here, There, & Over the Rainbow

> I was about to turn 33. I ran three magazines and a world-wide publishing house. Most days I actually fooled myself in believing it would last forever. Isn't that what being young is all about? Believing secretly that you would be the one person in the history of man who would live forever...
> —David Aames

   With the cowboy's "attitude" in mind, I want to explore (in detail) two other popular examples of Hollywood poetry in contemporary cinema in order to edify the notion that a "Hollywood of poetry" is not an uncommon phenomenon. Cameron Crowe's *Vanilla Sky* (2001) and Spike Jonze's *Being John Malkovich* (1999) both examine the phenomenal constitution of reality-production in a poetic manner similar to *Mulholland Drive*. *Vanilla Sky* is actually a remake of the Spanish director Alejandro Amenábar's *Abre Los Ojos* (1997). However, I do not want to explore the similarities and differences between these two films. Since *Vanilla Sky* supplements Amenábar's psychodrama with a larger exploration of the effects of mass-mediated reality-production on both personal and collective desires in American culture, I want to address how Crowe's film specifically becomes a poetic meditation on both the powers and dangers inherent in such simulated reality-productions.

David Aames (Tom Cruise) is the primary simulator of *Vanilla Sky*'s dream-like narrative a la Betty/Diane in *Mulholland Drive*. In fact, the film only makes sense if we interpret all of its narrative elements through the *filter* of David's own perceptual processes. Crowe's film is a Poetic-becoming a la Betty/Diane's in *Mulholland Drive*, and is, therefore, not a 'representation' of David's actual-life in a pre-determined space-time. Since the film takes place entirely from the perspective of David's own perceptual processes, the film can freely explore the virtual possibilities that can generate alternative, poetic possibilities. As we shall see, those poetic possibilities allow David to overcome the deceptions inherent in both his personal life as well as the virtual-media environment surrounding him.

David Aames is a curious product of mass-media culture in that his father was a domineering and distant media mogul who controlled a magazine-publishing empire in New York City. When his father died, David inherited the company. David is not only literally involved with mass-media production, but he believes that he is living a mythically-ideal life as presented and constructed by such popular media: he has everything from money, fame, and power to the sex appeal of a Hollywood star, which he uses solely for his own narcissistic ego-inflation. He often treats women as debased sexual-objects for gratifying his passing whims. The fact that mega-star Tom Cruise plays David is revealing of the fact that Crowe's film is a critique of the *power* that audiences/fans often equate with the glamorized personas of Hollywood stars.

In fact, David is more of a child of the mass media than 'actual' parents; as his life flashes before his eyes at the film's end, we witness how simulated media-images—especially from popular TV and film—are more meaningful to him than his actual childhood memories. His apartment is adorned with media technology, and even the image of his father on his apartment wall is a larger-than-life drawing—not an actual photograph, which implies that David never knew his father as an actual person. David has grown up in a life that resembles an idealized fantasy more than any actual life; at one point in the story he even admits to his best friend: "I'm living the dream, baby." However, we know from the outset of the film that there is something really wrong with David's dream-esque life: he has a revealing dream in which he awakes and then drives down New York City streets at 9 a.m., but there is no one else in the city but him. He gets out of his car in Times Square and runs frantically, but the only other life forms around him are the media billboards frantically flashing about. Those advertisements take on a sinister air in that they have replaced all human beings in a hyper-real simulacrum of Baudrillard-esque proportions, which have been severed from any productive connections to David's actual-life in the empirical world. This scene also foreshadows the key problems David must overcome in his life, i.e. his narcissistic and arrogant desire to be an ideal 'representation' that exists above any of the contingencies/limitations inherent in the empirical world (see below). In fact, Crowe's camerawork makes David's solipsistic 'reality' overtly obvious when it literally does a 360 degree pan around David, which implies that David's problem is that he truly believes the world itself 'revolves' around him alone.

Regardless of how charmed David's life appears on the surface, we get a clear look at how problematic things actually are when his use and abuse of women comes back to haunt him. In the first act of *Vanilla Sky,* David uses Julie Gianni (Cameron Diaz) for his own sexual gratification even though he has no desire for her as a singular person in her own right. Julie's jealousy reaches epic proportions when she watches David fall for another woman at his birthday party, to which she was not even invited; David instantly is attracted to Sophia (Penélope Cruz), who came to the party as his best friend's, Brian Shelby (Jason Lee)'s, date. After the party, Julie, who wants vindication, follows David as he walks Sophia home and waits outside her apartment to confront him. David, who leaves Sophia's apartment on "cloud nine," then attempts to sweet talk Julie out of stalking him; he gets into her car in order to talk it over, oblivious to what is about to happen. Julie's ulterior motive is to teach David an important lesson about the wrong way to treat people; she has experienced first-hand that she is effectively insignificant and meaningless in David's world; she, in effect, wants David to feel the pain and insignificance that she feels. After Julie claims that her version of happiness "is being with [David]," she runs her car 80 miles an hour over a bridge so that they can die together. However, only Julie dies; David is left with his face disfigured, and he must then confront just how non-ideal his life has become. This is perhaps an unsettling notion to ponder: such a terrible event is perhaps the only thing that can remind David of his own limitations in the actual world.

A la *Mulholland Drive*'s second act, when Betty/Diane must face the reality that her ideal dream is an utter impossibility, *Vanilla Sky*'s second act showcases David's inability to accept himself as anything other than the ideal figure he believed himself to be at the film's beginning. In fact, David's impossible desire to stay 'ideal' becomes a death wish as well when he tries to kill himself by swallowing a lethal dose of pain-killers. However, like Betty/Diane's story that perhaps ends with her suicide, David's death is not exactly an actual event in *Vanilla Sky*'s story-poem. At this point in the narrative, after David 'dies', we switch into David's lucid dream—a cryogenic simulation in which he is in charge of living any hallucinated reality that he desires; he had previously signed a contract with the company Life Extension in order to continue believing the fantasy that he was a limitless/ideal form even after his 'biological death'. This company, which combines 'high-tech' science and entertainment, assumes problematically that they have fantasmatically 'solved' the mortal, limited, and contingent nature of life. Life Extension, as David experiences it, then becomes a living nightmare precisely because his subconscious refuses to let him effortlessly possess the ideal life he still willfully demands for himself. Life Extension is also a serio-comic bit of social criticism in the sense that it is the ultimate mass-media 'promise' that ideal representations are possible if you can afford such a company's particular commodity/brand-of-wish-fulfillment. In this sense as well, *Vanilla Sky* is similar to *Mulholland Drive:* both Betty/Diane and David cannot effectively deceive themselves into having a perfect, idealized fantasy that escapes all the worldly snares of the empirical world. Both idealized fantasies utterly and completely fail because they are incongruent with a contingent/adaptable world.

Furthermore, *Vanilla Sky* exposes how David's actual, subconscious desires are ultimately more powerful than any idealized or glamorized media images/desires. David's desire to uncover his actual memories (he possesses this power as the author/simulator of *Vanilla Sky*'s narrative) is what leads him ultimately to let go of those alienating, idealized desires. However, in order to see how David's self-affirmation/overcoming comes about at film's end, we need to look more closely at how his subconscious desires poetically undermine and effectively overcome his own idealized mis-perceptions of both himself and the world around him. There are productively poetic elements of David's lucid dream, a la the virtual characters that aid Betty/Diane in *Mulholland Drive*, which possess the virtual powers to transform his self-deceptions.

In his lucid-dream state, David's guilt over treating Julie as solely a debased sexual-object has now placed him in a mental institution because he has been charged with her 'actual' murder; his mind keeps switching Sophia with Julie, which thematically implies that David's guilt won't let him forget about Julie's death. Furthermore, his subconscious won't let him have a stable relationship with a woman until he confronts his own chronic and problematic mis-treatment of women. Throughout the movie, David must confront all such self-deceptions with a psychologist, Dr. Curtis McCabe (Kurt Russell). David must even work through the fact that his ultimate love-object in his lucid dream, Sophia, is now solely a narcissistic hallucination of his own creation (a la Betty's projected love object in Rita). In fact, David's memories of Sophia prior to the lucid dream turn out to be more powerful than any ideal desire or possession that she may appear to 'represent' in his lucid dream (see below). By the end of David's story-poem, he becomes capable of seeing Sophia as a separate subject with a complete will of her own. However, in order to do that, he must first choose to see his own life as it actually exists in a contingent world.

David, therefore, must struggle to realize the alienating and nihilistic nature of his own idealized lucid-dream. After watching a commercial for Life Extension on TV, David and his psychologist visit the Life Extension corporation and watch a simulated demonstration—L.E'.s commodified "revolution of the mind"—which explains how such lucid dreams are overly-manipulated, narcissistic fantasies. Rebecca Deerborn (Tilda Swinton), a company representative, explains how such lucid dreams work:

> resurrected into a lucid-dream, you will continue in an ageless state, with a future of your own choosing. [. . .]. Your life will continue as a realistic work of art painted by you minute by minute. And you'll live it with the romantic abandon of a summer day, with a feeling of a great movie or a pop song you always loved—with no memory of how it all occurred, save for the knowledge that everything simply improved. And in any instance of discontent, you'll be visited by technical support—it's all just around the corner—the day after tomorrow. Another chapter begins seamlessly—a living dream. Life Extension's promise to you—life pt. II—a living dream.

For Ms. Deerborn, and Life Extension, a lucid dream means that "anguish, discontent, [and] even your death are no longer necessary." The comically-inflated arrogance inherent in such a company's idealistic fantasy (which is solely a poetic simulation that postures itself as the fruition of a timeless-human-wish like the desire for immortality), becomes, instead, a disaster waiting to happen. As if to hint that such solutions are truly impossible, she warns David: "the subconscious can always play tricks on you—the subconscious is a very powerful thing." David has begun to acknowledge how his 'splice' was never seamless at all, and his subconscious has been forcing him to remember his actual story, i.e. his suicide, which was supposedly wiped from his memory. In fact, David struggles against this realization for most of the film and, at one point, he even admits to his psychologist: "I don't want to remember," which thematically implies that he desires not to remember, but that he actually does remember.

However, David's simulated dream, fueled by the forces of his subconscious, which he has lost poetic control over precisely because he has been trying to repress them, are pushing him in a different direction altogether. It is at this point in the narrative that Dr. McCabe offers David an important perspective on the creative powers inherent in the subconscious: "you must remember what your heart and soul won't allow you to forget." Dr. McCabe further comments: "the subconscious is a powerful thing—you treated Julie carelessly didn't you?" This statement implies that David's feelings of guilt are too powerful to be adequately repressed or disowned; it also implies that even when David was living a charmed life at the film's beginning, he actually knew there was something wrong with how he treated women like Julie. Since David is the primary simulator of his own reality-production, he does have the power to re-write the story. However, he must first remember what precisely needs to be re-written. It is a refreshing and fascinating notion to entertain, therefore, that subconscious desires (as Crowe's film treats them) can never be wholly or completely 'trapped' or controlled by representing them in overly-idealized or simplified manners. The subconscious, as a generator of multiple possibilities for poetic Sense-events, is always-already more powerful than any abstracted or idealized system of representation.

David is seeking the 'truth' of his own story-poem that had been 'magically' wiped from his memory, which means that after acknowledging he is in a lucid dream, he can then be in a position to overcome or poetically re-write those fears and anxieties. After Deerborn's presentation, David runs screaming "Tech Support" out of her office. Robin Ventura (Noah Taylor), from L.E'.s tech support, then appears on the scene as promised. It is this moment in the film that is David's "true moment of choice." He can either re-enter the actual world a hundred and fifty years after his suicide because science can (in this story) actually re-animate his frozen body, or he can return to a new and improved lucid dream with all the glitches supposedly 'smoothed out'. What is at stake in David's symbolic choice is key: for David, if he chooses the actual world it means that his money won't last long and that Sophia will be dead—in effect, everything that was 'ideal' about his life will then be lost absolutely in a future world of fresh possibilities. If he chooses the lucid dream, he must do as Ventura instructs: "you must overcome your fears and regain control." However, as the simulator of his own story-poem, David must acknowledge that his desire for such an absolute, god-like power is what alienated him to begin with. We spectators, therefore, witness that L.E'.s lucid-dream-option is solely an alienating/nihilistic solution to David's actual problems.

David begins to realize that he cannot 'represent' himself out of his problems when he tells Ventura: "it's the little things—there's nothing bigger, is there?" This statement implies that David is now aware that he lives solely within the contingent world of simulation, and he now realizes that particularities like himself can never be copies or imitations of ideal/'big' forms that supposedly exist beyond the empirical world. 'Big things' are solely illusions like the magician's simulated message to Betty/Diane at Club Silencio in *Mulholland Drive*. David's self-realization, at this point in the film, implies that he must now let go of the idealized illusions that previously wreaked such havoc on his identity and desires.

David, confronted with the key choice of his life, can now decide to overcome the illusory natures of the idealized representations he previously bought into; in David's own story-poem, every event (especially the traumatic and difficult ones) has led him to this possible moment of self-affirmation/overcoming. After David demands an explanation from L.E., Ventura describes David's lucid dream in terms of the media productions that generated his identity as well as his desires:

>you sculpted your lucid dream out of the iconography of your youth—an album
>cover that once moved you—a movie you saw once late at night that showed
>you what a father could be like or what love could be like—This [i.e. Sophia]
>was a kind woman—an individual.

Confronted with the fact that all the key elements of his lucid dream, i.e., Sophia and his psychologist primarily, are simulations/hallucinations, he must acknowledge them as solely that if he is to have any chance at a productively-poetic self awareness. After Ventura echoes Julie's previous question—"what is happiness to you, David?—David can finally answer: "I want to live a real life—I don't want to dream anymore." He even acknowledges his actual memory: "I remember, somebody died—it was me." This is no minor moment in David's story-poem in the sense that he can now acknowledge something akin to the cowboy's message to Adam in *Mulholland Drive:* David's attitude can now "go some ways." This is the moment when David can begin to author a new story-poem for himself that is congruent with the contingent forces of the world around him—even if it is 150 years later and he will know no one, i.e., he won't have the 'ideal' life he once had.

This key moment also implies that the mass media images/productions that have constructed his life and desires are only as powerful as he re-authors or re-mediates them to be. They only become sources of alienation and discontent when one demands that they possess ideal meanings a la Betty/Diane's tragic plight in *Mulholland Drive*. *Vanilla Sky* also implies that if such media phenomena are used solely for escaping the actual world or as vehicles for desiring power over that world, they will lead only to a nightmarish self-alienation.

At this point in David's story-poem, he can even overcome his ultimate fear, i.e. his fear of heights. This fear is symbolic of how David never wanted to live an actual life with actual limitations—what he feared most was being in the same mortal boat as everyone else (his 'spliced-over' suicide earlier in the film harkens to this fact). On the top of the Life Extension building, looming high over the Manhattan sky-line of a future world, David can finally say good-bye to the idealized illusions he used to cling to obsessively. He acknowledges that Sophia is now an impossible desire when he tells her simulated-self: "I'm frozen and you're dead." He even acknowledges that his actual-life desire for her the night they met at his birthday party is more significant than any ideal desire he projects onto her; to edify this realization, he then echoes what she had previously told him: "every passing minute is another chance to turn it all around." He even says goodbye to Sophia with these serio-comic words: "I'll see you in another life when we're both cats." David acknowledges that it is useless to put one's hope in another, transcendent/ideal reality that can promise impossible solutions to actual-world conflicts and anxieties. David's serio-comic desire to be 're-incarnated' shows that his hope or faith no longer rests on a fantasized or ideal form he must represent. Rather, it now rests on the productive possibilities the actual world around him can generate, which have no absolute/ideal/timeless capacities. David's future, in effect, is no longer solely up to him, which means that he has become a life-affirming agent in the contingent world.

David is now willing to put his hopes and desires into an actual context that he does not have an idealized ability to overly-control. Ventura phrases this realization in the following manner: "even in the future, the sweet is never as sweet without the sour." And David does choose to come back down to the actual world when he jumps off the building in his lucid dream. This gesture symbolically implies that when he awakens from his crionized state (or the dream that both begins and ends the film's narrative), he will be able to be a productive agent capable of *action* in the world around him. The film itself ends with that self-awakening and affirmation: we watch David's eye open for perhaps the first time ever to a new, *poetic* relation to the forces of the actual world around him.

Vanilla Sky's cautionary-tale about the powers inherent in media simulations deserves further comment in that the entire film can be read like *Mulholland Drive* as acknowledging the actual limitations inherent in all such reality-productions. David learns what perhaps Betty/Diane could not realize about herself, i.e., such media productions possess a poetic (not an ideal) power that is absolutely dependent on how the viewer/perceiver re-creates or re-mediates such media-perceptions. Nevertheless, such virtual powers can and do transform one's relation to the actual world a la David's choice to re-enter the contingent world at the film's end.

In this sense, both *Vanilla Sky* and *Mulholland Drive* expose that the desire to be imitations or copies of ideal forms is an alienating desire outright, one that needlessly limits or immobilizes one's creative/interpretive powers. No one, these films imply, has such a power in a purely-unmediated capacity. *All reality is mediated reality*, which further implies that we must interpret all our perceptions of the actual world primarily for ourselves and our own Becomings. Both David and Betty/Diane serve as wake-up calls to the dangerous and alienating illusions inherent in media 'representations' that seek to disown actual-world contexts or stagings. Poetic or virtual simulations can become, a la Wittgenstein's philosophy, *the therapies-of-illusion* that we need in order to productively acknowledge the actual limitations inherent in the contingent world around us.

'Fame': the Pitfalls of Voyeurism & Vicarious Living in Being John Malkovich

In *Being John Malkovich,* Craig Schwartz (John Cusack) must confront many of the same illusions/self-deceptions that tormented both Betty/Diane and David Aames. Craig also suffers from a pathological narcissism, i.e., he wants his creative powers to have ideal capacities to control the world around him. In this sense, he is even more willful than Betty/Diane (who destroys herself in the face of her impossible desires), and David Aames—Craig (unlike David) ultimately refuses to give up the fantasy that he can possess such absolute, god-like power. Craig, aware of the impossible nature of his ideal-wish, still attempts throughout the film to violently control the people around him so that they will be puppets of his whims, regardless of the effects on either himself or anyone else.

Although Craig is the main protagonist in *Being John Malkovich*, he is not the sole simulator of the film's narrative a la Betty/Diane or David Aames. The primary generators of *Being John Malkovich*'s reality-production are the film's writer Charlie Kaufman and its director Spike Jonze; they simulate the story from multiple subject-positions (even a chimp's at one point and John Malkovich's subconscious at another). Kaufman & Jonze explore a more objective perspective on their film's reality-production than either *Mulholland Drive* or *Vanilla Sky*, which both present their narratives from more subjective positions, i.e., they can be better understood as *persona* story-poems. In effect, the main persona in Jonze's film is John Malkovich's, which is the ironically idealized one that many of the characters aim for but fail to attain. Nevertheless, many of the main characters in *Being John Malkovich* must go through the vicarious experience of 'being John Malkovich' like Craig does, and the poetic commentary of the movie arises from the fact that the characters in the film all learn very different lessons from such fantastic and absurd experiences (see below). As I will show in what follows, each of the main characters winds up either better or worse as individuals due to these simulated, vicarious experiences. It is crucial here to articulate exactly what is at stake both philosophically as well as aesthetically in such fantastical media-simulations.

Being John Malkovich is first and foremost a brutal satire of the idealizations that are common in mass-media culture; the film mocks/undercuts the often ludicrous expectations that constitute idealized recognitions like Hollywood fame and stardom. It also mocks the power people can project onto such 'representations' through idealizing their poetic/figurative power in an impossible representation, i.e. John Malkovich's body portal, which allows a person to take a 15-minute fantastic-trip whereby they can experience Malkovich's life from his exact perspective. This desire for idealized, vicarious experience is a common theme in mass media today because famous people are often hounded by reporters and fans who solely want to covet their lives as if some ideal-secret were waiting there to be exposed. This child-like, vicarious tendency also implies many people in mass-media culture resent who they are and would rather hijack the 'power' that stars possess than explore their own creative potentials.

In addition, audiences' covetous/voyeuristic desires for idealized forms can be seen as socially destructive. Such desires can easily yield to the desire for vengeance against life itself because it appears to only 'privilege' a select few with an 'idealized' legitimacy. Betty/Diane's hiring of a hit man to kill Camilla in *Mulholland Drive* exposes a similar violence inherent in such vicarious desires. Craig, like Betty/Diane, desires an idealized, vicarious experience but, when he doesn't get his way, he desires to get revenge on everything and everyone.

At the beginning of *Being John Malkovich*, Craig is steeped in resentment against the world around him. What he desires most is to be seen and praised by others as a brilliant puppeteer; in this film, Craig's obsession with his puppet-fantasy-world implies that he is not seeking artistic creativity at all, but a dominating *control* over the world and its 'objects'. The film's self-conscious, postmodern aesthetic even mocks Craig through his puppeteer-foil, Derek Mantini (Ned Bellamy), who is shown early in the film doing an absurd, televised puppet show, "The Belle of Amherst," with a 60-foot Emily Dickinson doll. In the face of Mantini's success, all Craig can do is groan: "gimmicky bastard." Since Emily Dickinson was a reclusive poet, Mantini's portrait of her is completely at odds with her historical life. Craig, however, takes such media recognition absolutely seriously, and revealingly tells his wife's chimp:

> you don't know how lucky you are being a monkey, because consciousness is a terrible curse. I think, I feel, I suffer, and all I ask in return is the opportunity to do my work. But they won't allow it, because I raise issues.

Craig has erroneously constructed other people as his obstacles to a god-like power, i.e., he is obviously the one who is deceiving himself with his own misunderstanding of the nature of power (see below).

Craig's asbsurdly self-righteous attitude takes on an even more comical air when we witness his street-side rendition of the 12th century love-story of *Héloïse & Abélard*: his performance only gets him punched by a little girl's father after she watches the puppets engage in sexual-pining for each other. Nonetheless, the actual story of Héloïse and Abélard offers a poetic insight into Craig's idealized/narcissistic world-view: since Abélard was castrated for his erotic desire for Héloïse, this fact implies that Craig's impossible demand for recognition as a brilliant puppeteer has actually rendered him impotent and 'castrated' in his responses to the world around him. His world-view is the diametric opposite of Abélard's, who, even though he was literally castrated, still loved and wrote letters to Héloïse regardless. Since Craig feels the world has punished him by not offering him the ideal recognition he desires, he solely wants power over that world in order to spite it. The film implies here that Craig's narcissism/lust-for-an-impossible-fame leaves him truly powerless to act productively or to love another person in a wholly-contingent world. In addition, the issue of unconditional love that Craig raises with his puppets can be seen as ironic since he doesn't want humility of any sort: he reveals himself to be a total hypocrite when we take a look at his marriage with Lotte (Cameron Diaz), since he does not have anything close to an unconditional love for his wife.

Craig constantly dismisses and ignores Lotte because his desire for fame is wholly self-centered and all-consuming. Lotte is therefore forced to sublimate the love she desires from Craig into her love for her pets. Their apartment resembles a zoo more than a happy home. Craig also does not want children with Lotte, and he uses their monetary troubles as an excuse to ignore and dismiss her most cherished desire. Even after Craig gets a job as a filer at Lestercorp., he still does not want children with Lotte. Instead, he becomes instantly attracted to a woman co-worker there, Maxine (Catherine Keener), because she 'represents' a more attractive image to the insecure and 'impotent' Craig (plus, she has power over him—a revealing insight into Craig's problematic world-view). He even claims that he has never felt the way he feels about Maxine for anyone else ever, which overtly reveals that his Héloïse & Abélard puppet show about unconditional love was an elitist sham he used in order to feel superior to the people around him.

Being John Malkovich takes an even more radical and absurd turn when Craig discovers a hidden 'body portal' into John Malkovich's mind and body behind a filing cabinet where he works at Lestercorp. The body portal, in *Being John Malkovich*, is *the* impossible or ideal 'gateway' that can satisfy people's desire for vicarious-experience/escapism-through-privileged-identities like Hollywood stars. It 'implausibly' offers Craig the impossible power he has been seeking. The poetic play of the movie here implies that Craig should be careful what he wishes for, since that impossible power he desires can only lead to further alienation from, and resentment against, the contingent forces of the actual world. The 'morality tale' of the portal also reveals many peoples' desires to escape themselves and their own unhappiness through fantasizing that ideal or transcendent 'gateways' actually exist in idealized forms (i.e. in the cultural-ideal of fame). The joke in the movie, however, is that the trip only lasts for 15 minutes, which harkens to the notion that everyone only gets '15 minutes of fame', and which further implies that fame and stardom (two of our key cultural ideals) are always temporal and fleeting.

Being John Malkovich also portrays the corporate America of everyday business machinations as propagating the illusory notion that 'transcendent-ideals' are attainable in everyday life. Lestercorps is on the 7 ½ floor of the Mertin-Flimmer building in Manhattan. Its workers are asked by the company to buy into the notion that their inconvenience is necessary for the company's well-being. In effect, they are truly subordinated to the company's bottom-line that is 'everything' in their pursuit of the 'ideal' and 'almighty' dollar. The poetic commentary here is that such businesses can justify any and all of their arbitrary and ludicrous limitations they impose on their own workers: the company has cut its own overhead by locating its offices on the 7 ½ floor, a business decision they justify through a ridiculously mythic-story that Craig watches on the company's orientation video-tape. Supposedly an Irish ship-captain had fallen in love with a dwarf and, since he owned the building, he wanted to make a structural accommodation to the building as a gift to her; he built a miniature floor between the 7th and the 8th that was more to her comfort. In effect, all Lestercorp. workers are asked to be continually humiliated by working in such uncomfortable conditions that are rationalized through the guise of a hokey, P.C. story that allows the company to make even more money. The joke here is that since most people are so afraid of not having money and the cultural legitimacy that goes along with it, they will put up with anything at all; they can often be manipulated and deceived like helpless puppets. The business world of *Being John Malkovich* is shown to be just as absurd and ludicrously arbitrary as the Hollywood-business-world of *Mulholland Drive*.

Being John Malkovich exposes the ludicrous nature of a cultural myth like an impossibly-transcendent fame by ironically actualizing it. Malkovich's body portal allows Kaufman and Jonze to explore other, brutal social satires as well. Since Craig has found a potentially 'magical' solution to his own resentment and misery, he only wants to use the portal for his own selfish interests; at one point he even tells Maxine that the portal is "a metaphysical can of worms;" however, he quickly dismisses any of those implications. Craig, in turn, begins to wonder how the portal could be used to control the people around him. Craig first tries to impress Maxine with the portal but, since she is coldly practical and worldly in all respects, she only wants Craig to help her make money off it: Maxine and Craig quickly commodify the Malkovich portal; they create J.M. Inc., which offers 15-minute, vicarious rides to anyone who has $200 after closing time at Lestercorp. Sadly, the portal and how it might profoundly affect people quickly yields to Craig's childish desire to control and manipulate the world around him. Craig tragically continues to trick himself into believing that he can possess the portal's impossible, anti-contingent-life power.

However, not every character sees the portal in the egotistical manner that Craig does. His wife Lotte actually feels transformed after her 15-minute ride. Lotte experiences empowerment from becoming a man for a moment. In fact, she feels that the portal has offered her an insight into an aspect of her personality that she has been repressing. She goes to an extreme, however, and tells Craig that she now wants to become a man. She's even willing to go through sexual reassignment surgery. Craig, in a moment of clarity, warns her: "you shouldn't be so quick to assume that switching bodies is gonna be the answer to your problems." This statement implies that Craig actually does understand that the portal is not a solution to anyone's problems but, because he is so self-centered, he still believes that he can control it for himself alone. In fact, the sexual implications that the portal raises are rather fascinating to explore critically.

Lotte discovers the vicarious sexual thrill of being in the portal when he is actually having sex with Maxine who, at one point previously in the narrative, fearlessly looked up John Malkovich and asked him on a date. However, the joke in operation here is that, for Maxine, it's only a thrill to have sex with Malkovich when Lotte is also there in his body portal. Maxine explains the power she feels to Craig: "do you have any idea what it's like to have two people look at you with total lust and devotion through the same pair of eyes?" Kaufman & Jonze's film is ironically commenting on how some people only take sexual pleasure from using someone or from being in a position of power over another person. Sexuality, in effect, becomes tragically and problematically conditional upon domination or manipulation. It perhaps goes without saying that the real victim throughout the film is John Malkovich himself, since his own subjectivity gets utterly robbed from him (via the megalomaniac protagonists that are metaphors for the fans of celebrity culture). Most of Malkovich's 'fans' solely see him as the vessel for their own narcissistic thrills/ego-trips. Thus, the idealized 'representations' in the film can also be seen as analogous to many viewers' desires to strip away actors' subjectivities on screen and 'project themselves' into the film in question. No one in the film cares much for Malkovich as an actual person, which renders him completely dehumanized; plus, it also reveals that the power fans often project onto such stars is actually nihilistic and anti-contingent-life.

However, Malkovich himself catches on to the fact that he is being used against his will for others' selfish desires, and he attempts to put a stop to it by visiting his own portal. When he does this, we witness the portal's nihilistic and destructive nature clearly. Malkovich sees the portal as a nightmarish, solipsistic hell in which all difference has been replaced by carbon-copies of himself. He is, like in David's dream at the beginning of *Vanilla Sky*, the only human being 'left' on earth. When Malkovich comes out of the portal, he tells Craig: "I've been to the dark side, I've seen a world that no man should see." The film's poetic image of the dark side of humanity is a narcissistic or idealized fantasy that one can become the center of the world itself. Therefore, we viewers witness the poetic fact that if the portal's power were actually 'real', it *would* create hell on earth. Malkovich phrases that realization as follows: "that portal is mine and must be sealed forever for the love of God."

Moreover, a key joke operating in the movie is that John Malkovich's 'actual-life' is presented as dull, drab, and barren; we see him perform such mundane chores as eating dry toast and ordering periwinkle hand-towels. It is ludicrous outright for anyone who takes the Malkovich trip to idealize his 'actual' life as possessing a magical or fantastical significance; in fact, most characters can't even remember what movies he starred in. Sadly, Craig refuses to heed Malkovich's advice: Craig feels that he must now attempt to step up his initiative and use his puppeteering skills to take over Malkovich's actual-life once and for all; this vicarious desire exposes how Craig's 'true nature' is comprised of a curious mix of megalomania and self-disgust.

Despite Craig's desire to erase Malkovich's subjectivity outright, other characters such as Maxine and Lotte attempt to solve their alienation through acknowledging their feelings for each other as well as their desires to have actual-world lives; those actual desires become more significant and meaningful than the 'impossibly-ideal' portal and its illusory 'promises'. However, Maxine must first overcome her desire for power and control that aligns her with Craig for much of the film's second act. Craig is more than willing to do whatever it takes to possess Maxine; Craig even locks Lotte in a monkey cage so she cannot interfere (this ironically gives Lotte the chance to live like the animals she loves, which then allows her a new self-awareness that can cathartically break free from her old, meek self). Craig, unfortunately, can now use his puppeteering skills to completely take over Malkovich's mind and body, which means that he has learned how to stay in the portal for as long as he wants (he, in effect, puppets the portal, thereby hijacking the film itself). Maxine even rejects Lotte when she realizes Craig's ability; she openly rationalizes her choice to Lotte: "Craig can control Malkovich and I can control Craig."

However, Lotte, who feels just as rejected as Julie Gianni in *Vanilla Sky*, chooses to get some answers to her problems. Earlier in the film, she had found a shrine to Malkovich in Dr. Lester (Orson Bean)'s house, so she decides to ask Dr. Lester about it. Dr. Lester then shockingly reveals that he is not Dr. Lester at all but captain Mertin who, 90 years earlier, discovered a portal to vessel bodies in the Mertin-Flimmer building. He discovered that he could leap from vessel body to vessel body, thereby escaping mortality. Dr. Lester was the previous vessel, and Malkovich will become ripe for Capt. Mertin's next transmogrification on his 44th birthday. It is here that Kaufman & Jonze's film takes a mocking jab at other Hollywood narrative ploys: Dr. Lester takes out a book that neatly explains this impossible scenario. The book's implausible, authorial power presents itself as a rational explanation of the impossible events in the film. *Being John Malkovich* thereby undercuts such an impossibly absolute or ideal authority by foregrounding its utterly arbitrary subject matter.

In addition, Dr. Lester warns Lotte that one must enter Malkovich's portal by midnight on his 44th birthday or s/he will be diverted into the subconscious of the next infant vessel (Maxine's yet-to-be-born child), thereby becoming trapped there "forever doomed to see the world through another person's eyes." It is perhaps obvious that Kaufman & Jonze's film is offering a further cautionary-tale here, i.e., if one is not careful about such power, one may have to suffer a powerlessness a la viewers like Craig who buy into impossibly-ideal/cinematic illusions. Lester/Mertin's explanation to Lotte is equally as absurd as L.E'.s assumption that they have found the way to immortality, and is equally as problematic. *Being John Malkovich* hints here that if one desires such a power over another human being, one will create only alienation and self-torment precisely because that power is actually impossible in a wholly-contingent world.

Since Craig uses Malkovich's fame in order to become a puppeteer that is also a media star, Malkovich must give up his acting career. The film here takes another brutal jab at the entertainment industry and mass-media idealizations in general. Since Craig uses Malkovich to "further his puppeteering career," we watch fans and other celebrities like Sean Penn admit that they want to do the same thing. This imitative tendency in popular culture is laughable here, in the sense that if something gets arbitrarily imbued with an idealized power, many people will fawn over it regardless of what it actually is. The film even runs an *Entertainment Tonight-esque* summary of Malkovich's transformation from an actor to a puppeteer. Craig's previously-mentioned pretentiousness takes center screen here in that Craig (as Malkovich) rattles off many pompous and arrogant claims about the idealized power he possesses in his own art. This ridiculously-inflated elitism reaches "gimmicky" proportions when Craig/Malkovich performs Swan Lake for Manhattan's 'upper-crust' entirely with a male puppet as one of the leads.

However, a problem arises in Craig's newfound/hijacked 'ideal' life of fame and stardom when Lester/Merton kidnaps Maxine and threatens to kill her if Craig won't leave the Malkovich portal. It is here that the love triangle between Craig, Lotte, and Maxine takes center stage again. Lotte even takes Craig's gun and tries to kill Maxine for her mistreatment of her; Lotte chases Maxine into the portal and into Malkovich's subconscious. However, they get knocked out when their 15 minutes are up; surprisingly, Craig also chooses to also leave the portal in order to save Maxine. Maxine, who had become quiet and withdrawn after her pregnancy and marriage to Craig/Malkovich, then reveals to Lotte: "I kept the baby because I knew you were the father, the other-mother, whatever." Since Lotte was in Malkovich when Maxine conceived her baby, Maxine chose to keep the baby because she really did have romantic feelings for Lotte. Therefore, now confronted by a newly-empowered Lotte, Maxine can finally admit that her previous desire to solely manipulate/control other people was alienating and bogus. Maxine re-creates or re-authors her actual desire for Lotte, which has now become more important to her than any ideal. The couple chooses, in fact, to reconcile, deciding to stay together and raise their child as a family unit in the actual, contingent world. Maxine and Lotte, therefore, are the thematic answers to the self-despising world-view (i.e. the desire for an impossibly-transcendent fame) that Craig embodies in the film.

Unfortunately, Craig has no such self-realization; when he exits the portal to impress Maxine, he sees that Lotte and Maxine are together as a couple. Unfortunately, all he can do is think about going back into the portal to make Maxine "love" him again. This reveals that Craig has learned nothing at all in the film because he still desires a willful/violent control over others. However, poetic justice catches up to him when he enters the portal after midnight, thereby being diverted into the next vessel, Maxine and Lotte's child, Emily (Kelly Teacher). Craig will therefore be stuck in her subconscious forever a la Lester/Mertin's prior warning. Lester/Mertin, who is now in control of Malkovich, also refuses to give up his impossible quest for immortality; he does not care at all that he has robbed another person's life for his own selfish reasons. In addition, he will voyeuristically stalk Emily till she is ripe for his next transmogrification. Lotte and Maxine are the only characters who author for themselves actual chances at happiness in the contingent world. The cautionary-tale/allegory of Kaufman & Jonze's story-poem can therefore be delineated as follows: *if one desires an impossible control over other people, one may get stuck in an alienating and impossibly-ideal simulacrum like Craig, who has been forever imprisoned by his own desire to imprison others.*

Just like *Mulholland Drive* and *Vanilla Sky*, *Being John Malkovich* is a poetic call to acknowledge the actual limitations that are inherent in a contingent world. It is no accident that all three of these films expose the dangerous illusions of timeless, ideal forms that are problematically operating within and informing much of mass culture. These films, therefore, *attempt to re-write idealized illusions through poetically re-interpreting them to be congruent with the forces of the actual world.* All three films are vital examples of media poetry, which possesses a figurative power that can re-write or re-mediate any deception/illusion that promises to 'solve' contingent life itself. Hopefully, many more filmmakers will also fearlessly attack and re-write idealized, cultural myths—like an impossibly-transcendent fame—which generate the resentment and alienation that plague many peoples' lives in our current, mass-mediated culture.

Other Films that Make You Think

> There's no such thing as realism in film or there's no such thing as truth. I'm only concerned with the poetry of realism, a supposed realism, and that's what *Gummo* is. That's why it's confusing to certain people. That it has this element. That it's organic. That everything seems like it's really happening but at the same time I'm tricking and I'm manipulating everything. It's made up. I'm genre-fucking...
> —Harmony Korine (*Interview* by Steve Ramos)

If we take a look at other classical and contemporary films, many filmmakers and film viewers have, in fact, embraced *a new birth of the poetic* in narrative cinema. If cinematic poetry primarily re-mediates/writes any transparent/naturalized representational-realism, there are a host of other films that do similar poetic-work as the films explored above. Many Hollywood and foreign films (regardless of their particular genres) highlight the fact that all reality-productions are dependent on simulation, not representation; they include but are not limited to: *Requiem for a Dream* (2000), *The Manchurian Candidate* (2004), *Bamboozled* (2000), *Dracula: Pages from a Virgin's Diary* (2002), *The Scent of Green Papaya* (1993), *What Is It?* (2005), *Heathers* (1988), *Bad Education* (2004), *Memento* (1999), *eXistenZ* (1999), *The Shape of Things* (2003), *Vertigo* (1958), *Throne of Blood* (1957), *Valley of the Dolls* (1967), *Bladerunner* (1982), *The Tesseract* (2003), *Pi* (1998), *American Psycho* (1999), *A Clockwork Orange* (1972), *American History X* (1998), *Bowling for Columbine* (2002), *Natural Born Killers* (1994), *My Own Private Idaho* (1991), *Starship Troopers* (1997), *Chungking Express* (1994), *Dark City* (1997), *Naked Lunch* (1991), *Lost Highway* (1997), *Brazil* (1985), *The Pillow Book* (1996), *Edward Scissorhands* (1990), *The Eye* (2002), *Ed TV* (1999), *The Eternal* (1999), *Pleasantville* (1998), *Citizen Kane* (1941), *Julien Donkey Boy* (1999), *Eternal Sunshine of the Spotless Mind* (2004), *Videodrome* (1983), *Eraserhead* (1977), *Hero* (2002), *Total Recall* (1990), *The Shining* (1980), *Sunset Boulevard* (1950), *The Truman Show* (1998), *Delicatessen* (1992), *Do the Right Thing* (1989), *The Butterfly Effect* (2003), *Session 9* (2001), *Leolo* (1992), *The Lady from Shanghai* (1947), *The Others* (2001), *Far From Heaven* (2002), *Salò* (1976), *Sex, Lies & Videotape* (1989), *Bolivar Soy Yo* (2002), *The Devil's Backbone* (2001), *Beetlejuice* (1988), *Harry Potter & the Sorcerer's Stone* (2001), *Titus* (1999), *The Sixth Sense* (1999), *Blue Velvet* (1986), *Halloween* (1978), *The Double Life of Veronique* (1991), *The Hunger* (1983), *X-Men* (2000), *Big Fish* (2003), *Willard* (2002), *Harry Potter & the Chamber of Secrets* (2002), *Heavenly Creatures* (1994), *Gattaca* (1997), *The Million Dollar Hotel* (2000), *Twin Falls, Idaho* (1999), *Cecil B. Demented* (2000), *Talk to Her* (2002), *Harry Potter & the Prisoner of Azkaban* (2004), *Hamlet* (2000), *Twister* (1989), *Twin Peaks: Fire Walk with Me* (1992), *Northfork* (2003), *The Bride with White Hair* (1993), *Star Maps* (1997), *28 Days Later* (2003), *Se7en* (1995), *Baraka* (1993), *The Crow* (1993), *Wings of Desire* (1988), *Johnny Suede* (1992), *Apocalypse Now* (1979), *Gift* (1992), *The Fifth Element* (1997), *The Seventh Seal* (1956), *12 Monkeys* (1995), *Gummo* (1997), *Kill Bill Vol.1* (2003), *Suture* (1993), *Strange Days* (1995), *The Village* (2004), *The Boondock Saints* (1999), *Virtuosity* (1994) *Tales from the Gimli Hospital* (1988), *La Femme Nikita* (1991), *Get Shorty* (1995), *The City of Lost Children* (1995), *Nadja* (1995), *The Player* (1991), *Kill Bill Vol.2* (2004), *Abre Los Ojos* (1997), *Medea* (1969), *The Princess & the Warrior* (2000), *The Professional* (1994), *Land of the Dead* (2005), *Tank Girl* (1994), *Deconstructing Harry* (1997), *Donnie Darko* (2001), *Swimming Pool* (2003), *Best Laid Plans* (1999), *The Butcher Boy* (1997), *The Matrix* (1999), *Fight Club* (1999), *Scarlet Diva* (2000), *The Cell* (2000), *Ken*

Park (2002), *What Dreams May Come* (1998), *What the Bleep Do We Know?* (2004), *Adaptation* (2002), *Demonlover* (2003), *Napoleon Dynamite* (2004), *Side Streets* (1998), *Ghost Dog* (2000), *X-Men 2* (2003), *Audition* (2000), *Teorema* (1968), *The Machinist* (2004), *American Beauty* (1999), *The Saddest Music in the World* (2004), *Hustle & Flow* (2005), *Serenity* (2005), *Fresh* (1994), *V for Vendetta* (2006), *Mysterious Skin* (2004), *I ♥ Huckabees* (2004), *21 Grams* (2003), *High Tension* (2005), *Toolbox Murders* (2004), *Ma Vie En Rose* (1997), *The Skeleton Key* (2005), *Rushmore* (1998), *Week End* (1967), *I Want You* (1998), *The Discreet Charm of the Bourgeoisie* (1972), *Palindromes* (2005), *Happy Here and Now* (2002), *Garden State* (2004), *True Stories* (1986), *Finding Neverland* (2004), *When Night is Falling* (1995), *The Real Blonde* (1997), *She's So Lovely* (1997), *The End of Violence* (1997), *The Last Temptation of Christ* (1998), *Wag the Dog* (1997), *Human Nature* (2001), *Gods & Monsters* (1998), *Trust* (1990), *Man Bites Dog* (1992), *The House of Yes* (1997), *A life Less Ordinary* (1997), *Brick* (2005), *Nurse Betty* (2000), *Broken Flowers* (2005), *Notre Musique* (2004), etc., etc.

These films' individual-merits, i.e. their productive re-mediations of the forces/Sense-events that give rise to our *reality-productions,* must be explored on a case by case scenario; to explore each of the above films in detail would take too long to do effectively here. It is currently, nevertheless, an exciting moment for narrative cinema because the poetic re-formulation of the cinematic medium itself is a potentially popular phenomenon as well, which reveals that the films that make us think are not necessarily doomed to the outskirts of culture. *Each of our attitudes can truly go some ways...*

3.
Bourgeois Myth Versus Media Poetry in Prime-time: Re-visiting Mark Frost and David Lynch's Twin Peaks

From the light in my window he can see into me
But I cannot see him until he is close
Breathing, with a smile at my window
He comes to take me
Turn me round and round
Come out and play   Come play
Lie still   Lie still   Lie still.

Little rhymes and little songs
Pieces of the forest in my hair and clothes
Sometimes I see him near me
When I know he can't be there
Sometimes I feel him near me
and I know it is something just to bear.

When I call out
No one can hear me
When I whisper, he thinks the message
Is for him only.
My little voice inside my throat
I always think there must be something
That I've done
Or something I can do
But no one no one comes to help,
He says,
A little girl like you.
                    (*The Secret Diary of Laura Palmer* 12)

The above poem, written by Jennifer Lynch in the persona of 12-year-old Laura Palmer (Sheryl Lee), foreshadows Laura's murder when she's 17; this unsettling murder also introduces prime-time audiences to not just Laura's tormented life and memory, but what her death reveals about the social milieu of Twin Peaks, Washington. It is perhaps obvious that what the young Laura is attempting to communicate in her poem is the 'private' and traumatic experience of sexual abuse. While such an unsettling subtext to a TV show is not often found in prime-time serials, *Twin Peaks* daringly brought this 'private' phenomenon into plain view during its second season. *Twin Peaks,* created by Mark Frost *(Hill Street Blues)* and film director David Lynch (*Eraserhead, Blue Velvet, Mulholland Drive)*, became a cult phenomenon on network television during its 29 episode run between 1990 and 1991. Nominated for 14 Emmys in 1990 and named the year's best show by The Television Critics Association, *Twin Peaks'* 3rd episode even got a "5.1. on the Nielsen and a 10 share" (Lavery 2).

Lynch/Frost's series has commonly been described as a nighttime soap opera/murder mystery, which combines a postmodern pastiche of the soap opera genre with a disturbing exploration of the phenomena of family violence and father-daughter incest. It has no doubt attracted much critical attention because of its unorthodox nature for prime-time. Critical responses to it are also intriguing not only because of the wide-ranging and contradictory reactions, but because many have expressed confusion or even an inability to flesh out an organizing social and political agenda in the series; for example, Jonathan Rosenbaum comments: "Lynch[1] has never shown the slightest inclination toward social commentary" (25). I will argue in what follows that the show's social and political readings to date are plagued by confusion precisely because no one has yet effectively mapped out *Twin Peaks'* critical attitude toward the social myths that give rise to American, middle-class social order as it's commonly portrayed in mass media.

To flesh out exactly what Frost and Lynch accomplish with *Twin Peaks'* critical perspectives on American social order, I want to draw a distinction between media poetry, which is the virtual generation of Sense-events/Becomings (the main theory of which is mapped out in chapter 1), and Roland Barthes' theory of bourgeois myth. Lynch and Frost's series will be examined here as a radical critique of what Barthes, in *Myth Today,* refers to as bourgeois myth, which can be defined as "a mode of signification, a form" (93) that "leaves its contingency behind" (103). Such myth is the essentialist tool of bourgeois ideology:

> bourgeois norms are experienced as the evident laws of a natural order—the further the bourgeois class propagates its representations, the more naturalized they become [. . .]. The function of [this type of] myth is to empty reality: it is, literally, a ceaseless flowing out, a hemorrhage, or perhaps an evaporation, in short, a perceptible absence. (129, 131)

Barthes' theory describes more of a mentality or world-view than a strictly income/class phenomenon, i.e., many who are not literally bourgeois can still look at life in the terms of bourgeois myth. Paul Breslin, in more tangible terms than Barthes, defines bourgeois, mythic discourse as:

> [a] predication of a world in which *not much happens,* apart from the private events of falling in and out of love, [and] forming and dissolving friendships [. . .]. This privatized world [. . .] rests on very large exclusions. Within it, one is unlikely to encounter hunger, violence, or injustice [. . .]. [. . .]. High-flying adventures are as unlikely as descents into the lower depths [. . .]. [. . .] the undifferentiated expanse of adult, middle-class life [. . .] becomes [. . .] a vast featureless plain on which no destination looks worth a pilgrimage.   (215, 216)

My primary concerns in this chapter are what then happens when such mythic discourses are forced to interact with the virtual potentialities (the percepts & affects) that media poetry generates and, furthermore, how those percepts & affects can most effectively re-write/re-mediate a static world-view with emotional and empathic meanings *that can still Become. Twin Peaks* I will argue below, succeeds in disrupting any 'safe', bourgeois discourse with what it seeks to deny and suppress, i.e. the poetic contingencies that can continually re-write or re-mediate any such 'timeless/transcendent' myth.

Media poetry, in the context of an open-ended, TV-serial narrative, operates in a slightly different manner than media poetry in the context of popular narrative film (see chapter 2). There exists no single poetic speaker in *Twin Peaks*; rather, there are a myriad of poetic speakers/perceivers that form an identifiable community, which means that such speakers/perceivers can re-write any bourgeois myth from singular as well as multiple perspectives. Such poetic perspectives, I will show below, expose that what bourgeois myth most seeks to 'empty out' is anything singular; as Walter D. Mignolo describes this phenomenon, bourgeois myth creates a "metaphysics of alterity as negativity" (177). What is interesting concerning Lynch/Frost's overt incorporation of singular, poetic discourses into *Twin Peaks* is that Barthes, in *Mythologies* (109-111), sets up poetic signification as the discourse that exists in direct ideological opposition to bourgeois myth. Since poetic signification resists bourgeois discourse's ability to "[summon] subjectivity" and to "occupy [or territorialize] it," it can productively re-mediate or overcome any such myth's 'coercive power' in language use as well as all other mediums of communication (Friedman 18).

The creators of *Twin Peaks*, a la Charlie Kaufman and Spike Jonze in *Being John Malkovich*, can best be thought of as the show's primary poetic simulators; Lynch/Frost possess an "autonomous" or objective relation to the show's subject matter, and they do not have to abide by any strict regime of representational or common-sense realism (bourgeois myth); Lynch/Frost are, therefore, poetically free to re-write the show's reality-productions with a vast amount of artistic license. Critical confusion over *Twin Peaks'* ideological agendas, I will further argue, arises from Lynch/Frost's ability to poetically blur the dichotomy between bourgeois myth and what it 'hemorrhages', in order to re-mediate any such illusory/'representational' duality.

The Social Make-up of Twin Peaks

> Some ideas, like men, jump up and say 'hello'. They introduce themselves, these ideas, with words. Are they words? These ideas speak so strangely.
>
> All that we see in this world is based on someone's ideas. Some ideas are destructive, some are constructive. Some ideas can arrive in the form of a dream. I say it again: some ideas arrive in the form of a dream.
>
> —the Log Lady's fireside intro to *Twin Peaks'* second episode.

Twin Peaks is a fictitious town of approximately 5,000 people in the northeast corner of Washington state, near the Canadian border. Its main industry is a saw mill, and its principal economic developer is Benjamin Horne (Richard Beymer), who is attempting to modernize the town by building resort estates using the capital of foreign investors. The predominately blue and white collar workers experience a trauma to their apparently-serene social world through the brutal rape and murder of high-school-student Laura Palmer. The investigation into her murder also brings the show's central protagonist, F.B.I. special agent Dale Cooper (Kyle MacLachlan), into town. Laura's murder puts Twin Peaks' social order and stability into radical question because bourgeois myth cannot absorb and 'naturalize' this unsettling event.

In order to effectively define the social milieu on *Twin Peaks*, we must confront not only the social make-up of the town but, since it was aired on network TV, we must also explore its interconnection with the standard bourgeois ideology central to prime-time shows. A typical negative reading of *Twin Peaks'* social and political agendas is Rosenbaum's *Bad Ideas: the Art and Politics of Twin Peaks*. Rosenbaum narrowly reads Lynch/Frost's "social orientation" as co-extensive with an obsession for the middle-class America of the 1950s (25). Rosenbaum assumes that *Twin Peaks'* aesthetic wholly emanates from an adolescent's fascination with "dirty little secrets," a "view of women that essentially regards them as either madonnas or whores," and the "nostalgia" inherent in such an idealized, regressive world view (25). These trends, for Rosenbaum, represent "the sum of Lynch's social agenda" (25). Rosenbaum accepts the social in *Twin Peaks* as a blatant endorsement of bourgeois myth, one that accepts uncritically its media images as its own 'metaphysics of presence', i.e. as secure 're-presentations' of that society's 'naturalized' nature:

> with a sheriff and a federal agent as its principal charismatic male buddies, a sentimentality about homecoming queens that borders on gush, a Reaganite preference for the wealthy over the poor (and WASPs over everyone else), and a puritanical *Peyton Place* brand of sociology, *Twin Peaks* is ideologically no different from other prime time serials.   (25)

Rosenbaum takes Lynch/Frost's portrayal of Twin Peaks' social reality at face-value, leaving no room for irony or social commentary. His analysis, in fact, totally disregards the commonplace critical appreciation of Lynch's film-art as paradigmatically 'postmodern'. Slavoj Žižek, in his summary of the standard critical reactions to *Twin Peaks* and Lynch's art in general, describes it in blatantly non-mythic terms: as "thoroughly artificial, 'intertextual', [and] ironically clichéd [. . .]" (3).

William Spanos provides a useful working-definition of postmodernism's political and theoretical dimensions that can also help to illuminate Lynch/Frost's 'postmodern' project. The following passage defines the postmodern against bourgeois myth; it is:

> [a] marginalized, parodic impulse of the folk imagination which seeks to mock and de-stroy the utterly completed, linear yet circumscribed, monoglotic, distanced, hierarchical, and timeless world of official genres and the sociopolitical authorities that legitimate them.   (paraphrased in Conte, 10)

In this sense, postmodernism refers to something quite different than linguistic descriptions of postmodernism that treat every mode of signification in terms of arbitrary and equivalent codes. In light of Spanos's definition, *Twin Peaks* can be read as incorporating bourgeois myth into its notion of the social in order to put its mythic structures and forms back into poetic/virtual play, and not to reify or naturalize them. In this sense, *Twin Peaks* acknowledges that when dealing with theories of the social, one cannot ignore or dismiss the socio-political discourses that give rise to bourgeois myth.

Alternatively, Lynch/Frost's postmodern aesthetic seeks to generate new Becomings/Sense-events out of what *bourgeois myth represses* within the context of a problematic bourgeois-social-reality (see below). Moreover, postmodernism, in the social mediums of popular film and TV, has quite a different vitality than theorizations of it based solely in "major," linguistic theories:

> it is the visual crisis of culture that creates postmodernity, not its textuality. While print culture is certainly not going to disappear, the fascination with the

visual and its effects that marked modernism has engendered a postmodern
culture that is most postmodern when it is visual.   (Mirzoeff 3)

While Mirzoeff's statement creates a binary between the visual and the verbal,
which my theorization of a media poetry rejects outright, one can nevertheless
read his assessment as acknowledging how any theory of postmodernism based
on linguistic theory is currently problematic and dated. Spanos's definition of
the postmodern as primarily a multi-modal, ideological critique is valuable here
because it does not seek to privilege any one medium of sensory expression over
another.

      Nonetheless, Rosenbaum does raise the important question of how we are
supposed to react to Lynch/Frost's incorporation of sentimental, clichéd, and
'gushy' subjects in *Twin Peaks*. Take, for example, Laura's heart-shaped gold
necklace, the other half of which she gives to her secret boyfriend James Hurley
(James Marshall) as a symbol of their undying love, or the over-the-top soap
opera everyone on *Twin Peaks* watches religiously: *Invitation to Love*. Exactly
how these clichéd phenomena function in *Twin Peaks* will be addressed at the
end of this chapter. For the discussion at hand, a more ideologically postmodern
approach to understanding the social in *Twin Peaks* is provided by Marc Dolan.

      In his essay, *The Peaks and Valleys of Serial Creativity*, Dolan cunningly
fleshes out the logic behind the two most commonly given responses by viewers
for the show's cancellation; furthermore, he exposes the social assumptions
about artistic productions that they both problematically entail; "it ran too long"
and "it took itself too seriously" were the common reasons given in a *TV Guide*
poll for the show's demise. Dolan reads these social attitudes as arising from
"well-established, 'legitimate', aesthetic doctrines—in the former case, Anglo-
American Romanticism; in the latter, postmodernist theory" (31). Dolan equates
the former formalist complaint with Coleridge's notion of 'aesthetic
organicism'. The underlying assumption operating here is that *Twin Peaks*
violated the Romantic 'vision' that art's primary purpose is "to idealize and to
unify" (31), which the show undermines by calling into question the assumed
stability or 'essential' nature of personal identity by incorporating phantom
characters who can inhabit other characters like the killer BOB (Frank Silva),
and by refusing to provide closure to many of its central mysteries: e.g., after
Leland Palmer (Ray Wise) dies, BOB does not disappear from *Twin Peaks* (see
below). Consequently, *Twin Peaks'* rejection of any such Romantic ideal or
unified artistic form reveals that the show's social reality itself radically negates
the idealized totalizations inherent in bourgeois myth.

      The other viewer complaint arose not from postmodern art in general, but
from postmodern art in the context of a TV serial/soap opera narrative. Taking
itself 'too seriously' by 'parading itself' as art in prime-time TV, *Twin Peaks*
appeared to some as a threat to established practices, which could potentially
alter audience expectations as to what constitutes the 'norms' of its pop culture
medium. Warren Rodman's essay, *The Series that Will Change TV*, encapsulates

perfectly this view (193-44). Dolan equates this defensive attitude of viewers with the "self-fulfilling idea that 'just' creating a television series can never be [properly] artistic [. . .];" to be 'art', "it must go against the grain of the medium" (32). It appears that *Twin Peaks* bumped up against the inertia inherent in bourgeois ideology, i.e., TV's supposed function is primarily one for codifying, not radically undermining, bourgeois myth. If viewers and TV executives were willing to accept the show as germane to prime-time, it would mean that they'd have to question not only the constructed nature of bourgeois myth, but also the role TV plays in both creating and protecting the bourgeois status quo. So attached are many viewers to TV's 'naturalized' nature that they disallow the multi-media/poetic potentials for *Becoming* that Dolan sees as inherent to the "open-ended medium of televised serial narrative" (32). Since *Twin Peaks* began as an experiment for ABC (its first season ran in the dead slot on Thursday night monopolized by NBC's *Cheers)*, its later demise was a victory for the 'normal', bourgeois codification of middle-class values that dominate network TV. The refusal of ABC to support the show beyond a second season speaks to the reality that *Twin Peaks*, for many viewers, could not adopt an ironically-postmodern approach to bourgeois values and be a prime-time series at the same time.

Twin Peaks' portrayals of white and blue collar citizens, which incorporate prime-time norms, nevertheless challenged at the same time the network standards that often uncritically propagate bourgeois values. This often-unexamined duality is actually a common phenomenon in TV shows; many prime-time characters flaunt feelings of misery and alienation whenever they buy wholeheartedly into bourgeois values; TV shows such as *Married with Children* have overtly foregrounded how its characters often willingly suffer extreme amounts of alienation, all the while refusing to reject idealized ways of perceiving the world. Furthermore, *Twin Peaks'* desire to toy with genre and social myths also makes it similar to other shows that aired around the same time such as the *X-Files*; however, whereas the *X-Files* based its primary mysteries and government conspiracies on aliens and larger-than-life secrets to which only government elites have access, *Twin Peaks* put its emphasis on everyday, middle-class society as *the mystery* to be deciphered (see below); in fact, David Duchovny's first FBI-man role was on *Twin Peaks* as a cross-dressing agent named Denise!

The depiction of the social on *Twin Peaks*, therefore, challenges viewers' assumptions about not only prime-time TV, but its dynamic, historical interface with actual-world, social norms. Diane Stevenson directly addresses this issue:

> the normal [on *Twin Peaks*] is defined in terms of the white, middle-class, heterosexual, patriarchal, nuclear family. The edge of parody with its declaration of artifice, implies the artificiality of this constructed normality, of the equation between the normal and the real, of the division between the normal and the abnormal. (74)

Perhaps some viewers' negative reactions to *Twin Peaks* arose from the show's undermining of bourgeois stability through foregrounding its arbitrary distinctions between 'normal' and 'abnormal': "in *Twin Peaks* the abnormal wins out but it stakes its claim at the heart of the normal, in the body and soul of Agent Cooper, so that in the end normal and abnormal are seen to merge indissolubly" (Stevenson 74). Stevenson is referring to the series' final episode when the phantom killer BOB, who can inhabit 'normal' people and who helped to murder Laura Palmer, is the face staring back at Agent Cooper in his hotel bathroom-mirror. Cooper, the one who supposedly restores communal order through solving Laura's murder, harbors the same potential threat to bourgeois social reality as BOB does. Thus, *Twin Peaks* can be read as demolishing two key bourgeois illusions/myths, i.e. the notions that the middle-class home is secure from the threat of incest and abuse, and that social control mechanisms (like F.B.I. Agent Cooper) guarantee communal faith in such myths.

Christy Desmet echoes the notion that *Twin Peaks* embodies such a productive and unsettling merger of the 'normal' and the 'abnormal': all its characters "lead double lives, two-timing their lovers and presenting a false face to the world" (99). This duplicity in *Twin Peaks'* social reality reveals an inherent deception in bourgeois values that prime-time TV dramas often present as 'eternal'. Slavoj Žižek's theory of *inherent transgression* is useful here. According to Žižek, 'the abnormal' and 'the immoral' in bourgeois society constitute the supposedly-hidden fantasies/foundations of bourgeois social reality. This phenomenon of inherent transgression, "far from effectively threatening the system of symbolic domination, [. . .] [is] its unacknowledged, obscene support" (7). The fact that bourgeois myth needs inherent transgressions to function properly exposes how it completely fails in its attempts to naturally 'represent' all that life has to offer. Žižek uses adultery as an example of inherent transgression in his discussion of the film *The Bridges of Madison County* (1995), noting that far from challenging the 'naturalized' assertion of family values, "Francesca's adulterous affair [. . .] allows [her] to endure the marriage with her boring husband" (7). According to Žižek, adulterous affairs can, in actuality, provide the fantasy support and perhaps the erotic desire that allow the institution of marriage to present itself as 'eternal'. Inherent transgressions, as well as bourgeois norms, are purposefully predicated upon such irreconcilable dualities.

Such dualities have commonly been exposed in TV shows and films that attempt to critique American social myths. The femme fatale in post-World War II film noir can be seen as the inherent transgression of

> the patriarchal symbolic universe, as the *male* masochist-paranoic fantasy of
> the exploitative and sexually insatiable woman who simultaneously dominates
> us and enjoys her suffering, provoking us violently to take her and abuse her.
> (Žižek 10)

This female figure and her threat in such a paradigm must be continually objectified and controlled in order to re-establish social order. Therefore, without this misogynist, fantasy support that constructs this mythically-powerful female as an obstacle, bourgeois social reality would not have enough 'fantasy support' to function in its present, 'eternal' state. The infamous tag-line from *Twin Peaks, who killed Laura Palmer?*, reveals just how complicated the show's murder mystery becomes since Laura, in part, played the ironic role of the mythic obstacle to both 'male mastery' as well as 'social stability', which also implies that her status as a threat to such 'order' is directly coded into bourgeois myth. Laura, throughout the series and, especially after her death, possessed the *femme fatale's* sublime, fantasmatic "aura" in spades (Žižek 10). The tragedy of her life comes from the fact that this idealized or mythic power people often projected onto her actively dis-empowered her own attempts to construct a productive, poetic identity for herself. Diana Hume George notes, paraphrasing Nicole Ward Jove in her case study of the Yorkshire Ripper Peter Sutcliffe, "the end product of cultural misogyny [can lead to] sexualized murder," which indicates that Laura's murder can also be viewed, in part, as an "extreme [. . .] outcome of normal, masculine enculturation" (113). Žižek, in his discussion of Lynch's film *Lost Highway*, theorizes that fantasies of domination and sexual power can become common inherent transgressions, which allow "the despair of our drab, 'alienated', daily life of impotence and distrust" to continue in its 'naturalized' form as middle-class America (13). Such an 'undifferentiated, featureless' plain's only places *worthy of pilgrimages* are often *fantasies of power and control over life itself.*

It's a sad fact that bourgeois myth continuously disowns its stake in generating such potentially-destructive fantasies. Bourgeois myth and inherent transgression can be viewed as directly connected through a complicitous dichotomy, whereby inherent transgression provides no challenge to social authority because it never disturbs the stable, surface appearance of bourgeois values; its fantasies can then compensate for the 'empty' natures of bourgeois myth in a 'private' realm that displaces and contains any threats to that society in fantasmatic/mythic terms—enter the *femme fatale* of film noir. The horror of sexualized murder thereby becomes 'hemorrhaged' by social authority to the realm of personal fantasy, allowing the social order to appear disconnected from such offenses by virtue of the fact that they are punished by social law. Therefore, bourgeois society can still appear 'natural' and 'eternal' since individuals become the ones who fail its myths, and not vice-versa. Symbolic, patriarchal law purposefully and problematically leaves its contingent, fantasy supports behind in all such individual matters. The paradox here becomes, therefore, not that *Twin Peaks* threatened bourgeois social reality through social criticism (i.e. the "depicting [of] a grim social reality"), but by nakedly exposing the fact that its citizens present a 'normal' appearance to the world all the while actively denying that appearance in their 'private' lives (Žižek 41). Žižek explains how Lynch's art confronts social attitudes through the "staging [of] its fantasies openly, more directly, i.e. without the 'secondary perlaborations' [or distortions] which [mask] their inconsistencies" (41). Such naked portrayals of bourgeois myth's exclusions on national TV arguably explode the dividing line between 'normal' and 'abnormal', 'high' art and prime time TV, more effectively than any overly-didactic or intellectualized social criticism. Such 'masks' of normalcy (including what they hide) on *Twin Peaks* become transformed by Lynch/Frost from signs of camouflage to ones of *conspicuousness* (see below).

Twin Peaks portrays the forces that primarily threaten bourgeois myth as arising from the dualities inherent in bourgeois social reality itself; bourgeois myth, therefore, is shown over and over again to be more problematic than 'empty'. Lynch/Frost's series expands its notion of the social by portraying how the realm of inherent transgression, contrary to Žižek's claim, refuses to stay safely contained as solely a fantasy support, especially in the case of Laura's murder. The most shocking and obvious form this threat takes is the 'lower-class' drifter/phantom killer BOB. He is the horror to middle-class normality as the murderer of Laura Palmer, the homecoming-queen, and he is a phantom-like inhabitor of 'normal' citizens. BOB is the personification of sexual and physical abuse that aids Leland Palmer, Laura's lawyer-father, when he abuses and murders her; however, the show portrays Leland in a rather ambiguous light. On one hand, Leland is also a victim, since he is the one who alerts Agent Cooper in episode 16 to the fact that BOB was his neighbor when he was a child and had abused him as well; on the other hand, Leland (possessed by BOB) is revealed to be the one who raped and murdered Laura, *his own daughter*. Moreover, BOB plays a rather paradoxical role throughout the series because he also guarantees the continuation of bourgeois myth in that he 'silences' anyone who can expose the fact that such myth is his *perfect cover*.

Since BOB embodies the cycle of sexual abuse (most abusers were previously abused themselves), *Twin Peaks* does not isolate the social plague of abuse solely in the 'lower-class' or the problematic consciousness of Leland Palmer, since many other characters also recognize BOB's 'true face', which further implies that sexual abuse is not reducible to an isolated, individual problem that can be effectively banished from bourgeois society. In fact, BOB gains an apparently unlimited power by operating in the fantasy supports that 'stabilize' bourgeois culture; by ignoring the fact that he actually exists in middle-class America, such a society problematically 'represents' him as 'unreal' and therefore unstoppable in a particular sense:

> abuse as Lynch represents it, as most of us tend to imagine it, wears the garb of unclean low life, from which the middle class home supposedly provides a haven; but in fact abuse lives in the middle class home as much as anywhere else. (Stevenson 74)

If we read Stevenson's problematic description of the 'low class' as 'unclean' as an attempt at irony, her comment can expose *Twin Peaks'* poetic use of what bourgeois myth disowns. By playing on a common audience fear, *Twin Peaks* reveals that the bourgeois myth of the middle-class home as a safe haven from abuse is a mythic chimera. In fact, *Twin Peaks* radically calls into question the stability of the mythic nature of social reality itself, when, in its previously-mentioned final episode, Dale Cooper winds up being inhabited by BOB himself. BOB appears to be able to inhabit anyone who disowns his/her own poetic/productive potentials for re-writing/mediating the inherent transgressions of bourgeois social order. It's a shocking notion to entertain that even Cooper, who is so adept at reading social problems, can succumb to such a personal alienation. Lynch/Frost's series, nonetheless, reveals that no absolute safety or stability exists anywhere.

While bourgeois myth attempts to empty out social reality by coding problematic people as threats or obstacles to that reality, inherent transgressions of fantasized violence and domination nevertheless keep disturbing such 'featureless and stable' bourgeois appearances. This notion implies that bourgeois society's posturing as stable and eternal masks its own fragility, since many, like Leland, actualize its fantasies (i.e. one can and should 'master' or dominate another person if they 'deserve' it). If someone embodies a threat to those people invested in the complicity of inherent transgressions and bourgeois myth, s/he is potentially very threatening. As we shall see, Laura embodies such threats perfectly, just as BOB embodies the hidden, destructive aspect of how bourgeois myth leaves its contingency behind and becomes 'timeless' and 'naturalized'. Even BOB's common name foregrounds this 'naturalized', horrifying dichotomy. By blurring the abuser (Leland/BOB) as coming from both the middle and 'lower' classes, Lynch/Frost refuses the bourgeois myth of 'the unclean lower class' because BOB, in Lynch's own words, is not a supernatural presence but a poetically-contingent or expressionistic "abstraction in human form" (Rodley 178).

Lynch's art in general, as Žižek discerns, is not interested in exploring supernatural realities a la *The X-Files*, but in de-mystifying the non-personal aspects of symbolization and social myths that constitute the discursive and political realities that shape American social order, which further implies that social problems are never reducible solely to the psychological profiles of problematic individuals (25). This is the domain where bourgeois myth is created or, as Lacanian theory describes it, the Big Other, which can be defined as "the dimension of non-psychological, social, symbolic relations *treated as such by the subject*—in short, the dimension of symbolic INSTITUTION" (Žižek 26). Since the Big Other is the imaginary ideal of social authority/language, to change its reified form as bourgeois myth means social attitudes themselves must poetically challenge and re-write the imaginary power inherent in any such totalized authority. *Twin Peaks*, which is a dynamic form of media poetry that generates contingent percepts & affects on network TV, subverts any mythic authority outright in multiple ways (see below).

To sum up how the social is presented in *Twin Peaks*, we can define it as the bourgeois standard (its middle-class, white, heterosexual nature) in which its symbolic authority must function as "the performative aspect of the subject's activity" (Žižek 26). However, the majority of the characters in *Twin Peaks* lead double, secret lives. In order to seek the fulfillment of their desires in a realm where those desires don't count for the Big Other, they must still complicitly "act as though they believe in it" so as to not provoke the disintegration of bourgeois society's dichotomous foundation (Žižek 26). A perfect example of this phenomenon is Ed Hurley (Everett McGill) who stays married to his wife Nadine (Wendy Robie) all the while continuing his affair with Norma Jennings (Peggy Lipton), his high school sweetheart. Lynch/Frost's twist on bourgeois social reality and its 'secret' inherent transgressions is to then go a step further by re-incorporating and foregrounding forces in the social fabric that have been hemorrhaged or emptied out. The two most significant forces are poetic signification and the central role adolescent characters play in the town of Twin Peaks. These forces are unique in that they possess the virtual potentials to transform not only the mythic nature of bourgeois society, but its fantasy supports as well.

Adolescence and the Poetic in Twin Peaks

> Letters are symbols. They are building blocks of words which form languages. Languages help us communicate. Even with complicated languages used by intelligent people, misunderstanding is a common occurrence.
>
> We write things down sometimes—letters, words—hoping they will serve us and those with whom we wish to communicate. Letters and words, calling out for understanding.
>
> —The Log Lady's fireside intro to episode 10.

While other critics, including Desmet and Dolan, have mentioned that there are strong poetic elements in *Twin Peaks*, many relate them to Julia Kristeva's theory of semiotic signification. However, no critic has yet given a thorough account of poetic signification's radical significance in the show. Kristeva's semiotic signification is "articulated by flows and marks: facilitation, energy transfers, the cutting up of the corporeal and social continuum, as well as that of signifying material [. . .]" (*Revolution in Poetic Language* 40). The semiotic relates to bourgeois myth in that these myths are the end results of the beaten/outworn pathways of the semiotic; bourgeois myth is the ultimate codification of the symbolic, which Kristeva defines as "a social effect of the relation to the other, established through the objective constraints of biological (including sexual) differences and concrete, historical family structures" (29). Bourgeois myth, in the terms of Kristeva's theory, can be seen as a radical denial of the semiotic's role in the creation and continual re-creations of social reality. Semiotic forces, however, precisely because of their transformative potentials, can still create change in social contexts through their emotionally-charged, disruptive sources of pleasure that pluralize/cut-up mythic homogeneity. They can challenge and complicate the 'essential', 'naturalized' appearance of American bourgeois society as well as its transgressive underpinning.

However, the semiotic significations on *Twin Peaks* are not vague, unknowable, Romanticized, or mystical phenomena as Kristeva's theory may problematically imply. Therefore, whenever I refer to the semiotic from here on, it should be read as an analogy for the simulated potentialities (media poetry's percepts & affects) inherent in a multi-modal, virtual mode of Becoming. Media poetry creates virtual phenomena/Becomings that arise from non-organic perceptual processes, and that always take on specific meanings in particular/interpretive contexts. Despite such key differences, I still want to incorporate several key aspects of Kristeva's insights. The semiotic in Kristeva's theory has been traditionally related to the mother and to pre-Oedipal experiences that are never wholly governed by the patriarchal, symbolic law of the father (the Big Other). Lynch/Frost's portrayals of women on *Twin Peaks*, and especially adolescent ones, still deserve careful analysis. In fact, many or the poetic speakers/perceivers on the show are both adolescent and female.

It is significant that adolescence, often demonized by social control mechanisms, becomes a fundamental make-up of the prime-time phenomenon of *Twin Peaks*. In fact, pop culture has always been fascinated by adolescent characters; many shows airing around the time of *Twin Peaks*, including *The X-Files*, often centered individual stories around alienated adolescents, especially white, middle-class ones. In addition, *Twin Peaks* can be seen as a more extensive re-mediation of the rite-of-passage from childhood to adulthood in middle-class America that his film *Blue Velvet* also explores. *Twin Peaks*, however, is rather singular in pop culture in its foregrounding of the social problems surrounding female adolescence. According to Susan Hayward, youth in Western society are often "visualised as deviant, as a spectacle of otherness" (83). She further explains that what plagues adult perceptions of youth

> is a fetishization of youth, a spectacularisation of youth-as-violence (breaking
> bounds) which says more about our fears of the very real changing boundaries
> of class, gender, and race that 'surround' us than it does about the youth class
> as a fundamental threat to the social order of things.   (83-4)

Youth becomes the site whereby such social fears are "displaced and contained,"
rendering youth "unreadable" to adults in order to protect those adults from
perceiving the actual-world crises in their social existences (83). The fear and
mistrust associated with youth in this social paradigm problematically 'justifies'
their marginality. Youth, just like the femme fatale in film noir, are therefore
coded as people who must be controlled in a social milieu supposedly stabilized
by a mythic smoothness.

Alternatively, for Kristeva, adolescence is not inherently dangerous to
social 'order' but is a profound developmental period that can re-connect one to
poetic/virtual signification and Becoming, since the psychological make-up of
the adolescent has not yet been 'fixed' by a codified social identity:

> the adolescent moment in Kristeva's account has a porousness in which the
> boundaries of sexual difference and identity, fantasy and reality, are more
> easily traversed, and which lends itself to a range of 'post-adolescent' cultural
> uses.   (Fletcher 2)

These cultural "uses" involve disruptions in the mythic 'smoothness' of
bourgeois society. As adolescence re-introduces a mobility of desire and identity
into the symbolic, mythic nature of bourgeois society, such adolescents must be
suppressed or coded as dangerous/deviant by bourgeois myth so that they will
not possess the power to overturn its codifications/totalizations.

However, *Twin Peaks'* adolescents' psychic potentials still maintain the
capacities to re-write/mediate mythic illusions. Of particular relevance to
bourgeois myth's exclusions and repressions is Kristeva's definition of
adolescence:

> I understand by the term 'adolescent' less an age category than an open psychic
> structure. Like the 'open systems' of which biology speaks concerning living
> organisms that live only by maintaining a renewable identity through
> interaction with another, the adolescent structure opens itself to the repressed at
> the same time that it initiates a psychic reorganization of the individual—
> thanks to a tremendous loosening of the superego.   (*The Adolescent Novel* 8)

The in-between-nature characteristic of adolescents in Western society implies
that they are in the unique position of not possessing totalized, subjective
identities for the Big Other of a 'normal' symbolic order. This phenomenon may
help explain why adolescents can more easily traverse bourgeois myth as well as
why prime-time audiences were initially captivated by *Twin Peaks'* central
mystery: *who killed the 17-year old Laura Palmer?* Laura's life-and-death

struggle for a poetically-productive identity more than likely provided audiences with a vicarious trip back to the more open, adolescent relation to a social reality that has been mythically 'emptied out', i.e., *Twin Peaks* implies that we viewers must also confront *who killed the adolescent in us*.

In addition, all of Laura's adolescent friends become central to the mysteries of *Twin Peaks* because they search for answers on their own outside of social control mechanisms. Laura's best friend Donna Hayward (Lara Flynn Boyle), her once-secret boyfriend James Hurley, and Laura's drug-dealing, captain-of-the-football-team 'official' boyfriend Bobby Briggs (Dana Ashbrook), all choose to confront Laura's death in their own ways, outside of the adult ways of mythically 'handling' such a tragedy. Desmet explains that problematic figures such as Laura can unfortunately be absorbed into the cultural myth of 'sin and redemption' in adult society, whereby she has achieved 'transcendent' peace in death through the end of her suffering, which had become a dangerous affront to bourgeois order:

> Lynch utilizes but also comments satirically upon the ways in which communities heal, or at least cover up, their social wounds by absorbing a dangerous woman like Laura Palmer into a conventionally pious narrative of redemption and transfiguration. (99)

However, this 'pious' narrative is a fundamental evasion of what Laura's life entailed; she suffered from the cultural wound of incest, and her life is a testimony to how bourgeois myth's fantasies, which must cover such cultural wounds with idealized/pious narratives, can be easily actualized in social reality itself (such idealized narratives can be seen as calling BOB's powers into reality a la a "return of the repressed"). By leaving his contingency behind, BOB exposes the violent logic of bourgeois myth's 'eternal/empty' appearances that can only appear that way through a fantasized and mythic power/control over anything that threatens to expose its illusory 'authority'.

BOB is not the only character who has a double existence in the symbolic order. It has often been noted that Lynch/Frost also created Laura as a character who embodies cultural contradiction: she was a sexually promiscuous cocaine addict; however, at the same time, she attempted to make a positive impact on her town: she organized a meals-on-wheels program for elderly shut-ins; she tutored the Chinese immigrant Josie Packard (Joan Chen) in English; she visited the developmentally disabled Johnny Horn (Robert Bauer); and she was attempting to deal with her own psychological plagues through visiting psychologist Dr. Lawrence Jacoby (Russ Tamblyn). However, as Diane Stevenson notes, due to her sexual abuse, "Laura lacks the resources—the self-esteem, one might say, the sense of good in herself [. . .]" to overcome such a trauma effectively (79).

Consequently, *Twin Peaks'* other adolescent characters must grapple with Laura's 'private' struggle on their own terms: they too can be seen as attempting to create for themselves a productively-poetic awareness of the social world around them in the wake of Laura's traumatic murder. Donna expresses this notion in her monologue on Laura's grave in episode 11: "we were always trying to solve your [i.e. Laura's] problems, and you know what, we still are." James, Donna, and Maddy Ferguson (Laura's look-alike cousin also played by Sheryl Lee) all begin their own investigations into who killed Laura separate from the adult/police investigation, even risking their lives to find clues. The adolescents in the town intuit that Laura's death directly relates to their struggles to also create productively-poetic identities; they also attempt to understand why her death is something that the adults might not be able to solve or even interpret on their own terms (i.e. in mythic terms).

Since the adolescents in *Twin Peaks* reject the mythic re-writing that Laura was troubled but 'her soul is now at peace', they perceive her death itself as a cultural lesson they must discern for their own well-being. Their attempts to comprehend Laura's subjective struggle implies that it is an attempt to bring back virtually-re-writable or poetic significations/Becomings into adult, mythic society. Because her culture does not openly acknowledge her suffering, Laura (who wrote a secret diary about her traumatic life) cannot effectively communicate her experience through mythic language. The poem that serves as this chapter's epigraph, written by David Lynch's own daughter Jennifer Lynch in Laura's persona, reveals that Laura used poetry to express what could not be communicated through bourgeois myth, i.e., how Bob was going to kill her and that no one could 'read' her suffering effectively enough to help her.

Kristeva's notion of how adolescent writing differs from conventional writing is illuminating here, especially in how it relates to creative re-mediations of empirical experiences:

> I will see writing as a semiotic practice that facilitates the ultimate reorganization of psychic space, in the time before an ideally postulated maturity. The adolescent imaginary is essentially amorous [. . .]. Adolescent fantasy (written sign + fantasy filtered through the imaginary codes) reactivates the process of the appearance of the symbol. (*The Adolescent Novel* 17)

Only the adolescents in Twin Peaks can still re-organize, in an amatory fashion, their psychic potentials around such a traumatic event as the 'empty' category of Laura's death, whereas the majority of the adults either ignore it or adopt a conventional myth like 'her redemption and transfiguration'. The adolescents on *Twin Peaks* are the only ones who appear willing to keep alive Laura's struggle to articulate the failings of bourgeois myth and its potentially-destructive fantasies so her death will not be 'in vain'.

Lynch/Frost's foregrounding of this potentially creative connection between adolescents and a codified social order appears in several important ways throughout the series. Laura's secret diary, because it expresses what Laura could not say openly in her social environment, becomes a key factor in her murder investigation. The adolescents in the town struggle for access to—and possession of—what they assume is a cathartic text. Laura had hidden it with an agoraphobic Harold Smith (Lenny Von Dohlen) on her meals-on-wheels route, so BOB would not find it again; Leland/BOB had once found it and ripped out all the pages that mentioned BOB's name. This fact reveals that adolescent writing, especially *female* adolescent writing, is a threat to bourgeois 'values' that must be erased and re-ordered into mythically 'empty' narratives so that 'order' can remain intact. In fact, in the *Twin Peaks* cinematic prequel *Fire Walk with Me,* Laura writes her way to the realization that her abuser (in the guise of BOB) is actually her father, and tells him authoritatively: "stay away from me." Her realization, unfortunately, is what precipitates her murder, i.e., she is killed so that she will not be able to expose her actual abuser.

Nonetheless, Laura's best friend Donna, who takes over Laura's route after her death, discovers that Harold has Laura's diary and enlists James and Maddy's help to steal it back from adult hands in episode 13, i.e., she hopes to return it to its rightful adolescent owners (who can still wrest new potential meanings/Becomings from it). Since Harold did not take it to the police, the only function the diary served in adult hands was as a fetishized object that Harold could use to vicariously covet Laura's wounded/open identity in the 'safety' of his own home. In episode 14, he selfishly rips up the diary on the night he commits suicide so no one else will ever be able to read it. The diary appears to have a poetic/vital significance and a potential to reveal social repressions or denials only in the hands of those whose creative potentials are not yet determined by a mythically-stable social reality.

Donna Hayward's younger sister Harriet (Jessica Wallenfels) is portrayed in the series as a poet like Laura, and Harriet's method of dealing with Laura's death is to write a poem and use her creative imagination to transcend the adult 'sin and redemption' myth that only neutralizes the challenge Laura poses to society's mythic structure. Harriet intuits that Laura's struggle is a poetic one for a productively-open identity in an otherwise 'empty' environment. Harriet even reads this poem at a family dinner party that the Palmer family also attends in episode 8 (she therefore reads the poem to Laura's actual murderer). Although Desmet reads Harriet's poem as evoking only clichéd images from a stereotypical hagiographic stock, the poem nevertheless reveals the constructed/virtual nature of symbolic production unlike the 'naturalized' adult-myth of Laura's redemption in death. Harriet's poem begins as follows:

> It was Laura,
> And I saw her glowing in the dark wood;
> I saw her smile;
> We were crying and we were laughing,
> In our sadness I saw her dancing.
> It was Laura
> Living in my dreams.

What differs most from the adult re-writing of Laura's life is the amatory, empathic bond Harriet develops from her own—as well as Laura's—struggle in adolescence. Even in a naïve poem such as this one, Kristeva's "open structure" for creating potentials outside of socially-codified myths becomes apparent *even when it uses the same hagiographic images as bourgeois myth.*

Harriet's version of Laura's memory is not empty because Laura becomes, in effect, Harriet's poetic muse. If we contrast Harriet's poem to the bourgeois myth that the middle-class home is a safe haven from sexual abuse, we see how Harriet uses Laura's struggle as a potentially-inspiring force that can "see" beyond Laura's tragic life (see below). Harriet's poem, therefore, re-writes Laura's beauty in emotional and empathic terms, i.e. "our sadness," and never in idealized terms like the femme fatale's 'threatening' beauty. Laura's struggle to contact semiotic/poetic forces outside of the 'empty' ones of her bourgeois upbringing, which could not protect her in life because incest has been 'hemorrhaged' from the middle-class home, is still a possibility for others. Harriet, therefore, transforms bourgeois myth's hagiographic imagery from an empty category into a productively-poetic one:

> the filtering [. . .] [from available ideologies or codes of representation][. . .] can become a repression of unconscious contents and give rise to a stereotyped writing of clichés; on the other hand, it can permit a genuine inscription of unconscious contents within language [use]. (*The Adolescent Novel* 9)

Adolescent writing can return a vitality and inspirational desire to re-mediate social reality back into Laura's memory and traumatic life. Her death for most of the adults in the town, a la Harold, becomes not a potential for creative discovery, but a fetishized tragedy for which they have no writing other than mythically-empty clichés.

We can demise a lot about Lynch/Frost's view of adolescence through their rendering of Harriet and Laura as writers. In Harriet's poem, she desires through language-use an active, reciprocal relation between her adolescent life and Laura's. Laura's vitality in the poem is an invitation to an inter-subjective understanding of the transformative nature of adolescent identity. Through this poetic-vitality or virtual-potentiality that expands out from Laura's memory, Harriet's writing re-inscribes her desire to stay in contact with such Sense-events/virtual powers. Such powers can create an empathic relatedness to traumatic lives like Laura's, and they can also potentially counteract the difficulties and isolation common to adolescence.

An adolescent imagination like Laura's refuses to deny even the destructive/dangerous forces like BOB, i.e. the violent truth of a repressive bourgeois society that always disavows Leland's 'true nature'. Laura had to learn on her own that BOB is (in part) an actual, unsettling manifestation of adult, destructive social-myths, which harbor violent fantasies of mastery over those who 'must be controlled'. If we read Laura's desire to write out her traumatic life-experiences as an attempt to find a language of relatedness between herself and others not based on domination or any norm, this notion helps to explain why the adolescents around her desired her diary, i.e., they wanted a poetic interface with her experience, which could then allow them to potentially re-envision social interaction in general in non-mythic terms.

Here is another poem from Laura's secret diary that the other adolescents in the town risked their lives to find:

> Inside me there is something
> No one knows about
> Like a secret
> Sometimes it takes over
> And I drift back
> Deep into darkness.
> This secret tells me
> I will never grow older
> Never laugh with friends
> Never be who I should if I ever reveal
> Its name.
>
> I cannot tell if it is real
> Or if I dream of it
> For when it touches me
> I drift off
> No tears come
> No screams
> I am wrapped up
> In a nightmare of hands
> And of fingers
> And of small tiny voices in the woods.
> So wrong
> So beautiful
> So bad
> So Laura.

(*The Secret Diary of Laura Palmer* 20)

Laura's poem struggles to come to terms with what threatens to annihilate her singular identity in a cultural space that demands that she be silent about her suffering. It is because of her fear that she only expresses such struggles in a secret diary. Adolescent writing, nonetheless, possesses the virtual power to see through and overcome mythic emptiness for an inter-subjective, poetic openness to experience—especially traumatic experience.

However, Leland/BOB relives Laura's murder through killing her look-alike cousin Maddy in episode 14; this double murder reiterates how "Lynch invalidates with devastating finality *Twin Peaks*' [ironic incorporation of the] master narrative of sin and redemption" (Desmet 99). Through the double murder, Lynch/Frost reveal how Laura and Maddy's deaths cannot fit into any 'naturalized' myth, for *Twin Peaks'* social reality will not stay empty. In fact, Leland/Bob kills Maddy because she is planning to leave Twin Peaks. She had come to help out her aunt and uncle after her cousin's death, but Leland/BOB uses that occasion to fetishistically re-live 'their' *silencing* of Laura. Leland even calls Maddy "Laura" over and over as he tortures and beats her in one of the most disturbing scenes ever aired on network TV. For Leland, Laura—who symbolizes the writer as well as the image of female-adolescent desire—must be killed over and over because she keeps threatening the smooth and undifferentiated plain of a mythic social reality, i.e., she is a free subject/individual in a repressed/Bourgeois society that fears freedom as a disruption of its order. Lynch reiterates that what truly threatens bourgeois reality, in the mocking form of BOB's 'timeless' nature, is an outcome of social repressions that are often 'secretly' complicit with forces such as BOB. Bourgeois myth, unfortunately, desires both Laura and her desires as a corpse whenever they rebel against its 'empty' authority. Since there is a double erasure of female writing inherent in such myth, Lynch/Frost imply that Laura therefore 'requires' a double elimination.

While Desmet does not invoke Laura's struggle for a poetic/semiotic capacity for self-expression, she still interprets BOB's nature as arising directly from social myths themselves, i.e. as the embodiment of the male paranoid-desire to possess and abuse young women, especially those who assert their individuality:

> Laura Palmer refuses to fit neatly into her social role [. . .]. In committing the murders, then, Leland expresses not only his own incestuous rage but also the community's outrage at Laura's refusal to submit to the classic American script for beautiful Homecoming Queens and at Maddy's failure to be a dependent daughter. Bobby's melodramatic statement that 'we all' killed Laura Palmer, delivered at her funeral [in episode 3], is therefore accurate. (101)

Even Bobby, the drug-dealing adolescent thug, reveals Lynch/Frost's emphasis on adolescence as a creative time with a special capacity for insight into society's mythic structure (the Big Other), and how such myths seek to marginalize all those who challenge codified social roles. The adolescents of Twin Peaks openly flaunt their incapacity to fit into adult society, as Bobby's disruption of that social ritual attests. Unfortunately, Bobby's insight falls on the purposefully-ignorant adults at Laura's funeral. Even though adolescent *re-writing* calls into question the imaginary nature of social authority, there is no cultural space in Twin Peaks for an actual dialogue between the forces of bourgeois myth and the virtually re-writeable forces of media poetry (the adolescent poems described above as well as Bobby's above statement are key examples of such non-empty percepts & affects).

Kristeva's theory of the poetic has articulated how adolescents expand the codified relation between social myths and their more shadowy side of inherent transgressions through the link between perversion and artistic creativity. Perversion, in a psychoanalytic context, is not exactly a pejorative term. As Renata Salecl states, "the pervert is the subject for whom castration has not been fully operative" (155). Since castration, in psychoanalytic theory, occurs when one becomes a speaking being, his/her identity is always limited to the discursive or performative make-up of that subjectivity. In more semiotic/poetic terms, castration becomes, a la the philosophy of Luce Irigaray, a heterogeneous, relational, and wholly-transformative position in language-use, which rejects any essentialized/naturalized homogeneity. To have a perverse or heterogeneous psychic make-up implies that the Big Other is not the sole authority over one's subjectivity

The adolescent, therefore, can be seen as possessing a perverse (i.e. open) capacity for relation in a 'foreclosed' social-order, one that seeks to allow "something new and changed [to be] revealed" (Deleuze, *The Logic of Sense* 206). Perversion becomes, in *Twin Peaks'* paradigm, a bridge between bourgeois myth and the forces that it either rejects or does not control. Such adolescent

'open structures' find themselves immediately echoing the fluidity, i.e. the inconsistency, of a mass media society. The adolescent is found to represent *naturally* this structure that can be called a 'crisis' structure only through the eyes of a stable, ideal law. (Kristeva, *The Adolescent Novel* 9)

Adolescents can approach cultural inconsistencies through their more playful, open relation to mass-media images/signs/Becomings; alternatively, adults often do not possess this creative ability and only attempt to mask bourgeois myth's exclusions with either 'private' fantasies or pious narratives. Žižek's problematic definition of perversion "as a defense against the Real [. . .], against the threat of mortality as well as the contingent imposition of sexual difference" does not possess the same notion of evasion for adolescents as it does for adults, because the adolescent still maintains a potential connection to the multiple or heterogeneous potentialities of poetic/semiotic Becomings (36). Adolescent creativity situates itself "around writing and the 'open structure' of the adolescent—'the innocent and justified pervert'—the psychic sources and dimensions of literary and symbolic creativity" (Fletcher 3). Perversity can be seen, therefore, as a force that transcends mythic codifications because it can create virtually-re-writeable forces/Sense-events that explode such myths.

We have already noted the 'perverse' nature of the adolescents in Twin Peaks who refuse to cooperate with the adult investigation into Laura's death, believing that they can solve it on their own terms outside of any social law. While this borders on being another pop culture cliché, in the vein of *The Hardy Boys* or *Nancy Drew*, the *Twin Peaks* adolescents' openness to drugs, sexual experimentation and even self-annihilation in prime-time TV reveals an openness (even if it's a problematic one) to sensory experience that's lost to many adults.

The character who perhaps best embodies the perverse/creative stance toward the adult bourgeois social order is Audrey Horne (Sherilyn Fenn), the daughter of Benjamin Horne. In *Twin Peaks'* pilot episode she takes perverse pleasure in undermining her father's business deal with Norwegian investors by seductively parading her body for them. After one investor asks "is there anything wrong, young pretty girl?," she proceeds to tell them how sad she is that her good friend Laura Palmer had been murdered the day before. As the Norwegians exit Twin Peaks, Audrey laughs in the background not only because she thwarted her father's will, but because she *spoke the truth* about his attempt to keep the Norwegians 'in the dark' about Laura's death.

Nonetheless, the adolescent view of sexuality on *Twin Peaks* can often be considered overtly perverse. Laura and Ronette Pulaski (Phoebe Augustine) often sent fantasy letters to the porno magazine *Flesh World*, which is the clue Agent Cooper uses to connect the two girls to a prostitution ring. While Laura and Ronette's sexual experimentations lead to Laura's murder and Ronette's near death, what has to be understood here is what these girls were attempting through their perversity. Kristeva speculates about this notion: "the pornography of the young and immature [. . .], [is] the effort to name, to make an uncertain meaning appear at the frontier of word and drive" (*The Adolescent Novel* 22)? Arguably, these characters were attempting to contact productively-poetic forces often repressed by the patriarchal social order that attempts to codify adolescent girls' sexual and imaginative potentials. The violence these young girls encounter arises not from their acting out of adult behavior, but from the adult mal-adjustment to such unformed subjectivities, which can problematically become re-ordered into the female image of the masochist/fantasy support of a bourgeois society, i.e., such girls can then 'appear to deserve abuse and to be controlled'. For example, Leland Palmer, the wife-abusing drug-dealer Leo Johnson (Eric DaRe), and the drug dealer Jacques Renault (Walter Olkewicz), all embody this paranoid fantasy that views women as "untrustworthy and [who] must be controlled"; in fact, each of those men exhibits sexual aggression towards Laura the night she is killed in Lynch's *Fire Walk with Me* (George 113).

While *Twin Peaks* tragically renders the plight of Laura and Ronette's perverse quest to contact poetic/semiotic forces outside of mythically-codified ones, Audrey Horne is more successful in her quest for her own productive identity. Her crush on Agent Cooper provides her with the challenge to *become* more mature and self-assured, for she believes that this is the type of woman Cooper desires. She even takes on the role of Cooper's helper, providing him with important clues that aid him in his investigation into Laura's death, including the location of One-Eyed Jack's where Laura was staying as a prostitute, as well as the fact that her father was also Laura's lover, making him a suspect in Laura's murder investigation.

By uniting Audrey's desire for sexual maturity with Agent Cooper's quest to stay in constant contact with poetic/semiotic forces that can aid him in his investigation into Laura's death, *Twin Peaks* reveals that Cooper's intuitive quest for knowledge and perception outside of bourgeois myth connects him with adolescent perversity, making him the rare exception for adults in *Twin Peaks*. Cooper takes continual delight in sensory pleasures throughout the series, from the Douglas firs surrounding Twin Peaks to the cherry pie and coffee he consumes continuously. All experiences, in effect, contain the possibility for further exploration and joy in Cooper's interactions with the empirical world. Desmet elucidates how the poetic/semiotic on *Twin Peaks* and its relation to pre-symbolic/textual forces threatens the symbolic order with its own contingent nature: "the ruptures, revisions, rhythm and echolalia that characterize the semiotic also mark the visions and enigmatic messages used to unravel the mystery of Laura Palmer's murder" (Desmet 104). *Twin Peaks* often presents viewers with bizarre phrases, such as "the owls are not what they seem" and "that gum you like is going to come back into style," which not only become unlikely clues that point to Leland's guilt throughout the series, but that undermine the logocentrism inherent in the patriarchal social order. Desmet problematically situates the semiotic as "the origin of the knowledge sought by Dale Cooper as well as the source of BOB's evil" (95). BOB, in my reading of the series, is instead the force that secures the authority and domination of the symbolic system; he is not a poetic evil since he destroys any attempts at such meaning, as is evident when he rips out the pages that identify him in Laura's diary.

Cooper, like Laura, uses a poem from a dream in episode 2 to also grapple with what BOB 'means' in Twin Peaks' social reality. The poem is spoken by MIKE/the one-armed man (Al Strobel) to Cooper as follows:

> Through the darkness of future past,
> The magician longs to see.
> One chants out between two worlds:
> FIRE
> Walk with me.

The message in the poem implies that poetic/semiotic signification is the force that longs to see alternative aspects of reality that are not territorialized by a violent/repressively-rational common sense. As Martha Nochimson explains, "Cooper longs to see [but] Bob yearns to control [. . .]" (86). Or, in terms of Laura's murder investigation: "Cooper values feminine experience, BOB devours it" (Nochimson 87). The poem hints that there is a destructive force operating in Twin Peaks' social reality that wants to destroy peoples' connections to poetic signification: "fire walk with me." In fact, other adult women in the community, who are also in touch with poetic capacities for meaning, aid Cooper through several poetic and serio-comic premonitions they have. Sarah Palmer sees a vision of BOB in her daughter's bedroom and even gets a policeman to make a sketch of his face. The Log Lady, an eccentric denizen who receives communications through a special piece of wood, gives Cooper continual warnings about forces outside of rational understanding like "the owls are not what they seem;" she even warns Cooper in episode 14 that something bad is going to happen on the night that Maddy is murdered.

Hence, the forces that exist outside bourgeois common-sense can take one of two paths: they can either become productively poetic or they can generate an anti-life desire to control and dominate whoever or whatever seeks such alternative capacities for knowledge/perception. Lynch is offering an interesting gender commentary here; as Nochimson explains: "Lynch sees an imbalanced priority on aggression and control in [rational or common-sense] knowing—or [even] seeing. By contrast, in *Twin Peaks* the dominance of phallic power is represented by Bob, the annihilator of meaning" (88). Here again we see how BOB is an agent of bourgeois myth that makes sure social reality stays poetically empty. In addition, there is no strict gender binary in operation in *Twin Peaks*, since poetic signification is available to both men and women equally, as Agent Cooper's example attests. The critic Dolan, as well, reads the poetic/semiotic signification in *Twin Peaks* as Lynch/Frost's attempt to offer a "semiotic rather than hermeneutic reading of Laura's murder," which implies that her murder can never be mythologized away and has itself become a perverse and creative potential for personal/cultural meaning (38).

One of *Twin Peaks'* most startling poetic-percepts, which occurs throughout the series, and which we first see in Cooper's dream in which MIKE reads the above-mentioned poem, is the Red Room. The Red Room in *Twin Peaks* is a place that exists wholly outside the show's codified/adult social reality: it's a border-space "between two worlds" as MIKE's poem describes. The Red Room is a poetic reality in which anything can be virtually re-written/mediated. According to Lynch, it overtly functions as a multiplicitous/virtual Sense-event, i.e. "anything can happen. It's a free zone, completely unpredictable" (Rodley 19). It is also referred to as a "waiting room" by the Man from Another Place (Michael Anderson), who is a dwarf that serves as its intermediary; the dwarf even speaks reversed-backward-speech, which undermines for audiences the 'naturalized' notion of language use as a transparent vehicle for common-sense; Lynch filmed the actors speaking backwards in the Red Room, so when we watch the scenes in actual-time, their voices become distorted and awkward for bizarre/comic effects. The Red Room is also referred to in the series as the entrance to the White and Black Lodges, which are two very powerful gateways to different/alternate realities. Deputy Hawk (Michael Horse) explains to Agent Cooper that, in Native-American mythology, the white lodge is ruled by forces of love that want to explore alternative realities, whereas the black one is ruled by fear of such realities. Therefore, the characters in the show that desire phallic/logocentric power over others seek the mythic power of the black lodge, whereas those who desire poetic knowledge and understanding seek the virtual powers inherent in the white lodge. Since the Red Room comes about in the show through the involuntary dreaming of Cooper, it must not be read as a metaphysical space, but as a dream-esque one that can re-shape events/forces in the actual world from alternative, creative perspectives.

The Red Room embodies both poetically-productive potentials as well as mythically-destructive ones (i.e. BOB) just like *Twin Peaks'* social reality. The Red Room is decorated by luscious, flowing, red-drapes and art-deco chairs and couches. Its floor has a zig-zag, black-and-white design that poetically implies that the white and black lodges are actually "one and the same," as The Giant (Carel Struycken) states in the show's final episode. This poetically implies that the person who enters the Red Room either perceives it as a place dominated by either fear or love, and their perceptions of such a poetic reality determine what they can gain by entering it. In fact, this explains why Cooper leaves the Red Room in the show's final episode haunted by BOB, since he only entered the Red Room to heroically rescue his girlfriend, Annie Blackburn (Heather Graham); Annie had been kidnapped and taken there by his nemesis and former partner Windom Earle (Kenneth Welsh). Cooper, because he fears what will happen to Annie, ignores everything but his rational will to rescue her, thereby becoming shut off from all other possibilities for experiencing such a poetic reality (see Nochimson's *Desire Under the Douglas Firs* for an excellent analysis of this final episode).

However, it must be noted that the show's final episode is not nihilistic at heart, since it only implies that, for the moment, a BOB-esque aspect of Dale Cooper has won out precisely because he has let fear become the most powerful emotional reality in his life. Therein lies one of the show's key messages to its audience: *how one perceives the world around one creates what that world can signify/Become. We all have the violent and destructive capacity to see the world like BOB sees it.* In the Red Room's free-zone or virtual space-time, the possibilities for open-ended meanings directly reflect the perceiver's ability to poetically construct what such a space can offer. In this case, Cooper has momentarily contacted an unsettling aspect of his personality that contains the potential (a la BOB) to eradicate all capacities for poetic meaning and perception.

Twin Peaks, therefore, can be read in its entirety as germane to prime-time TV through openly exposing and re-writing bourgeois myth; in addition, it is also a singular phenomenon in TV history in that it foregrounds many poetic forces that challenge such myth with its own contingent nature. Herein reside *Twin Peaks'* political potentials. Barthes explains:

> there is therefore one language which is not mythical, it is the language of man [and woman] as producer: wherever man speaks in order to transform reality

and no longer to preserve it as an image, wherever he links his language to the making of things, metalanguage is referred to a language-object, and myth is impossible. This is why revolutionary language proper cannot be mythical. Revolution is defined as a cathartic act meant to reveal the political load of the world: it *makes* the world; and its language, all of it, is functionally absorbed in this making. It is because it generates speech which is *fully*, that is to say initially and finally, political, and not, like myth, speech which is initially political and finally natural, that Revolution excludes myth. (*Myth Today* 135)

Through viewing bourgeois myth as a social form of oppression, Lynch/Frost's series posits that these myths oppress any capacity for *productively* poetic meanings that can operate beyond or in opposition to common sense—especially female writing like Laura's in her diary. Such forces are what can vitally and virtually transform the cultural repressions/self-denials inherent in bourgeois social reality. In this sense, media poetry in the context of TV is always-already more powerful than bourgeois myth whenever one takes full advantage of such poetry's productive potentials. Mythic order, when seen from this perspective, is precisely what generates social alienation, and its claims to 'represent' the pinnacle of human potential is a leveling and destructive fantasy of power and control over a dynamic and fluctuating world. If one buys into bourgeois myth, the price one pays may just be the world itself. Gone will be any further possibilities or Becomings of any significant kind.

Can we therefore read the adolescents on *Twin Peaks* as successfully changing and overcoming the mythic order of their town? Because the show was canceled, a definitive answer is not possible. Nevertheless, Twin Peaks' adolescents' abilities to reject bourgeois myth succeed in leaving Laura's murder with an open potential for meaning, which implies that the show at the very least brings out this realization for viewers. The show's adolescents, along with agent Cooper's unorthodox detective methods, succeed in revealing mythic society's inability to 'naturalize' Laura's death. TV audiences, by extension, are also offered an opportunity to contact poetic forces outside of 'normalized', prime-time ideologies. Through Laura's death and her society's inability to mythically empty-out her death, audiences can confront the inadequate relationship between social myths and the poetic/semiotic forces that not only created them but that still possess the virtual potentialities to re-create them.

Twin Peaks' Ironically-clichéd Universe

A poem as lovely as a tree:

As the night wind blows, the boughs move to and fro. The rustling, the magic rustling that brings on the dark dream. The dream of suffering and pain.

Pain for the victim, pain for the inflictor of pain.
A circle of pain, a circle of suffering. Woe to the
ones who behold the pale horse.
—the Log Lady's fireside intro to
episode 14.

Since poetic/semiotic signification achieves a powerful presence on *Twin Peaks*, how then should we read Lynch/Frost's previously-mentioned incorporation of 'gushy' and clichéd subjects like Laura's gold heart charm and *Invitation to Love* that everyone in *Twin Peaks* watches? Do these examples prove that Lynch & Frost are only mocking the sentiments of their characters? Do these clichés undermine Lynch/Frost's poetic/semiotic elements in *Twin Peaks*? In order to understand the phenomena of clichés on *Twin Peaks*, we must view them in relation to their social function in an empty status quo. Perhaps the key in interpreting these clichés is to understand whether they are empty, cynical comments on the inert status of human creativity or naïve vehicles that nevertheless can still invoke poetic/semiotic potentials in bourgeois society.

Perhaps the only connections many adults and even adolescents have to semiotic/poetic forces are clichéd versions of those semiotic forces. Thereby, a cliché can become a semiotically re-charged (i.e. *productive*) vehicle for connecting people back to the creative imagination *if it flaunts its constructed/artificial nature and not a naturalized/empty one*. The cliché could then be ignited with new potentials for emotional-expressions/Sense-events through its perversely-naïve make-up. Žižek also lends support to the fact that the clichés in Lynch's film-art have a "redemptive value" in themselves (3). However Žižek's reading is limited by the fact that he does not relate them to the virtual potentialities (the percepts & affects) they can also generate.

The previously-mentioned, clichéd nature of Harriet's poem to Laura after her death is an effective example of how poetic/semiotic potential can recharge an empty mode of expression; her entire poem reads as follows:

It was Laura,
And I saw her glowing in the dark wood;
I saw her smile;
We were crying and we were laughing,
In our sadness I saw her dancing.
It was Laura
Living in my dreams.
The glow was life;
Her smile was to say
It was alright to cry.
The woods was our sadness,
The dance was her calling.
It was Laura,
And she came to kiss me good-bye.

While Harriet uses the "available ideologies" to express "an uncertain meaning," her invocation of Laura's desire to transcend her own traumatic life becomes the *productive* potential of the poem. Although Harriet could not have known that Laura was an incest victim at the time she wrote it (in episode 8), Harriet nevertheless intuits that Laura's "crying" is anything but "empty." The "glow" of life in the poem, therefore, becomes the empathic bond that results when Harriet poetically/semiotically identifies with Laura's problematic struggle for a poetically-productive identity. Harriet's poem can be read in this light as an attempt to see beyond Laura's suffering in a repressively-logocentric, hyper-rational social order. Harriet's adolescent psychic potential transforms Laura's struggle into a positive source of poetic meaning/Becoming for herself. Through incorporating this poem into the narrative of *Twin Peaks,* Lynch/Frost reveal that cliches are not automatically cynical but, can, through their own perverse naïveté, invoke other creative potentials for meaning. In this sense, Lynch/Frost suggest that nothing can be rendered 'empty' once and for all through cliches.

Harriet's poem is not the only example of *Twin Peaks'* use of semiotically/poetically recharged cliches. If we view the previously mentioned examples of Lynch/Frost's cliches, they fare in a similar manner. Laura's half-gold heart charm can also be seen to invoke semiotic forces. It can be viewed as an actual symbol of the fact that, due to her being an incest victim, her heart has permanently been 'broken' in half. *Invitation to Love,* alternatively, although it does not invoke semiotic forces because it parodies the already clichéd nature of soap operas, can be seen as a "cry for help" because what is often missing in its adult audience is the productively-emotional charges (the affects) of poetic/semiotic significations; *Twin Peaks* offers one solution to such culturally-empty portrayals of people's search for poetic potentials through its semiotically-re-charged percepts & affects. The "ironically-clichéd" pulp narratives like the mafia conspiracies, twisted love triangles, contract hits, etc. that give rise to Lynch's later film *Mulholland Drive,* also expose how all cliches are *ironic* in Lynch's simulated-universes.

Twin Peaks continually undermines not only the empty natures of cliches but the 'featureless', phenomenal ground of the bourgeois plain. The show is a testimony to TV's potential for bringing in other voices into bourgeois culture. The fact that a bourgeois, mythic social order is not the sum total of human meaning implies that undermining bourgeois 'naturalization' can have productive results for escaping its tyrannical hold on cultural meaning. Ironic cliches are more desirable than cynical claims that a hyper-rational common sense already occupies the total potential for cultural meaning. Since *Twin Peaks* became wildly popular in its first season on ABC, it serves as a symbol that undermining bourgeois values and attracting prime-time audiences are not always mutually exclusive.

1 It has become a critical commonplace to refer to *Twin Peaks* as part of David Lynch's movie career. The show's co-creator Mark Frost has had his contribution wholly subsumed into Lynch's auteur status, as have all of the other writers and directors of the individual episodes. Since all of the criticism on *Twin Peaks* refers to it as Lynch's creation and usually relates it to Lynch's other films, this chapter will attempt to correct that critical convention.

4.

"It's Rather Poetic": Buffy the Vampire Slayer & Deleuze's Becoming-art

> So that's why time went all David Lynch?
> —Buffy, "Dead Things," Season 6.

****

> Buffy: I wanted to tell you how much I enjoyed this class. I
> mean I know I wasn't the best student, but I really learned a
> lot, and I really like poetry, I really do. [. . .]. I wish I had
> time for it. [. . .].
>
> Her Poetry Professor: Well, maybe short poems.
>
> Buffy: Yeah, like those Japanese poems that sound like a
> sneeze.
>
> Her Poetry Professor: Haiku?
> —Buffy talking to her poetry professor about
> dropping all her classes, "Tough Love," season 5.

The above conversation between Buffy Summers (Sarah Michelle Gellar) and her English professor may at first appear to be a random scene foregrounding Buffy's difficulties with balancing her college career and her demon/vampire fighting, but it's rather significant that the only professor she is shown conversing with is her poetry one (Buffy had to withdraw because she was overwhelmed by both her demon-fighting duties as well as the death of her mother). The implication in the above scene is that Buffy's poetry class has been the most vital for her life experience and education; although Buffy may lack a traditional knowledge of poetry as an academic object of study, her life still has a lot to say about poetic ways of interacting with the forces that make up the actual world (see below).

What is most curious about Buffy's conversation with her literature professor is that printed poetry is given a privileged place in Buffy's rocky education even though it is not a mainstream art-form in our current, virtual-media environment; revealingly, Buffy also gets kicked out of an "Images of Pop Culture" Class for being a disruption the first day of her freshman year in season 4, which thematically implies that her learning needs something more than just re-hashed 'images'. The irony in operation here is perhaps obvious since *Buffy the Vampire Slayer* (*BtVS*)[1] is a prime-time TV serial that aligns its heroine's education (a la Laura Palmer in *Twin* Peaks) with a more marginalized art-form than the TV one that her character is actually a significant part of. Joss Whedon's *BtVS*, therefore, implies that Buffy's identity and relation to the world around her do not necessarily fit the sensationalized norms/ideals commonly lauded in contemporary TV and mass media. It also implies that poetic signification is desperately needed in multi-media environments, and it should not be fetishized as solely printed code on white pages.

BtVS often portrays its characters discussing the cultural significance of different media and artistic phenomena, usually from rather self-conscious, postmodern perspectives, so musings about how literature and popular media effect culture-at-large are not uncommon in the show; in the 1st-season episode "I, Robot...You, Jane," a conversation occurs concerning virtual media; one radically-extremist student, Fritz, serio-comically exclaims: "the printed page is obsolete. Information isn't bound up anymore, it's an entity. The only reality is virtual. If you're not jacked in, you're not alive!" Fritz's comment is a rather over-the-top take on how quickly new media can change social modes of communication.

Even though Buffy does not have much 'private' time for studying poetry and its 'intellectual' relations to new media, her life as a pop-media heroine is nevertheless a poetically-rich and complicated one; for example, Gregory J. Sakal describes Buffy's challenging duty to the world around her in the following manner: "it is not for her to decide who is redeemable and who is not. Her task is to protect and help—not to judge" (250). Buffy's magical birthright and power as a demon fighter render her responsibility to the world around her a difficult, poetic duty more than a sensational, 'media-image'. Since not all demons are evil in the Buffyverse, and not all humans are life-affirming agents, Buffy must continually and productively re-mediate her knowledge of all that life and art have to offer. Throughout the series, Buffy does not see the world in sensationalized or idealized terms at all, but as something contingent in nature that must be protected and productively nurtured so human potential can overcome all that threatens to block it; as Scott R. Stroud describes this notion: "Buffy is a vigilante hero with a scrunchy—a seemingly ordinary teenager who is charged with an extraordinary task of protecting the community from demons and its own ignorance" (185). It goes without saying that this is not the average responsibility of an attractive, blond, adolescent/young woman in contemporary American culture.

More often than not, Buffy is placed in the position of having to be a marginalized outsider who must reject the normalcy and shallowness inherent in the social world surrounding her. The artistic or poetic image of the world Buffy must fight for as the slayer, who protects the ignorant and the oblivious, is incongruent with any mythically-ideal, bourgeois world-view or mentality. Buffy's poetic world-view, alternatively, is perhaps best described by another demon-fighter, Angel (David Boreanaz), in his own spin-off series:

> there is no grand plan, no big win [. . .]. If there's no great, glorious end to all this, if nothing we do matters, then all that matters is what we do. 'Cause that's all there is—what we do—now, today. [. . .]. I wanna help because people shouldn't suffer as they do. Because if there isn't any bigger meaning, then the smallest act of kindness is the greatest thing in the world.   ("Epiphany," *Angel*, season 2)

Both Angel and Buffy fight to protect other people's rights to enjoy the poetic contingencies of actual, mortal life. Buffy and all her demon-fighting friends must continually overcome any escapist notion of a safe/empty/idealized reality that 'can' supposedly exorcise all its threats once-and-for-all.

In fact, what makes *BtVS* a fascinating cultural commentary is that Buffy's life before her calling was dominated solely by such bourgeois interests, i.e., she used to only care about boys, idealized appearances, and avoiding all complicated, actual-world concerns. Once bestowed with her 'magical' slayer-powers, Buffy had to effectively overcome any and all idealized or egotistical notions of herself and her relation to the world around her. By extension, Buffy's home, Sunnydale California, is also a seemingly idyllic mid-sized town whose 'ideal' appearance is dramatically confounded by the fact that its "suburban paradise is but a storm drain resting over the cauldron of hell" (Hibbs 52). Hibbs is referring to the fact that Sunnydale has its own Hellmouth, a portal that is literally under the high school and that can open Sunnydale's reality to demon dimensions of all varieties. Buffy's demon-fighting job is often rendered even more difficult by the fact that the 'ignorant' adults around her often view her as a rebellious threat who brings trouble to their 'safe', bourgeois/dualistic way of life.

By extension, Whedon's series can be read as implying that fantastic, media/poetic productions can also be exiled by such a normalized, bourgeois world-view, and Buffy must also thematically fight for the freedom to engage the actual world in traditionally 'unreal' artistic/creative manners (a la the adolescents on *Twin Peaks*). Buffy and her friends all willingly choose to complicate their lives by entering into such a difficult, daily struggle for a 'creative' relation to the world-at-large. Since Whedon's show acknowledges that Buffy "really like[s] poetry," it therefore foregrounds that any poetic world-view's main threats are the idealized, bourgeois myths that seek to 'empty out' all of life's fabulations/complications/Becomings. The demons/vampires that come from the Hellmouth are, therefore, more than just campy versions of age-old Hollywood villains; they are 'materially-embodied' metaphors for what the adults in the town often disown about themselves and their social reality. Thus, *BtVS* is a curious mix of hokey fluff and profound social commentary.

Whedon's *BtVS* and its spin-off *Angel* are much more than just campy re-presentations of conventional story lines and conflicts from the histories of American film and TV; both shows seek to poetically re-write many conventional and normalized assumptions about artistic production and the actual world itself. As Whedon states in his audio commentary on the episode "Innocence" (season 2), *Buffy* is about the poetic/singular effects of "emotional resonance," and not about any strict, pre-determined realism. Carolyn Kersmeyer expounds on Whedon's claim: "the varied portrayal of emotions in this series signals an unexpected aesthetic depth in a show that might at first seem relatively fluffy entertainment" (170).

The often hokey appearances of the demons in the Buffyverse are, in addition, clues to not read them literally. As Tracy Little notes:

> even the show's title, *Buffy the Vampire Slayer*, is an ironic tribute to the show's premise of a blond, fashion-obsessed high-school girl having the supernatural power to defeat the forces of evil that lie in the world. Many critics dismiss the show off-hand because of this intentionally campy title, but they fail to grasp the irony as setting the premise of the story and providing a context for the very real social issues that lie just beneath the surface of the show's metaphors. (288)

Since the show uses poetic metaphors to discuss actual-world problems and conflicts in a more productive, fantastic capacity than any conventional or common-sense TV 'realism'/'idealism', it is perhaps no accident that the show's writers and directors have aligned *BtVS*'s mode of signification more with poetic production/meaning than 'empty'/sensationalized pop-culture-'images' or 'representations'.

Little describes below the show's mode of visual and narrative signification, and her description is uncannily similar to how media poetry operates as a hybrid, multi-modal artistic-mode-of-expression:

> researchers argue that as the fears and threats in a society change, so does the way that we [portray] such fears and threats as a culture. A new set of norms is often required to address and respond to these fears and threats, as well as to allow for the development of a common frame of reference and understanding. Metaphors are often utilized in this way because they allow us to communicate about events, fears, and emotions that may not yet be understood fully by

members of a society. Thus, metaphor serves as a way to discuss topics for which we do not yet have a language, or for which our vocabulary cannot reach in a one-dimensional way. Through making a comparison to something else, metaphor creates layered dimensions of understanding by which the speaker and listener can better communicate and through which a level of emotional or philosophical understanding can be reached that would not be possible with a straight description of the situation or feeling. (283)

BtVS's mode of artistic signification creates a hybrid media discourse through such fantastical metaphors, which allow for multiplicitous commentaries on vital personal and cultural issues that are often dangerously codified by pre-determined norms/conventions. Since most social threats are repressed or ignored by the 'normal' adults in Sunnydale, *it is no artistic accident that adolescents like Buffy must fight them in 'unreal' or fantastic forms.*
As Little goes on to explain, the desires of we viewers are also intimately implicated in *BtVS*'s artistic world-view:

the writers and producers of *BtVS* have utilized this [metaphorical] approach not just as an effective story-line motivator, but also as a valid way to appeal to viewers on several levels. In this context, such metaphors have the capacity to help viewers put their own fears and emotions into perspective, [to] deal with such fears and emotions in a more effective way, to provide a point of comparison with the reality of the viewer and that of the show, to recognize that the fears and the emotions played out by the show's characters may be similar to their own, and, finally, to legitimize the feelings of the viewer. The complex nature of such metaphors also allows for multiple interpretations on the part of the viewer, providing the viewer with a means of agency for interacting with the show on a deeply personal level. (284)

In fact, the diegetic world that Buffy and her friends inhabit is a poetically open-ended one in which such metaphors are always more than just symbolic/rhetorical figures of speech, i.e., they can 'ontologically' and virtually transform the show's diegetic reality itself; in the Buffyverse, any virtual entity can be made actual through magic, which implies that the virtual-actual phenomenon of magic is one of the most powerful forces in that diegetic world. In this sense, the show foregrounds the Nietzschean/Deleuzian notion of Virtual-becoming (or Becoming-art) that can transform the individual into a self-creating artist who productively sees art (the virtual) and contingent life (the actual) not as separate phenomena, but as intimately-interrelated forces that co-create what's possible. Time itself in the Buffyverse goes all "David Lynch," i.e. all multi-linear, quite often for productive and fascinating effects.

The Buffyverse: Magic as a Poetic Language

> We don't belong to ourselves, we belong in the world
> fighting.
> —Angel, concerning his relationship with Buffy;
> "Hero," *Angel*, Season 1.

It is perhaps ironic to consider that David Lynch's *Mulholland Drive* was originally slated to become an ABC-TV drama series and instead become a buzzworthy, independent film, whereas *Buffy the Vampire Slayer* started off as a less-than-hit film and actually became a popular, long-running TV series. Those facts reveal that in a virtual-media environment, different mediums have no purely essential or absolute qualities-in-themselves. Therefore, the diegetic reality that *BtVS* and its spin-off *Angel* inhabit is a rather curious one for prime-time TV, one that requires some elucidation. First off, its reality does not conform to any strict notion of representational or common-sense realism, since everyday citizens commonly harness or invoke magical/poetic powers; in addition, there are demons and vampires lurking in almost every shadow—facts that most of the citizens of both Sunnydale and Los Angeles Ca. choose to stay willfully ignorant of.

Herein lies one of the key ironies in the Buffyverse: most people continually choose to live in a mythically-ideal, bourgeois mentality that ignores not only dangers/threats but also the creative powers that the world around them allows. The fact that *BtVS*'s diegetic reality generates the possibility for magic/poetic phenomena also goes a long way towards securing a vast amount of artistic freedom for the show, which is indirectly correlated with the lack of poetic freedom in a bourgeois, idealized social reality. Magic in the Buffyverse (a la a Wittgensteinian, multi-media *language-game*) is portrayed as a dramatic, reality-producing Sense-event, which simulates the context/'spirit' in which the characters act or perceive the world around them.

Magic, in *BtVS*, is a *poetic language* that is capable of transforming actuality when its effects are congruent with the productive forces of the contingent world; Spike (James Marsters) edifies this notion in the episode "After Life" (season 6): "the thing about magic: there's always consequences—ALWAYS!" Magic acts that can poetically/virtually distort the show's diegetic reality reveal that both the characters as well as we viewers can benefit by re-writing/mediating the world in the contingent terms of creative simulations (the magic powers dramatized in the show), and not in the transcendent, 'fixed' terms of ideal representations (bourgeois myths). For example, to show exactly how *BtVS* exposes narrative itself to be a poetic process of virtual simulation, consider the 1st-season-episode "Nightmares," in which a young boy, Billy (Jeremy Foley), must communicate his physical abuse from a coma that his

Kiddie-League coach put him in; Billy's 'silent' suffering magically translates reality itself into everyone's worst nightmares. As everyone confronts their worst fears made actual a la Billy's situation, Buffy learns that such a magically-transformed reality points directly to Billy's actual abuse. Such explorations of virtual realities are similar to how Agent Cooper in *Twin Peaks* must come to understand Laura Palmer's 'silent' sexual abuse by entering a virtual dream-logic (the Red Room) where such suffering can find a communicative form; in addition, Buffy and her friends must continually confront such 'phantom'/actual forces like BOB on *Twin Peaks*. As such virtual transformations of a common-sense reality show, these 'unreal' phenomena must often speak for disowned/unsettling actual-life concerns.

As I discussed *Twin Peaks* in the last chapter as a hybrid-medium-example of media poetry, I also want to discuss *BtVS* in a similar vein; however, to avoid confusion, I want to re-iterate exactly what this term means in the context of a serial TV narrative. In the Buffyverse, simulation creates all signification: the magical and supernatural elements in the show are solely multi-media versions of Wittgensteinian *language-games* that do not have to reference a pre-existing reality to have productive effects; as Melissa M. Milavec and Sharon M. Kaye phrase this notion: "the supernatural premise of the series enables it to explore the nature of human relationships at a deeper level" (174). In fact, magical acts and artistic productions are virtually the same things in the Buffyverse. Like artistic production, magic imposes a new law on actuality that poetically distorts it in order to make it function by new rules, i.e., it taps into the multi-modal potentials for difference inherent in productive simulations. Such magical acts, however, to be poetically productive, must create hybrid language-games (meta-poetic commentaries) that are either directly or indirectly congruent with the productive forces of a contingent world.

Since the Buffyverse is radically open to multiple interpretations, and there have already been a myriad of articles interpreting the show, I want to add another way of reading it, i.e. as a productively-fantastic *media poetry*. This notion implies that for Whedon's series, art and actual reality are never separate phenomena; both contain the possibility for generating free and infinite capacities for difference in signification. In the Buffyverse, the particular narratives in individual episodes almost always revolve around poetic parables of Becoming, violence-as-catharsis, and the overcoming of actual-life conflicts. Even though *BtVS* exaggerates such conflicts in a comic-book/graphic-novel-esque manner, its metaphorical/poetic narratives are solely *language-game* hypotheticals that can create a virtual space-time in which all personal and cultural meaning can be put into virtual-play/Becoming. The serio-comic irony in operation here is that the characters treat all such transformations as actual phenomena, since the Buffyverse often productively erases the distinction between the virtual and the actual; this is the main reason why I'll be reading the show primarily as media poetry (or Becoming-art), and not as purely fluffy or hokey fantasy. In fact, what the Buffyverse's poetically-open diegetic reality can comment on in actual-world contexts is rather startling to explore.

As we shall see, the heroes and heroines of the Buffyverse continually seek to re-write/mediate any and all effects of dark-magic that are anti-contingent-life, and this further implies that in such an artistic world-view that rejects all timeless/ideal representations, everyone must become acutely aware of the fact that each person has a creative say in how the world itself functions. Little expounds on this constructive notion:

> today's teens live in a world where their classmates plot their murders, where the threat of gun violence is always present, where there is a high rate of sexually transmitted diseases, date-rape, and stalking. Now step into the world of [. . .] *BtVS*—here you will find that the monsters under your bed at night are real, that there actually are demons lurking outside your bedroom window. Also, more often than not it's the teens and young adults of the Buffyverse who see this reality for what it is, and it's the adults who are often the ones existing in a collective state of denial. (282)

Just like the adolescents of *Twin Peaks*, the Buffyverse's teens/young adults are open to non-mythically-ideal ways of perceiving and interacting with the forces and threats of the actual world. What is especially fascinating about the Buffyverse, as stated previously, is that many of its 'unreal' threats are materially-embodied metaphors for disowned, historical, and/or contemporary problems; the demons and vampires symbolize the myths/illusions that can dominate our fears and desires, e.g., the illusory notion that one can 'possess' a transcendent/timeless power over contingent life. If we look specifically at the vampires on the show, they are presented as the mocking ideal of current cultural wishes, i.e. they're the ones who are 'forever young;' however, they are more 'trapped' in a timeless alienation—which completely contradicts the Platonically-ideal vampire-form that 'promises' to redeem 'faulty' human beings.

Since the vampires are predominantly younger in *BtVS* than in many previous vampire tales, they are a revisionist version of the traditional, Freudian interpretation of the vampire as the mythically-powerful dead-father-figure (a la Bram Stoker's Dracula) who has escaped social limitations through death and who therefore can possess a God-like, fantastic, 'unlimited' access to the female population. In *BtVS*, the vampires possess powers that are much more ironic in that their 'ideal' existence is often sadly anti-contingent-life, i.e., they must feed off of such life to keep their 'ideal-state' going. It's rather revealing to consider that even though they're immortal, they can still be staked and killed; in addition, their 'ideal' natures do not at all overcome their *resentful* attempts to possess power over life itself. Most vampires in Whedon's show are constantly thwarted from having such an absolute/phallic power over life by Buffy and her renegade friends.

Whedon's *BtVS* implies, therefore, that it's the anti-life, ideal form that vampires/demons 'represent' that's truly evil and destructive, because even vampires like Spike and Angel realize this notion and reject such an anti-life idealism by aiding Buffy in her attempts to protect the contingent, mortal lives/desires around them. In addition, James Lawler explains that what a vampire 'represents' to we mortals is a metaphor for common psychological traps: "egotism, fear, and separation are the natural element of the vampire" (110); *BtVS* poetically implies that everyone in the audience has the potential to see the world like an a-social vampire. The challenge to the characters and audiences alike, therefore, is to complicate one's existence like Buffy in order to see actual-life as more dynamic than anti-contingent-life ideals.

In addition, there exist no strict, moral rules that govern the people who are evil and those who are not in the Buffyverse, since people's (and demon's) behaviors can often change unexpectedly and dramatically, which confounds any simplistic or ideal notion of evil. Mimi Marinucci explains how the Buffyverse rejects any reductive notion of an essential identity: "Buffy's treatment of Angel and Spike suggests that it is right for Buffy to kill vampires (when it is right) not because of what they are, but because of what they do" (64). In addition, "Angel, as viewers know, is a vampire with a 'soul', code in the show for moral conscience" (Miller 43). Since Spike is also granted a soul in the finale of season 6, this fact reveals that the human 'soul' portrayed in the series is not a purely timeless or metaphysical essence. The term 'soul' implies rather a sensibility or an artistically-expressive relation to the world a la Wittgenstein's theory of linguistic meanings as *language games*. The non-essentialized nature of the Buffyverse implies that the ultimate contest in the series is between anti-life agents and the productively-poetic, life-affirming ones, i.e., it is a battle between those who believe in life-as-representation (bourgeois myth or anti-contingent-life ideals) as opposed to those who believe in life-as-simulation (Becoming-art or media poetry).

Buffy's poetic role as the slayer, who must protect the contingent order of things, then, is one of a 'universal balancer' because she must stop any and all timeless ideals, i.e. the people, demons, and vampires that seek to escape all contingent forms and limits that, in their ultimate form, are also congruent with death. According to the spirit of the first slayer, Buffy's primary gift to the world around her "is death," and this is not an easy realization for either her or the show's audiences ("Intervention," season 5). Buffy, whose powers are a magical (or meta-poetic) gift past down from the distant past to protect mortal life, is the one who is burdened with propagating the often difficult, contingent-order of things from those who often seek to disavow that order. In this sense, Buffy's job is not morbid or nihilistic at all, but life-affirming in every respect, since she does not seek to deny the reality of death. For Buffy, the opposite of life is not death, but the fear of living, changing, and Becoming that characterizes most of the major characters' journeys in Whedon's series (see below). *BtVS*'s rhetoric, therefore, asks us, a la Buffy and her friends, to reject any anti-life ideals that disown mortal, contingent life. This is likely why Buffy is said to "really" like poetry, i.e., poetic production, according to Roland Barthes' theory discussed in chapter 3, *is the mode of signification* that seeks to reject any notions of the forces that make up the empirical world as 'representations' of timeless/transcendent forms.

One of the most striking examples of Buffy's poetically-contingent relation to the world around her occurs in the episode "The Body" (season 5), when Buffy's mother suffers an aneurysm and dies. Near the end of the episode, Buffy's unbelieving sister, Dawn (Michelle Trachtenberg), sneaks into the morgue to see her mother's dead body. As Dawn reaches to take the cloth off her mother's body, a vampire awakens in the morgue. Luckily, Buffy goes to find her sister and kills the vampire; however, the scuffle pulls the cloth off her mother's body, which now lies exposed. As the camera pauses on Buffy's face, it appears to register her awareness that her actual duty *is* to protect mortal and contingent life from all who threaten to escape it. The context of this scene implies that Buffy is truly fighting for her mother's right to die from natural causes; Buffy's gift to the world *actually is* death in this sense. As this episode reveals, Whedon's *BtVS* tackles some of the most challenging and difficult realizations life has to offer.

A Portrait of the Slayer As a Poetry-Fan: Buffy's Noble Ethics

> I don't want to protect you from the world, I want to show it to you.
> —Buffy to Dawn, "Grave," season 6.

> I got so much strength, I'm giving it away.
> —Buffy to Willow, "Same Time, Same Place," season 7.

> Giles—we get it—miles to go before we sleep.
> —Buffy, "The Prom," season 3.

The title of this chapter is taken from Giles (Anthony Stewart Head)'s serio-comic comment concerning the fact that Buffy has fallen in love with Angel, a vampire: "a vampire in love with a slayer, it's rather poetic." Giles, Buffy's watcher, who is in 'official' charge of her physical and 'spiritual' development as the slayer, hints with this statement at just how poetically rich the relationships are in *BtVS*, since they do not conform to any pre-determined notions of 'repressively-proper' behaviors or actions on the part of the characters. Therefore, I want to highlight Buffy's process of Becoming that *BtVS* charts for 7 seasons, in order to flesh out the specifics of what can be gained from the show's aesthetic portrayals of this young woman's maturation process. The issues of gender, and *how* to productively/pragmatically relate to the world-at-large that Buffy's development also foregrounds, are fascinating, poetic commentaries on many current socio-political issues/preoccupations. In addition, Buffy's self-creation is a compelling example of how one authors media poetry through re-writing/re-mediating one's life experiences; as Deleuze explains this phenomena: "only the creative artist takes the power of the false [what's creatively mediated or constructed] to a degree which is realized, not in form, but in transformation," i.e. Virtual-becoming or Becoming-art (*Cinema II* 146).

Joss Whedon has stated in several interviews that Buffy is a revisionist, mass-media character: she is the blonde, attractive young girl who is commonly helpless in the monster/horror movie-genre. Whedon created Buffy with the magical/media *power* to avoid such victim status, and to be able to kick the crap out of monsters with her own mental cunning and physical prowess. In addition, it is rather significant that she is an adolescent female at the start of the series. Female adolescence has commonly been portrayed throughout Western history as a battleground where forces vying for control clash, and where much of the cultural fear that is associated with young girls' transformations into young women threatens to become anti-contingent-life. Such young women like Buffy and even Laura Palmer have continually played a major role in much Western literature and drama since at least Greek times, and the Greek term for this female adolescent is the parthenos—a young, unmarried girl suddenly plunged into the disturbing and unsettling moment of sexual awakening.

According to Barabara Smith in *The Woman's Companion to Mythology*, the parthenos occupies the ambiguous physical/psychological/social state when a girl enters menarche, before she is married according to the customs of her society so that she will eventually become a mother (i.e. so the status quo can continue 'unthreatened') (87-88). In the Patriarchal tradition of Western culture, such male authorities have feared such adolescent females' powerful, 'unreadable' energies, and have traditionally sought to channel them into acceptable societal practices so that the foundation of Western/patriarchal society would not 'crumble'. More often than not, this irrational fear and the overbearing drive to control that it generates place the young girls themselves in danger, for parthenoi had only two options in life: marriage or obliteration. Buffy is a rather postmodern/folk-tale re-writing of the parthenos since she now possesses the traditionally-male trait of physical-dominance that has often guaranteed these young women's subordination to such a dis-empowering, cultural codification of their potentials.

In fact, Buffy's powers protect her society in ways that the traditional patriarchs of Western culture never sought to, since Buffy not only attempts to thwart evil but to also increase the productive potentials of everyone in her social reality. To re-iterate: it's truly a tragic irony that many adults in Sunnydale reject such productive potentials through buying whole-heartedly into bourgeois myths. Buffy foregrounds how media portrayals of young women are never pre-determined, and that everyone (males and females alike) can benefit by exploring *how* Buffy creates for herself a socially-constructive, empowered re-mediation of adolescent, female sexuality. Buffy, as a poetically-powerful parthenos, has the ability to not only re-create life in a biological sense, but to protect all the life around her from the anti-life threats that seek to limit people's poetic potentialities. Buffy, as we shall see, can especially inspire such desires in others.

I therefore want to interpret Buffy herself not only as an example of a socially-productive and life-affirming parthenos, but as a noble role-model as well. Nietzsche's notions of a Noble Ethics and Will-to-Power have traditionally been plagued by many critical mis-interpretations. For my purposes here, I will read both of Nietzsche's key tenets as wholly life-affirming enterprises, ones that foreground how an individual must become one's own moral authority and decision-maker and, therefore, resist subordinating oneself to any absolute, cultural/mythic authority. Whenever one submits oneself to such an absolute authority, one's potential to act in the world is often greatly and needlessly limited. According to Deleuze, Nietzsche's Will-to-Power is intimately tied to affect: "the capacity for being affected is not necessarily a passivity but an *affectivity*, a sensibility, a sensation. [. . .]. This is why Nietzsche always says that the will to power is 'the primitive affective form' from which all other feelings derive" (*Nietzsche & Philosophy* 62). It is perhaps obvious that Buffy reveals exactly why the Will-to-Power is tied to new ways of feeling and Becoming (i.e. a self-overcoming enterprise of artistic/creative transformation), since she always makes up her own mind about situations and is not afraid to go against both Giles, her mentor, and the patriarchal Watcher's Council that Giles 'represents'. Such a patriarchal, 'secret-order', which charts demon movements in the world, is often ignorant and oblivious as to what Buffy actually has to face. In fact, even Giles leaves the order and its mythic authority when he realizes that it only limits Buffy's development/Becoming.

Buffy is the sole authority over her choices in life, and she uses a rather simple but infinitely challenging poetic-awareness as her moral compass: anything that is life-affirming is worth protecting, and anything that threatens such life-potentials in the actual world must be re-written/mediated by the individual, i.e. Buffy herself. This tenant of the Will-to-Power has often been criticized because it privileges the individual to such an extreme, even potentially fascist, degree[2]. However, the Will-to-Power must always be opposed to a "*will to dominate*" (Deleuze, *Essays Critical & Clinical* 134). Nietzsche directly addresses this issue himself to avoid any such confusion:

the noble type of man [or woman] feels *himself* [or *herself*] to be the determiner of values, he does not need to be approved of, he judges 'what harms me is harmful in itself', he knows himself to be that which in general first accords to honour things, he *creates values*. Everything he knows to be part of himself, he honours: such a morality is self-glorification. In the foreground stands the feeling of plenitude, of power which seeks to overflow, the happiness of high tension, the consciousness of a wealth which would like to give away and bestow—the noble human being, too, aids the unfortunate but not, or almost not, from pity, but more from an urge begotten by a superfluity of power [. . .]. (*Beyond Good and Evil* 260)

The above quote is a great description of how *BtVS* continually foregrounds Buffy herself as a noble human being first and foremost, since her powers are never used for her own self-aggrandizement separate from how those powers aid her duty to the world around her; in fact, the responsibility she feels to help her fellow citizens is directly commensurate with the power that has been bestowed upon her.

Buffy's desire to protect the people around her can become quite a burden since what must often be sacrificed are her own personal interests and desires. As Deleuze explains, the Will-to-Power only flourishes in extra-personal contexts:

the will to power is essentially creative and giving: it does not aspire, it does not seek, it does not desire, above all it does not desire power. *It gives*: power is something inexpressible in the will (something mobile, variable, plastic); power is in the will as 'the bestowing of virtue', through power the will itself bestows sense and value. (*Nietzsche & Philosophy* 85)

It is striking to consider that the Will-to-Power is a fundamental preoccupation of *young women* (especially *teenage women*) in many mass-media shows like *BtVS* and *Twin Peaks*. Buffy whole-heartedly accepts such power/responsibility, and even inspires her friends to also re-create themselves in more productive, life-affirming capacities—regardless of how challenging such processes can often be (see below). In this sense, Buffy's burden never forces her to stay in complete isolation, which lessens the difficulty of her 'secret identity' that must stay as secret as possible because it puts the lives of those closest to her in constant jeopardy.

What is perhaps so "emotionally resonant" about Buffy's evolution/Becoming in the series is that nothing she learns in that process is ever smooth or easy for her. The show implies, therefore, that what she gains from most in her life are the experiences that deny her any safe or idealized world-view. In fact, during the first season of *BtVS*, she often seeks to disown her calling and birthright, wishing for nothing more than to be a 'normal' teenager. However, what wakes her up to her poetic duty to the world around her is what would happen if she did not fight off the demons/vampires that prey on an oblivious populous. Plus, Buffy becomes more and more aware that her job is not to re-enforce such an 'ignorance-is-bliss' mentality that the adults and many of the adolescents around her often choose; she, rather, must continually acknowledge the fact that she can transform the world around her in a more productive (not safer or easier) manner, and complicating both her life as well as the world itself is actually a life-affirming enterprise.

However, Buffy's first response to her calling is to view it solely in fatalistic and self-pitying terms; in the 1st-season-finale "Prophecy Girl," she assumes that an ancient prophecy signaling the slayer's death at the hands of the Master (an extremely old and powerful vampire) means that she must willingly offer her life, in a Christ-esque fashion, once and for all to this prophecy. Her mistake is to understand such prophesies in purely literal terms; when she does offer her life to the Master (Mark Metcalf), he bites her and throws her in a pool of water to drown—he too mistakenly assumes she will die as prophesied. However, Xander (Nicholas Brendon), one of Buffy's closest friends, refuses to believe the prophecy and luckily follows her down into the Master's layer, where, minutes later, he revives her with CPR; Xander's life-saving concern for his friend reveals how nothing is ever set-in-stone in the Buffyverse, and the individual can transform such a contingent world by productive/creative acts. In effect, there is no ideal or timeless 'representation' one must conform to once-and-for-all. Xander's desire to not believe the literal nature of the prophecy is an example of a poetically-productive act. To edify this notion, when a revived Buffy again confronts the Master and he exclaims "but you're dead—it was written," Buffy revealingly quips: "what can I say, I flunked the written." Such poetic re-writings of fate or pre-determined notions of life-as-representation have profound implications for the entire series, especially its final episode "Chosen" (season 7) when the entire mythology that gave rise to Buffy's powers gets such a re-writing (see below).

Throughout the many seasons of *BtVS*, Buffy has to face not only most of the challenges a young, female adolescent has to face in 'mythic' America, but just about everything else such an idealized-social-reality disowns about itself. In the series' finale, "Chosen," Buffy paints a serio-comic self-portrait in a conversation with Angel, one that sums up where all of Buffy's Becomings have been leading her throughout the series; in fact, this conversation implies that Buffy has completely overcome any bourgeois notion of her own identity for one based on the radically-open, productively-poetic processes of Becoming-art:

Buffy: O.K. I'm cookie dough—I'm not done baking—I'm not finished becoming whoever the hell it is I'm gonna turn out to be. I make it through this, and the next thing, and the next thing, and maybe one day I turn around and realize, I'm ready—I'm cookies. And then, you know, if I want someone to eat me——or——enjoy warm, delicious cookie-me, then, that's fine, that'll be then, when I'm done.

Angel: Any thoughts on who might enjoy——do I have to go with the cookie analogy?

Buffy: Not really thinking that far ahead, that's kinda the point.

It is rather striking that Whedon chooses to end the series without wrapping up who will be Buffy's key romantic interest; Whedon implies with this gesture that any romantic narrative is completely secondary to Buffy's actual process of Becoming the individual she creates herself to be. *BtVS* reveals to audiences, then, that any bourgeois, romanticized notion of what life has to offer must acquiesce to a dynamic/unpredictable process of Becoming. In addition, the serio-comic sexual pun in Buffy's above self-portrait implies that one can only fully enjoy the contingent pleasures that life has to offer *after* one has first created one's identity and desires in a productively-singular/noble capacity.

However, Buffy's above-thoughts on how far she has come in the series have been rendered possible only through her constant battles with all the challenging and difficult realizations contingent life has to offer. After having died for several minutes at the end of season 1, Buffy must face how season 2 does not render her life any simpler for having overcome that traumatic fact. At the beginning of season 2, Buffy has not overcome her 'death' at the Master's hands. In the episode "When She Was Bad," Buffy defensively hides in an emotionally-invincible and shut-off persona that alienates her from all her friends until she gets the cathartic chance to smash the Master's bones into dust and to thus overcome his traumatic memory.

Season 2 of *BtVS* continually charts how Buffy must still confront many of her often naïve and inexperienced notions about other people's motivations and inabilities to treat others in noble capacities. In fact, by the end of the season, Buffy gets kicked out of her house by her mother because Buffy defied her wishes and continued risking her life as the slayer; Buffy also gets kicked out of high school because her principal assumes (because trouble follows her around) that she is a rebellious and violent threat to everyone else. Buffy must also 'kill' the man/vampire she is in love with, Angel, because he had turned 'evil' again after a curse came true that stated if he ever achieved a moment of true happiness he would lose his soul (gypsies had cursed him with a soul—i.e. moral conscience—as punishment for the pain and suffering he caused when he was killing as a vampire). Sadly, Angel's evil-turn proves deadly for Giles' love-interest, Ms. Calender (Robia La Morte), since Angel's plan for truly hurting Buffy is to first kill all her friends and loved ones. It's rather unfortunate for Buffy that what has triggered Angel's descent to his old, murderous self is having sex with her (a true moment of happiness)—and on her 17th birthday no less!

In the 2nd season episode "Innocence," Buffy must confront the fact that a now soul-less Angel, after taking her virginity, only wants to destroy her physically and emotionally. Whedon's series, however, foregrounds how Buffy is not rendered powerless and demeaned by such a destructive, 'demonic' abuse of her desire to truly love another person (or vampire in this case). In fact, calling the episode "Innocence" implies that Buffy's innocence has momentarily been hurt, but not once-and-for-all, since the episode ends with a touching moment when Giles tells her that, regardless of what has happened, he still has only respect for the choices she has made; the touching conversation about Buffy's first 'hellish' sexual experience happens as follows:

> Buffy: You must be so disappointed in me.
>
> Giles: No, no I'm not.
>
> Buffy: But this is all my fault.
>
> Giles: I don't believe it is. Do you want me to wag my finger at you and tell you you behaved rashly. You did, and I can. I know that you loved him and he has proven more than once that he loved you. You couldn't have known what would happen. The coming months are going to be hard, I suspect, on all of us, but if it's guilt you're looking for Buffy, I'm not your man. All you will get from me is my support and my respect.

This conversation, which leaves Buffy in tears, implies that it is solely up to Buffy (and not anyone else) if she is still "innocent" enough to trust another person that way again.

To complicate matters further at the end of season 2, Buffy must 'kill' Angel even after Willow (Alyson Hannigan), Buffy's best friend, magically restores his soul because Angel had previously opened a portal that would allow demons to freely wreak havoc on the world, and only Angel's blood can close the portal; Buffy has no choice but to close it with Angel trapped inside. By having multiple, terrible things happen to her at the end of season 2, Whedon's series suggests, Buffy is not rendered a tragic victim because she's also given the chance to ultimately overcome them through poetically re-creating herself as a more self-actualized, self-reliant young woman. By extension, the show implies that one can only truly learn about contingent life through embracing and overcoming all the painful/fearful things life itself offers up. Through being stripped of some of her bourgeois illusions about how the world functions, Buffy is now able to create a more poetically-aware and empathetic world-view.

Much of season 2 showcases to audiences that in high school one must learn how self-reliance is not dependent on how other people view one, especially destructive/abusive people who solely seek to dis-empower and degrade others' potentials in the world. Many times in *BtVS* Buffy and the other main characters must learn that people are often not who they present themselves to be, and appearances are never ideal since most people manipulate them in order to derive egotistical advantages from them. Many people like Buffy have had to face the similar fact that someone has used/demeaned them sexually for their own egotistical gratification. Whedon, in his audio commentary to "Innocence," calls this fact the "baptism-by-adolescent-fire—the romance gone wrong." This is another example of how Whedon's series uses poetic/virtual metaphors to describe the often painful maturation process in adolescence that is seldom, if ever, ideal. As Little describes this awareness: "the metaphor of the loss of self-esteem and identity that so many teens go through is dealt with head on [in *BtVS*], and the underlying message is 'Be Yourself'" (292). The series implies that to productively become yourself, you first have to go through the difficult process of creating a personal/singular identity. Thus, it's a poetic truth to realize that, as Whedon claims in his audio commentary, Buffy, in season 2, "hasn't lost anything" at all.

The beginning of season 3 on *BtVS* introduces us to a traumatized and resentful Buffy; she has left Sunnydale for L.A. because of the havoc her slayer duties wreaked on her personal life. She takes her middle name, Anne, as her first name and becomes a waitress in order to escape her devastated life. In fact, her move is similar to Diane's in *Mulholland Drive*, since Diane 'moved' to L.A. to also become a new and hopefully 'more ideal' person (Betty); however, Diane's escapist wish turns out to be like Buffy's move—i.e., it's solely a willful desire to escape or nullify her 'actual' self. Luckily, Buffy's desire to escape her own identity ends on a more positive note than Betty/Diane's. Buffy/Anne runs into someone Buffy had saved in the past, Lily/Chantarelle (Julia Lee), who was involved in a vampire-worshiping cult in the episode "Lie to Me" (season 2); Lily is unfortunately now living on the streets of L.A. However, she still remembers Buffy's positive, life-saving potential, which does not please Buffy/Anne at first. Buffy/Anne has no choice but to help when Lily gets taken prisoner by a demon that uses young street kids in an underworld, slave-labor trade. Such a terrible event actually becomes what re-triggers Buffy's latent desire to help the less-fortunate, and it furthermore allows her to re-envision her own pain and suffering as inter-related with what she can do to alleviate others' pain.

In effect, Buffy momentarily succumbs to the common adolescent trap of feeling a radical loss of identity that Little describes above. The fact that Buffy can beat the crap out of those underworld demons who harvest young, street-kids to do their labor allows Buffy the catharsis she needs to break out of her problematic cycle of self-erasing/pitying behavior; the social commentary in operation here is the unfortunate fact that few people notice when such 'unwanted' kids go missing. To foreground this adolescent identity-loss, the demons in the slave-trade force all the street-kids to repeat the self-erasing mantra "I'm no one." However, when the demon asks Buffy/Anne who she is, she defiantly states: "I'm Buffy, the vampire slayer, and you are?" Both Buffy and the adolescents she then rescues benefit by Buffy's Nietzschean-esque self-affirmation; Buffy-the-prodigal-daughter can then return home to Sunnydale and to her relieved mother.

Lawler explains the poetic metaphor and social commentary in operation in this episode: "the ultimate logic of this world [i.e., anonymous urban life] is not the elusive happiness of 'ordinary life', but enslavement. [. . .]. [. . .] if we seek merely to satisfy our physical needs and desires, we become slaves in a mechanistic underworld founded on our own cowardly acquiescence" (109). Therefore, the demon-run, slave-underworld in this episode is also a poetic metaphor for how low-income, service-jobs can dis-empower and even erase one's personal identity. Buffy's power, therefore, is not just physical strength, but the poetic ability to re-write such outworn, destructive patterns of identity-loss.

Nonetheless, Buffy's power can also be used in ways that are not purely life-affirming. In fact, in season 3, Buffy must confront the socially-destructive tendencies that her power may also generate; by extension, as we shall see, other characters throughout the series (such as Willow) are also productively transformed through being dramatically confronted by their own potentials for self-erasing and socially-destructive tendencies (see below). Thus, Buffy is forced to acknowledge the 'dark side' of her powers when another slayer, Faith (Eliza Dushku), is magically called to duty after Kendra (Bianca Lawson) is killed; Kendra had been 'called' to be a slayer when Buffy momentarily died at the end of season 1.

Hedonistic Faith embodies, in many ways, everything that Buffy and her brand of Noble Ethics are not. Faith is portrayed, in effect, as Buffy's self-destructive alter-ego. For Faith, a slayer is better and more powerful in every way than an average person and, for her, this means the regular rules do not apply to slayers. Faith's perspective is, in effect, an anti-life version of Nietzsche's Will-To-Power, i.e. a Will-To-Dominate. Faith is willing to use men for sexual gratification and to steal whatever she needs; she even whole-heartedly believes the idea that a slayer must always work alone, since it is beneath a slayer to form legitimate attachments to others. For Faith, attachments solely imply a weakness on the part of a slayer's individuality. Principal Wood (D.B. Woodside), in "Chosen" (season 7), serio-comically refers to this tendency as "defensive, isolationist slayer-crap."

Faith, however, does wreak momentary havoc on Buffy's life when she convinces Buffy that they can do whatever they want, since, as slayers, they do enough good in the world to justify whatever less-life-affirming things they may desire. This dynamic perhaps makes the logic of the Buffyverse and how it portrays the processes of Becoming rather obvious, i.e., the way to transform oneself is to be confronted with the way *NOT* to productively live one's life. By experiencing such an anti-life actuality first-hand, one then has the potential strength and the desire to cathartically break-away from such a destructive cycle of behavior. For Buffy, this moment with Faith comes in the episode "Bad Girls" (Season 3) when they decide to kill vampires in style: they steal a whole bunch of expensive and flashy weapons, get arrested for it, and then break out of the police car that would have taken them to jail. The girls' 'lawless' night culminates in a very 'real' transgression when Faith accidentally kills a human being, the deputy mayor, who she mistakenly thinks is a vampire. For Buffy, this death implies that the one line she could never cross has been crossed, i.e., she has failed to live up to her own credo that anything which is a part of mortal, contingent life is worth protecting. Faith, who refuses to deal with the emotional consequences of what she has done, chooses to rationalize the killing through the fact that she has saved countless others. However, if we take a look at how both Buffy and Faith respond to this unfortunate event, we can garner a lot about the ethical structure and logic of the Buffyverse itself.

In effect, the moment when the deputy mayor is killed destroys the budding alliance between Buffy and her alter-ego Faith, and Buffy is forced again to re-envision her relation to the world so that it can be as poetically-productive as possible. Faith, who tries to avoid all personal responsibility, even tries to name Buffy as the murderer. Luckily, Buffy's friends choose not to believe Faith. But this fact only sends a thwarted Faith head-first into resentment because she then forms an alliance with the evil mayor of Sunnydale (Harry Groener), who is seeking to ascend to a Platonic state of pure demon-hood. Faith even tries to spite Buffy by attempting to kill Angel, who mysteriously returns in the middle of season 3 from some unknown hell-dimension where he had been tortured viciously by demons. As a poetic comment on such unpleasant events at season's end, Buffy must fight and overcome both Faith and what she symbolizes. Buffy mortally wounds Faith in this head-to-head fight, which thematically implies that Faith herself has become a threat to mortal, contingent life.

The end of season 3 also foregrounds more difficulties for Buffy: Angel leaves because he realizes that he cannot offer Buffy the actual-life-romance she desires, since he will never be able to have a sexual relationship with her without losing his 'soul' again. Angel, therefore, chooses to be selfless in the matter by leaving town so as to allow Buffy the chance at true happiness with someone else (and to start his own spin-off series). All these events point to how Buffy needs to make a mature leap into young adulthood by cathartically breaking with many of her outworn (adolescent) patterns of behavior.

In fact, Whedon's series offers Buffy and all her friends a rather dramatic and cathartic break with their high-school, adolescent lives at the end of season 3. The mayor, who is slated to be the speaker at Buffy's high-school graduation, has chosen this moment for his ascension to a state of pure and ideal demon-hood, whereby he will leave behind mortal life by literally feeding off the entire graduating class. Buffy and her friends have no choice but to blow up the entire high school in order to kill the mayor when he 'ascends' to his much larger demon form. *BtVS*, therefore, allows its adolescent characters one of the ultimate forms of catharsis in the history of American pop culture, since the break they make with the often torturous/adolescent high-school life is equivalent to productively destroying it; they effectively have no choice but to move forward in life.

In fact, this Dionysian cartharsis also prefigures the series finale when Buffy and her friends get to destroy the entire town of Sunnydale, which implies that they have no choice but to again make a 'clean break' and to become adults since they now cannot go backwards or regress at all—*as there's literally no place for them to go back to* (see below). Season 3, therefore, caps how Buffy has effectively overcome her capacity for using her powers as anti-life forces, and she must also make the difficult steps toward becoming a self-reliant, young woman. As might be expected, her confrontation with Faith is not over, since Faith does return in season 4; however, Whedon's series, which charts the Becomings of all major characters, now places Faith in a position to learn some difficult, experiential truths from Buffy.

Season 4, which charts Buffy's uncomfortable transition into college life, also showcases Faith's awakening from a coma; Faith now desires nothing more than to get revenge on Buffy for 'destroying' her life. Since Faith blames everything that happened to her on Buffy, she decides to make Buffy pay in the ultimate form: she was left a magical device by the mayor in case his plan for pure-demon-hood failed so they could get payback. This magical device allows Faith to switch bodies with anyone she desires and, since Faith's life is now, in effect, over (she is wanted by the law for murder), she can start anew by stealing Buffy's identity.

In the episode "Who Are You?," Faith gets the chance to vicariously experience life through another person's eyes. Unlike Craig in *Being John Malkovich*, Faith discovers such a phenomenon to be a humbling and eye-opening experience. In fact, what triggers Faith's re-evaluation of what is important in life is how Buffy is *recognized* or *regarded* by others. In order to keep up the illusion that she is actually Buffy, Faith (after she switches into Buffy's body) must keep protecting people's lives from vampires. One particularly grateful woman gushes over the fact that her life had been spared, which renders Faith incredibly uncomfortable by such a display of emotion. In addition, when Buffy's mother hugs what she thinks is her daughter, Faith recoils from that intimate recognition. In effect, Faith is beginning to realize that Buffy's lifestyle, which she once dismissed because Buffy was supposedly "a stuck-up tight-ass with no sense of fun," is actually more interesting and even more pleasurable than Faith's hedonistic one.

To edify this fact, the event that really strips Faith of her illusions/assumptions about life is when she decides to sleep with Buffy's love-interest in season 4, Riley (Marc Blucas); when Riley tells what he thinks is Buffy that he "loves her" after they have sex, Faith, in effect, freaks out, since she is completely incapable of handling such intense emotional gestures. Greg Forster describes this moment in terms Faith would understand: Faith is surprised to realize that Buffy "has a better sex life than she does" (17). In fact, as Faith is about to run away from Buffy's actual-life because it is too emotionally heavy, Faith hears on the news that a group of vampires have held up a congregation on a Sunday morning to mock the fact that their savior will not show up to save them (and to herald the coming of the season's Big Bad, Adam).

Faith revealingly chooses to stop the vampires, which implies that her sense of duty has now become comparable to Buffy's; Faith even tells them: "you're not going to kill these people, [. . .] because it's wrong!" This statement implies that Faith has been radically transformed by her vicarious experience of Buffy's life. As Faith is forced to do battle with not just vampires but with a pissed-off Buffy who wants her body back (in a church of all places), Faith's enemy becomes not Buffy, but herself. As Faith bashes in her own face, she begins to let loose her true feelings, even calling herself a "disgusting, murderous bitch." Luckily however, Buffy can use a magical counter-spell devised by Willow and Tara (Amber Benson) to switch back to her actual body, which then brings Faith's newly-poetic awareness of herself to a harsh and humbling fruition.

Such a vicarious experience does, in fact, lead to a productive transformation of Faith; after she leaves Sunnydale for L.A., she meets up with Angel, who, having been a killer in the past, can give her advice on how to overcome her own troubled past: she must take full responsibility for what she has done and face the actual and difficult consequences of her actions. On the *Angel* episode "Sanctuary" (season 1), Faith even turns herself into the police to begin paying for her crimes, which implies that she will attempt to re-create herself in a more noble capacity that's congruent with a contingent world. In fact, Faith is later called upon to help Buffy and Angel in the final stages of season 4 of *Angel* and season 7 of *BtVS*, which implies that Faith's actual-world 'conversion' is not just a momentary glitch. Faith's story in the Buffyverse reveals that Buffy's life itself can serve as poetic inspiration for others to engage the actual world in the terms of her own noble code, which is founded primarily on emotional openness and empathy for others; as Faith learns, even though Buffy's life makes the world more complex and challenging, it is inherently better than living one that is saturated with fear, ignorance, and a falsely-inflated notion of anti-life power. Buffy, it should be noted, gets the chance (by literally becoming Faith) to again overcome some of her own darker tendencies as well.

Seasons 5 and 6 on *BtVS* take Buffy to even darker places than ever before and, at the end of season 5, Buffy even sacrifices her life to save her sister Dawn from a demon-portal similar to the one Angel opened in season 2. However, in the context of Buffy's Becoming, all the unsettling events that have burdened her during these seasons ultimately allow her even more power, i.e. poetic capacities to re-write her own contingent, mortal life. At the end of season 5, Buffy is once again traumatized by an apocalyptic threat similar to the Master. This time she must face off against a hell-God from another dimension, Glory (Clare Kramer), who flaunts herself as the mocking, perfect/Platonic form of female desirability; in fact, Glory is a hellish-personification of a shallow, image-obsessed, and self-proclaimed "chicklet" who desires both a perfect appearance as well as power over the world itself ("The Weight of the World," season 5).

Throughout the story-arc of season 5, Glory, the anti-life, uber-narcissist (like all the other "big bads" on *BtVS*) is searching for the *key*, i.e. a mystical energy that has the power to open up a portal between dimensions, and that would allow her to return to the hell dimension she has been banished from; monks had been hiding this *key* but, when Glory moved close to discovering them, they magically turned this key into a young girl, Buffy's sister Dawn, since they believed Buffy has the actual power to protect this mystical energy from a threat like Glory. Here again we see that Buffy's power makes her life much more complicated than a 'normal' life, which perhaps reveals to audiences just how the nature of a productively, life-affirming Will-To-Power works, i.e., the more poetic power one possesses, the more responsibility one has to protect/nurture the contingent forces of the world-at-large (in addition, the archetypal female-names in the show like Dawn and Faith imply that young women have an intimate connection to this Will-to-Power).

Nevertheless, at the end of the season, in the episode "The Weight of the World," Glory (who desires only a Will-to-Dominate) succeeds in kidnapping Dawn, which traumatizes an already-weakened Buffy who is still reeling from the death of her mother. Buffy's guilt over not being able to protect Dawn sinks her into a catatonic state, one in which she loses all hope to fight the apparently too-powerful Glory; this reveals, a la Faith's past troubles, that there are times when even Buffy cannot handle the emotional weight of her responsibility. Willow, who at this stage is an advanced, extremely-adept witch, is forced to save the day by resorting to a very advanced magic technique—one that can reach Buffy through virtually entering her mind.

Inside Buffy's simulated mind-world, Willow discovers that Buffy has again chosen to quit her slayer duties over the guilt she feels concerning not being able to save Dawn. In fact, as Willow witnesses, Buffy's guilt has, in fact, become "the weight of the world." Buffy's mind has convinced herself that she is actually the one who killed Dawn. Buffy, whose despair has reached a truly nihilistic degree, uses the first slayer's statement that "death is [her] gift" to justify what happened to her sister, i.e., the slayer is nothing more than a killer so Buffy is essentially responsible. As Willow begins to see the actual psychic mechanism in play, she exclaims to Buffy: "snap out of it! All this—it has a name—it's called guilt." Willow acknowledges here how Buffy has momentarily succumbed to the desire to escape life itself because it has become too difficult. In effect, no one can fault Buffy for the extreme responsibility she must feel in such a dire situation but, as Willow reveals to her, such trauma is not the be-all-and-end-all in life; since such guilt is not actually 'real', Buffy must be made aware again that there are events in contingent life that no one can have absolute control over. Buffy, in fact, chooses to awake from her guilt-ridden catatonia and, as might be expected, this does not mean her life will be any simpler in the future.

As Buffy re-enters the outside world, she now has to face the unfortunate reality that the only way to stop Glory is to kill Dawn before Glory uses Dawn's blood to open the hell-portal. By this point in the season, Buffy has accepted the fact that Dawn is not her *actual* sister and, regardless of how Dawn came into being, she is a legitimate part of Buffy's life and the world-at-large, which means that Dawn warrants as much protection as anyone else; Dawn, a la Spike and Angel in the series, learns to relate to the world like a life-affirming human being and, in the eyes of Buffy, this makes Dawn equivalent to the poetic potentials that must be protected in contingent life. In a conversation with Giles in the season-finale "The Gift," Buffy admits to the fact that if her sister is killed, she may not (yet again) have the strength to continue as the slayer; in this moment of deep despair, she states: "I don't understand—I don't know how to live in this world—if these are the choices—if everything just gets stripped away—I don't see the point. I just wish my mom was here." No one could possibly fault Buffy for her momentary temptation to quit her difficult duty to the world around her.

Since Glory and her helpers succeed in opening the portal, Buffy realizes that she is too late to save Dawn; however, instead of sacrificing her sister, Buffy chooses to jump into the portal and let her own blood close it, as Dawn was, in fact, made from Buffy's DNA by the monks who were in charge of hiding the *key* from Glory. As Buffy is about to sacrifice herself, she does realize again something vital about contingent life; she explains to her sister:

> Dawn, listen to me, listen. I love you, I will always love you. This is the work I have to do. Tell Giles, tell—I figured it out and I'm o.k. Give my love to my friends. You have to take care of them now. You have to take care of each other. You have to be strong. Dawn, the hardest thing in this world is to live in it. Be brave, live for me.

In this touching good-bye, Buffy has not only confronted her fear of death, but has realized a rather significant understanding of the finite nature of existence. Buffy is willing to sacrifice her life so other people can live lives with greater potential; therefore, she is willing to sacrifice herself to life itself, which implies that she has truly achieved a noble understanding of her own self as only having significance in relation to others' potentials. Season 5 even ends on a shot of Buffy's tombstone but, as one might guess, even death is not enough to end Buffy's saga since she was killed by 'mystical'/magical energy; in the Buffyverse, a magical act can be re-written if it is not congruent with the most productive version of contingent reality.

In fact, in season 6 of *BtVS*, Willow and friends realize that they cannot fight demons on their own effectively enough; Willow (whose powers as a witch have rivaled if not exceeded Buffy's magical powers as the slayer by this point) is even forced out of grief to try a re-vivication spell on Buffy, which does, in fact, work because of the supernatural nature of Buffy's demise (as we shall see, there is no way in the Buffyverse to reverse a natural death). However, Buffy is not exactly happy to be brought back into the difficult world that asked her to sacrifice so much of herself (more than once, it must be added). Buffy even acknowledges to Spike that she had felt truly at peace in death. Throughout season 6, Buffy has trouble connecting to life itself again, and she even slides into some rather self-deprecating behavior when she starts a passionate but destructive sexual affair with Spike, which happens not out of true love for him but, as Willow phrases it, "just to feel" ("Two to Go"). Spike throughout the season is the only person Buffy can relate to (since he also died); Spike, in effect, empathizes with the extreme extent to which Buffy feels separate from life itself.

In addition, Buffy's mother's death has also placed a financial burden on Buffy, who is forced to get a fast-food restaurant job just to pay the bills. The burden of slayer-hood often reveals itself to be both an unglamorous as well as un-commodifiable job (like poetry, it should be noted!). It appears that Buffy's life has yet again reached a worse place than ever before. However, what snaps Buffy out of the difficult spot she finds herself in is the fact that someone else's self-destructive tendencies actually come to eclipse her own. Willow (during the course of season 6) has trouble handling the awesome amount of power she possesses as a witch. In fact, she begins to abuse such powers in an anti-life capacity; the metaphorical analogy *BtVS* draws here is that Willow becomes addicted to her own power as an alcoholic or drug addict becomes hooked on the escapist and self-nullifying high of drugs. In fact, Willow's slide into the "dark arts," which turns her desires anti-life, is the exact cathartic shock Buffy needs to re-write her life again in a more productive capacity; by being confronted with someone else's incapacity to accept contingent life as it is, Buffy fights for Willow to re-affirm the finite nature of existence. When Willow is, in fact, stopped at the end of season 6 (see below), Buffy can again re-awaken to a different and transformed world; she now becomes able to accept the role of mother-figure for Dawn in the wake of their mother's death. As the quote that introduces this section reveals, Buffy is once again willing to accept life as it is, and she now has the desire to "show" this challenging world to her sister/daughter.

Buffy's gesture to Dawn re-edifies the original desire that she had felt when she sacrificed her life for Dawn, i.e., living is truly the hardest thing in the world but it is nonetheless worth doing. The implication here is that one is only truly living life when one confronts its most challenging aspects. Buffy continually finds productive ways to re-orient herself so that her own life can become as noble as possible in the most difficult situations imaginable. Therein lies one of the key, fundamental messages *BtVS* offers to its viewers: Buffy's ability to poetically re-write her life and identity are worth emulating. The fact that life is never easy, and that Buffy often breaks down in the process, reveals how life itself is never hopeless because it also allows the possibility of re-inventing ever-new-capacities for re-engaging it productively.

BtVS's final-season 7 re-iterates many of the lessons previous seasons explore; however, as stated previously, the entire mythology of the show gets a rather fascinating re-writing in its final episode. The main story-arc of season 7 revolves around the First, a preternatural evil that is incorporeal but that can appear as the image of any dead person it wants; it is, in effect, the evil energy that gives rise to all other manifestations of evil, *which thematically implies that evil's actual power is often illusory in nature*. The First originally appeared in season 3 when it tried to convince Angel, through appearing to him in the visages of all his former victims, to kill Buffy (this also sheds light on how Angel could return from 'Hell' during this season). The First is perhaps one of the creepiest portrayals of evil in media history because it only works through suggestions and manipulations that prey on people's innermost fears and unresolved issues. In fact, most of *BtVS*'s final season portrays how Buffy and her friends attempt to prepare for their coming battle with the First and its legions of evil forces by training a bastion of potential, future slayers; yet again, the First, this season's "big bad," has the plan to open the Hellmouth and let demons have free reign on earth. As Buffy and her friends try to raise an army of powerful parthenoi, it appears that they are the definite underdogs in the impending battle.

As many earlier characters revisit the series in its final hours to help Buffy and her potential slayers, the two key characters that have the power to actually defeat the First are the two key parthenoi throughout the series, Buffy and Willow. This fact reveals how the entire series, and the fate of the Buffyverse itself, boils down to the powers inherent in two rather un-traditional/women-heroes who have the poetic/media powers to re-write any anti-life force or mis-perception. In fact, the First even begins to prey on Buffy's worst fear, i.e. the fact that she bears the burden of protecting the world alone as the 'one' slayer, doomed to forever feel such isolation from others till she is killed in the line of duty and another young girl steps into her difficult shoes. In fact, in the series finale, the First appears to Buffy in her own image (as Buffy had previously died) and flaunts this fact: "in every generation a slayer is born. She alone...there's that word again, what you are, how you'll die—alone!" However, being confronted with her greatest fear actually gives Buffy a rather poetic idea. A mystical order of women had sworn to protect life against such threats as the First, and they had magically created a rather powerful scythe, which they give Buffy. Buffy's poetic idea is to let Willow harness the magical power the scythe possesses in order to re-write the entire tradition of how slayers function; as the watcher's council only allowed one girl in each generation such mystical power in order to keep Patriarchal control over such a parthenos's power, Willow uses the scythe's mystical power in order to grant every potential slayer Buffy's (as well as Faith's) actual powers. In this sense, the burden of slayerhood, i.e. the weight of the world, will no longer rest on one or two girl's shoulders since all young women are now potential slayers.

Willow and Buffy in "Chosen" attempt to re-write the world itself to have greater potential for protecting mortal life from the big bads who solely want to possess control over the world through becoming anti-life representations of ideal forms (a la the Platonic First). In fact, such a setting-free of the parthenos's ability to creatively have authority over her own potential in the world allows Buffy and her renegade friends a multiplicity of powers with which to beat the First (which only believes that power arises from anti-life abilities to limit the poetic possibilities inherent in the contingent world). Nietzsche & Deleuze would likely concur with Buffy that the Will-to-Power is the most important aspect of everyone's Becoming.

Nonetheless, as the final episode in *BtVS* reveals, Buffy actually gets to see her noble efforts reach an actual and rather dramatic transformation of the world itself; no longer is Buffy just holding evil at bay, since she now has invented a more productive or multiplicitous way to actually overcome such dark magic. By extension, Whedon's series implies that what limits everyone's potentials is the tendency to cling to outmoded ways of mis-perceiving/disowning one's poetic relations to the contingent world. Buffy and friends effectively destroy the Hellmouth itself when Spike stays behind to make sure that a talisman with mystical powers wipes out all the creatures of the Hellmouth, therefore allowing everyone else time to escape. Spike's love for Buffy, which inspires him to perform this noble gesture, unfortunately means that such a mystical power burns him up as well (since he is still a vampire). Spike, regardless of this fact, realizes such a sacrifice is worth it in the big-scheme-of-things because it will increase others' potentials to live more poetically-open lives. His sacrifice is equally as noble as Buffy's at the end of season 5; since Spike joins the cast of *Angel* in its 5th and final season, his Becoming does not end here because 'supernatural' forces were also responsible for his death.

Whedon's *BtVS* ends on a rather un-cheesy or un-fluffy poetic insight, in the sense that all the characters now get to look at a destroyed Sunnydale (all its denizens except Buffy & Co. had run for the hills because of the First months before). Xander even states: "we saved the world," to which Willow adds a rather significant correction: "we *changed* the world." While the main characters are staring at the crater that once was Sunnydale, Willow speaks the final words of the series: "Buffy, what are we gonna do now?" The camera pans to Buffy smiling in response, which implies that they all will get to live fuller lives now that fighting evil is not solely their 'secret' responsibility. Finishing the series on this note implies that the entire show was leading toward such a poetic/re-writeable view of life and the world itself all along. All the pain and loss the characters suffered throughout the series never reduced their potentials in the world but, ultimately, allowed them a more poetic awareness which can then create ever-new relations to that world. Audiences as well can share in such a life-affirming edification that all of life, both the good things as well as the terrible things, deserve to be affirmed for what they are. Everyone's poetic capacities for self-creation/Becoming must include both for such Becomings to be truly life-affirming at heart.

"No More Hiding": Willow & Emotional Control

> Tara: Even when I'm at my worst, you always make me feel special. How do you do that?
>
> Willow: Magic.
> —from "The Family," season 5.
>
> You're the strongest person here—you know that, right?
> —Buffy to Willow, "The Gift," season 5.

Although there are many characters who go through rather dramatic Becomings in the Buffyverse—especially Spike (a poet before he became a vampire), Cordelia (Charisma Carpenter), Dawn, and Angel—the person who truly rivals Buffy in her heroic ability to keep re-writing her identity till she gets it poetically-right is Willow—another parthenos. Willow however, at the beginning of the series, does not have anything close to either the magical birthright or physical power that grants Buffy her uniqueness. In fact, to consider where Willow ends up in the series as opposed to where she began, Buffy's Becoming appears almost easy. What makes Willow's Becoming so fascinating are the extremes that she must go to in order to overcome what threatens to limit/destroy that Becoming. In fact, Willow's transformations in *BtVS* may be some of the most resonant with audiences because she is saddled with what many people can relate to: at the start of season 1 Willow is meek, geeky, and so socially-insecure that she even dresses in a rather androgynous manner as if to hide from how others see and judge her. Therefore, it is no accident that what helps Willow overcome such insecurities is productively re-mediating the processes of her identity-construction a la Buffy's life-affirming/noble world-view.

Willow's key setbacks are her insecurities about herself, which often render her productive potentials completely contingent on what she assumes is the socially-justified, 'normal' image of feminine attractiveness/social-worth. She, therefore, problematically buys into the notion that idealized, bourgeois myths such as a transcendent, static feminine-beauty are more significant and powerful than any poetic re-writing of such myths. In addition, Buffy's arrival on the scene, at first, only exaggerates Willow's insecurities because Willow must then deal with comparing herself to not only the 'normalized' image of feminine attractiveness, but the super-hero, empowered image of femininity in Buffy. It's safe to say that overcoming such insecurities are no minor feats for a self-effacing parthenos like Willow.

Nonetheless, Willow does possess a lot of intelligence and academic potential, and she is fascinated by the world and learning about it, which thematically implies that she has an extremely powerful connection to life itself; she states emphatically in the episode "Ted" (season 2): "I just wanna learn stuff." Even though she often jokes that she is a "spaz" and has problems with "emotional control," Willow's comments also foreground how she is open to experience in a more powerful and intense way than perhaps anyone else around her. However, her insecurities continually threaten to isolate her from her productive desires to learn and experience. In this sense, she does have the tendency (like Buffy it must be noted) to slide into self-pity. Fortunately, when Willow meets Buffy, Willow is given the opportunity to leave behind the shallow, clicky, and mythically-empty high-school-environment that demeans her desire for knowledge; she can now join a fight that is worthy of her potentials in the world.

Willow's greatest fear remains that she is not attractive enough to be 'worth' much to most 'normal' people, and this assumption is continually shown in the series to come more from Willow's own fear than how others actually see her. In the second-season episode "Halloween," Buffy convinces Willow to dress like a sexually-confident, rock chick, and she even gives her the compliment: "don't underestimate yourself, you got it in you," which, in this context, means she has the potential to be a sexually-desirable young woman if she is courageous enough to stop hiding from such a recognition. Buffy also edifies this notion when she tells Willow: "you're never gonna get noticed if you keep hiding." Nonetheless, what actually triggers Willow's Becoming in the series is when she must confront her own 'dark-side', i.e. her alter-ego, who is the diametric opposite of a weak, insecure, and fragile adolescent. While this narrative move is similar to Buffy's confrontation with her dark-side in Faith, it is humorous to consider that Willow's alter-ego is actually more violent and sexually aggressive than Buffy's.

In the third-season episode "Dopplegängland," we are introduced to a Willow who is finally getting fed up with how other people just use her as a doormat: Willow is bullied by Principal Snyder into tutoring a basketball player, Percy (Ethan Erickson), who may fail his classes without her help; however, Percy just connives her into doing all his work herself. Willow is also tricked by Anya (Emma Caufield) into casting a spell to re-locate Anya's magical amulet (which gives her power as a vengeance demon to wreak havoc on unfaithful men). But, the spell revealingly doesn't work because Willow, who is disturbed by what she sees in the alternative dimension where Anya lost it, actually stands up for herself and stops the spell before it is finished. Howęver, Willow brings back something else from that dimension: her own alter-ego vampire-self, a move that thematically speaks to just how pissed off she has become at herself for not Becoming who she wants to be, i.e. a powerful and confident young woman. Anya had previously lost her magical amulet at the end of an earlier 3rd-season episode, "The Wish," in which Anya granted Cordelia a wish to get back at Xander for cheating on her (by kissing Willow no less); Cordelia's wish in this episode that "Buffy Summers had never come to Sunnydale," turns out to be a rather disastrous one for everyone in that alternate reality.

In "The Wish," we get to witness a different Sunnydale that never had a slayer, one in which the Master has gained control of almost every aspect of Sunnydale; he even creates a mass-production line that mechanically harvests human bodies for blood. Humans, in this version of Sunnydale, are solely food for the now more dominant species of vampires; the social commentary in operation here is anything but subtle in that 'normal' life in regular America is also a rather violent hierarchy/food-chain to begin with. Willow and Xander in that reality have become vampire-henchmen of the Master, who are both not only ruthless killers, but rather sexually un-repressed. In fact, Willow-the-vampire is decked out in a leather dominatrix outfit, and she is unabashedly into both men and women. In this episode, we get to see that if things happened differently, Willow would not have wound up meek and insecure by this point in time. The thematic implication here is that Willow does, in fact, possess the strength and potential to be very self-confident if she can productively harness such potential. The vampire-Willow, who is brought back to the actual Sunnydale in "Dopplegängland," comes to teach actual-Willow an important lesson about how she mis-perceives herself and her own powers. As we shall see, this realization will give Willow the cathartic chance to overcome her self-effacing insecurities.

In "Dopplegängland," we audiences come to understand why Willow's inadvertent wish was for something so destructively-aggressive. The vampire-Willow, disoriented and now in a different world, goes to the Bronze (the high school kids' local hangout) and randomly bumps into Percy, the basketball player she is supposed to help tutor. Percy, however, only mocks her because of her outfit, and he arrogantly tells her: "till we graduate, I own your ass," to which the vampire-Willow calmly states "bored now" and then throws him across the room. This Willow is not going to put up with anyone's crap. In addition, we also get to see how Willow's friends truly *recognize* her when they think she has actually been killed and turned into a vampire. Giles states: "she was the best of all of us," to which Xander replies: "much, much better than me;" Giles comically retorts again: "much, much better." Such a scene implies that Willow is vital to their attempts to keep Sunnydale free of demons, even when she does not recognize this fact herself.

Buffy's 'Scooby gang' are nonetheless forced to go after the vampire-Willow before she threatens to turn Sunnydale "like it was" in the alternate universe of "The Wish." Regular Willow, however, only grabs a stun gun, which revealingly implies that she does not want her alter-ego killed. But, before she can catch up to Buffy, Willow is ambushed by her vampire-self, which leads to a rather funny and revealing scenario. The vampire-Willow jokes that maybe she should stay in this reality so they can "be bad," hinting that it would be a fun experience to have sex with one's own double-self from an alternate reality. Not only does this foreshadow Willow's acknowledgement in season 4 that she has in fact fallen in love with a woman, Tara, but, it also reveals that vampire-Willow does have something to teach and show Willow that she has not yet acknowledged about herself.

Willow's need for a more productive self-realization is edified thematically again when, at the end of the episode, Willow does not want Buffy to kill her vampire-self but to help cast a spell that would send vampire-Willow back to her own universe. What is rather curious about this fact is that Willow seems to understand why vampire-Willow came into her world to begin with, i.e., she came to remind Willow that she does in fact have a lot of power if she confidently accepts that fact. Willow even hugs her vampire-self and tells her to "try not to kill people"; in response, her alter-ego jokingly pinches her ass. They can only smile at each other, which acknowledges the fact that Willow is productively integrating vampire-Willow's potential for aggressive strength into her own personality.

Unfortunately, Willow almost does slip back into her old meek ways, when, later that day, she states how she doesn't feel like going out that night because between her and her vampire self she has "double-guilt coupons," and she also now "sees where the path of vice leads." However, as if to give her a reminder that she must incorporate the lesson of being self-confident like vampire-Willow, the episode ends when a newly-studious Percy actually gives Willow the homework he had done the night before—'she' had, in fact, 'put the fear of God in him' at the Bronze. Ironically, the vice-ridden vampire-Willow did manage to do some good in Willow's reality by teaching Percy a valuable lesson about how not to treat people. Willow then decides to go out on the town that night as if acknowledging the fact that there are times in life when one must be aggressive and willing to stand up for oneself. It's rather startling to think that this is the moment in the series when Willow really begins to become a confident, powerful young woman—one that, as we shall see, comes to rival or even exceed Buffy's power as the slayer.

Willow, throughout season 3, begins to make choices for herself and on her own terms. One key choice she makes is to stay in Sunnydale even though she has been accepted at a lot of top notch colleges throughout the country. In

Willow's mind, it is worth helping and protecting people like Buffy does, and she therefore decides to go to U.C. Sunnydale in order to continue aiding Buffy as a demon fighter; for Willow, such a fight is a more noble feat than getting a degree from a big-name college. In fact, in the context of the series, Willow is not losing anything by going to a 'lesser', state school, because her education and desire to learn have always been her own responsibility. This also implies that she is strong enough to make such a choice, when perhaps, if she were more insecure, she would choose a college solely because of its name recognition. Willow, as mentioned previously, is shown to have progressed significantly in magic and her ability to productively-transform the world in seasons 2 and 3; she succeeds in a major magic spell (using the notes of Ms. Calender) that grants Angel his soul back in season 2. In season 3, Willow even stands up to Faith and tells her off. To edify this newfound potential, as season 4 attests, Willow thrives much better in a more intellectually-stimulating college environment.

Willow even describes the intense desire she has to learn in college in serio-comically-sexual terms, which implies that she is coming into her own not just as an intelligent and self-assured young woman, but as a more sexually-aware one as well; her revealing conversation with Buffy in "The Freshman" transpires as follows:

> Willow: It's just in high school, knowledge was pretty much frowned upon. You really had to work to learn anything, but here the energy, the collective intelligence, it's like this force, this penetrating force and I can just feel my mind opening up, you know, and letting this place just thrust into—and spurt knowledge——and——that sentence ended up in a different place than it started out in.
>
> Buffy: I'm with you though. I'm all for spurty knowledge.

This conversation implies not only that, for Willow, knowledge and sexuality are both intimately connected (i.e. they are very intimate experiences of the world around her), but that she too has to have her 'baptism-by-adolescent-fire'. Season 4 charts how Willow loses her high-school love Oz (Seth Green), a werewolf who turns aggressive and deadly three nights a month around the full moon; unfortunately for Willow, Oz meets another female-werewolf, Veruca (Paige Moss), and their animal attraction is irresistible; Willow then has to confront the painful fact that Oz sleeps with Veruca. After this betrayal, Willow slips into a major funk that affects her ability to do magic (the episode "Something Blue" brings out this notion in a hilarious light).

When Willow meets another magically-inclined friend at her local Wicca group, Tara, Willow must also face the challenging realization that she is sexually attracted to Tara. This was a daring move on the part of the producers and writers of *BtVS* as the show had been "apparently the first long-term lesbian sexual relationship ever featured on a broadcast network television series"

(Pasley 255). Not only does this fact reveal how "tolerance has been promoted on *BtVS* and *Angel* not only for lesbians and nerds and witches but also for certain categories of demon [. . .]," it also implies that one of the main mission statements of the Buffyverse is the cultivation of a productive awareness and celebration of difference in all walks of life and art (Pasley 255). However, Oz returns to Sunnydale after figuring out a way to conquer his werewolf alter-ego, which complicates Willow's life in that she now has to choose between Oz and Tara. It is no minor thing that Willow chooses the riskier of the two choices, Tara. As we shall see, Willow's relationship with Tara opens her eyes in both positive and destructive aspects to much of what life has to offer. As season 4 unfolds, we viewers witness Willow coming into a new, singular awareness of her potentials.

As if to foreground this transformation through a counter-example, the season 4-finale-episode "Restless" (a dream-logic episode as surreal as anything on *Twin Peaks*), explores the unconscious fears of the four main characters in the series. The episode also sums up where they each are in their individual Becomings, and we get to see specifically that Willow's greatest fear is still how she might slip back into her meek and insecure ways of relating to the world like when she was in high school. In Willow's dream, we see her painting a Sappho poem in Greek on Tara's naked back, which edifies again the intimate connection Willow feels between sexuality and knowledge. However, Willow is made uncomfortable by some vague threat she feels to this safe, positive life she has found with Tara.

Willow's nightmare then revealingly switches into a high school setting where she must take a drama class: when she shows up for the first class, she is supposed to perform the lead on stage for everyone she has ever met. This turn-of-events reveals that Willow's key fear is still how others see and judge her as socially inadequate. As she escapes into the red curtains behind the stage (a la the curtains that flourish in the Red Room on *Twin Peaks*), Willow, like Agent Cooper, must face some truly scary aspects of herself. In fact, her nightmare reaches a fever pitch when she stands in front of a high school class to read a book report on "The Lion, the Witch and the Wardrobe;" however, her class only makes jokes about how nerdy she is. Xander even exclaims "Who cares?," and Oz and Tara are seen whispering romantically into one another's ears as Oz mockingly tells Tara "I *tried* to warn you." Willow's nightmare reveals that her insecurity over her social inadequacy has the potential to drain away all the progress she has made so far in her own Becoming. However, as season 5 and 6 attests, a la Buffy's rocky Becoming in the series, Willow still has a lot to learn about the dangers in mis-perceiving oneself and one's potentials in the world.

As far as the poetic peaks in Willow's development, one of the most touching moments ever on *BtVS* occurs when Willow, Buffy, and friends must confront Tara's 'ignorant' kin in "The Family" (season 5), in order to rescue Tara from them. Tara, at the beginning of the episode, feels like she doesn't quite fit into Buffy's Scooby-gang. Tara's dilemma becomes further confounded when her family shows up believing that the women in their family 'turn evil' on their 20th birthdays and must therefore be hidden away and controlled so as not to become full-blown witches. Ironically, for Tara to actually be accepted by Buffy's make-shift, Scooby family, Tara must first complicate their lives by almost getting them all killed. Since Tara believes her family's assumption that she is actually part demon, she casts a spell on Buffy and the rest of the Scoobies so that all demons will be invisible to them. However, Glory at the same time sends several demons to attack Buffy, which means that Buffy and Co. are then rendered pretty much powerless to fight them.

Fortunately, when Tara shows up she quickly breaks the spell. At this precise moment when her life could not get worse, her family arrives to claim her and take her away. As Buffy, Willow, and friends realize that Tara only cast the spell so that she could "hide" from her fear of not being accepted by them, Buffy and Co. put aside their anger to side with Tara against her 'short-sighted' family. As Buffy, Dawn, Giles, and everyone there tells Tara's family that they can only take Tara by going through them first, this gesture effectively leaves Tara in tears. What this scene implies is that Buffy's make-shift Scooby-family is a legitimate one for all involved because they all stick by each other and support each other no matter what. Tara is lucky to have found such friends and a 'new' family who will stick up for her own uniqueness. As the episode ends, Tara and Willow dance together in the Bronze, magically floating above the floor; this touching finale implies that the two lovers have created a truly-poetic moment for themselves.

However, in season 6, tension begins to mount between Tara and Willow concerning Willow's increasing addiction to magic. Tara, eventually, has to leave Willow after Willow casts a mind-control spell on Tara to make her forget a fight that they had. Willow's insecurity, therefore, can still be a destructive force in her life. Willow effectively loses, at this point, any productive connection with magic as a life-affirming art. She slips even further when another magically-inclined friend, Amy (Elizabeth Anne Allen), hooks her up with a dark-magic dealer Rack (Jeff Kober) who "likes little girls," and who unfortunately gets Willow so high (i.e. divorced from actuality) that she almost kills herself and Dawn in a car accident. After that crash, Willow is so shocked at her alienation from herself that she decides to quit magic completely. As she must face life without both magic and Tara, Willow reaches a definite low point. However, in the Buffyverse, this only means that even worse things are on the way.

Willow does, in fact, succeed at quitting magic for many months, so she eventually wins back Tara's trust. Unfortunately, this reunion is soon devastated when tragedy hits again. Warren (Adam Busch) and his two nerdy, wanna-be-evil friends (who have attempted to kill Buffy all season) get seriously humiliated and defeated by Buffy in the episode "Seeing Red," which then drives Warren to attempt a rather extreme payback: he walks into Buffy's backyard with a gun and shoots at Buffy several times; his wild shots unfortunately hit not only Buffy but a stray bullet comes through an upstairs window and hits Tara right through the heart. It is perhaps no surprise to say that after this, Willow will no longer be 'on the wagon'. She unfortunately cannot bring Tara back magically as Tara died a natural (not a supernatural) death. All that Willow can do about Tara's death is either grieve or seek payback on Warren.

Throughout the final episodes of season 6, Willow becomes the most powerful threat in the Buffyverse because her grief and fury are so extreme that she doesn't even care if the "black arts" she uses to avenge Tara's death will also destroy her life in the process. Willow reaches a similar anti-contingent-life point as Diane in *Mulholland Drive* when Diane takes out a contract on Camilla. Willow, like Diane at this point, feels that there is nothing left in the world for her to care about so it doesn't matter what happens in it. Willow even magically heals Buffy to help her go kill Warren, but Buffy refuses to help Willow's nihilistic mission; Buffy attempts to talk Willow down from her resentment before she "crosses a line." However, Willow has, by this point, become more powerful than Buffy, which means no one can really stop Willow.

In addition, the ethical issues Willow's quest-for-blood brings up are anything but clean-cut; indeed, Xander states in "Two to Go" that Warren is "just as bad as any vampire you send to dust-ville." Buffy, however, raises another significant point:

> Warren's human [. . .] so the human world has its own rules for dealing with a thing like that. [. . .]. We can't control the universe. If we were supposed to, then the magic wouldn't change Willow the way it does, and we'd be able to bring Tara back. There are limits to what we can do. There SHOULD be. Willow doesn't want to believe that. And now she's messing with forces that want to hurt her, hurt all of us. I will not let Willow destroy herself.

What Buffy's above comment reveals is that Willow-the-vigilante has effectively disowned the contingent nature of the world and would rather play the role of a transcendent judge who can decide over others' rights to live. However, what must be reiterated here is that Willow's extreme desire to effectively destroy herself is actually only a function of the pain and suffering she refuses to let affect her; in effect, Willow desires to destroy the world itself before that world can hurt her again.

When Willow does catch up to Warren, no one has the power to stop her from getting her violent revenge. She, in turn, tortures Warren with one of the bullets that he shot Buffy and Tara with. For added effect, Willow slows the bullet down for a slow death. Warren's hatred of women (he has killed two by this point) is then revisited on him ten-fold. As Buffy and Co. catch up to stop Willow, she is forced to speed up the process by effectively ripping all his skin off; as if to echo the dark power of her vampire/alter-ego self, Willow states "bored now" as she flays Warren alive. Unfortunately, getting revenge does not end Willow's pain because she then attempts to go after Warren's two oblivious, nerdy henchmen, Andrew (Tom Lenk) and Jonathan (Danny Strong).

Willow's rage, at this point, will not be contented until she ruins her own life by becoming a serial killer. As her friends both understand why she would kill Warren as well as the difficult notion that they are the ones who must stop her, Willow has effectively erased her own unique, singular identity with her "dark arts." They are her 'drugs' to momentarily numb the pain; as if to acknowledge that self-erasure, she tells Dawn at one point: "honey, I am the magics." In order to register the extremes inherent in Willow's Becoming throughout the series, Jonathan serio-comically states: "I just can't believe that was Willow [. .]. Willow was, you know—she used to pack her own lunches and wore floods and—you know, was always just Willow."

Willow-the-vigilante, unfortunately, is even willing to injure her friends if they get in her path of self-erasure and hatred. Buffy tries to plead with Willow and to get her to acknowledge the contingent world again: "the forces inside you are incredibly powerful. They're strong, but you're stronger. You have to remember you're still Willow." Here, Buffy is offering advice about the dangers of identity loss that she too went through when she became Anne. Unfortunately, Willow only replies:

> let me tell you a little something about Willow. She's a loser. And she always has been. People picked on Willow in Junior High School, High School, up until college with her stupid mousy ways. And now Willow's a junkie. [. . .]. The only thing Willow was ever good for—the only thing I had going for me were the moments, just moments, when Tara would look at me and I was wonderful. And that will never happen again.

Willow's feelings of social inadequacy have come center stage to halt her Becoming again, and she has problematically lost herself to the notion that she is only worth what others had 'recognized' her as being worth. In effect, this moment in *BtVS* implies that anti-life, dark *arts* come from such dis-empowered perspectives where resentment can run rampant; *BtVS* also implies that such alienation is rather easy to fall into. This traumatized-Willow has effectively lost any identity at all; she even fights Buffy near the end of season 6 and kicks her ass, mocking Buffy's life-affirming potential by stating: "I'm the slayer now."

Willow's dangerous, self-annihilating slide into the dark arts prompts Giles to return from England, where he had moved for most of season 6. Giles' plan to rescue Willow from herself is to show her the truly life-affirming nature of magic (i.e. media poetry) again. However, he must trick her into recognizing it; Giles had been imbued with borrowed power (the true 'essence' of magic) from a rather powerful coven, knowing that Willow is advanced enough to steal that magic from him. When Willow needs a re-charge and does steal Giles' magic, she gets more than she bargained for, as 'true' magic lets her intimately feel all the pain and suffering throughout the world at once. However, Willow's first response to this feeling is that such suffering must be stopped, and she is willing to do anything, even burning the world to a cinder, in order to erase so much pain. This nihilistic desire arises wholly from Willow's wish to erase herself.

Willow re-iterates her extreme self-hatred in the 6th-season-finale "Grave:" "Willow doesn't live here anymore. [. . .]. Nothing can hurt me now. This [she points to her face] is nothing." Willow is perhaps at the darkest place any character has ever been throughout the series. Luckily, Willow has effectively underestimated the power of 'true' magic. As Giles states that "no magic" can stop Willow now, Xander *magically* reaches Willow at the moment she is about to burn away the world's pain. *True* magic is the only thing that can now get Willow to recognize herself and her own suffering; Xander tells her at the 11th hour:

> I know you're in pain. I can't imagine the pain you're in. And I know you are about to do something apocalyptically evil and stupid, and hey, I still want to hang. Hey, you're Willow. [. . .]. The first day of kindergarten you cried 'cause you broke the yellow crayon and you were too afraid to tell anyone. You've come pretty far, ending the world—not a terrific notion. And the thing is, yeah I love you. I love crayon-breaky Willow, and I love scary-veiny Willow. So if I'm going out, it's here. If you want to kill the world, well then start with me. I've earned that.

What is so striking about Xander's plea is that his "pitch" is all about the contingent, singular experiences that make life poetically viable. These experiences are the events and phenomena that Willow's dark-arts seek to nullify and reject. As Xander repeats over and over that he loves her, Willow's dark-magic sputters out, since Xander has effectively reached the last touch of "humanity" she has left. The ultimate or true magic is being able to love people for the contingent moments that have made them the singular individuals they have become (regardless of any 'transcendent' or ideal 'form' one might use to judge someone's worth outside of such contingencies). Willow collapses in tears, hitting Xander in the chest over and over with her fists, as if to imply that she is now allowing herself to feel the pain and rage over what happened to Tara. Thus, Willow is now in the position to be able to poetically re-create her identity in a more productive manner a la a media poet.

Willow's dark-turn also brings Buffy and her sister Dawn together since they are forced to fight several demons side-by-side that Willow had sent in order to slow them down. This camaraderie inspires Buffy to both open up to Dawn as well as to edify to audiences that the main focus of *BtVS* has been to foreground the difficult nature of Becoming that every individual must go through; the logic in operation here is that everyone is a potentially better person for having gone through difficult/'hellish' experiences; in addition, everyone can benefit from realizing that *identity construction is a poetic process outright.* Buffy even tells Dawn: "I see it [. . .]. You. [. . .]. I want to see my friends happy again. I want to see you grow up. The woman you're gonna become. Because she's going to be beautiful. And she's going to be powerful." This moment of affirmation is a fitting way for Buffy to cathartically overcome her own inability to connect productively with life itself in season 6. The 'true' magic that has brought Willow back to herself *is* the poetic ability to see others' potentials as intimately inter-related to one's own process of Becoming.

Throughout *BtVS*'s final-season-7, we witness how Willow does, in fact, overcome her tendency for self-hating, self-nullifying, and even murderous ways of relating to the world. Giles succeeds in rehabilitating Willow in England so that she will have the potential to use magic as a life-affirming art again. Not only does she come back to the contingent world by becoming emotionally invested in it again, she moves on in other areas as well: Willow begins a new relationship with a feisty potential slayer, Kennedy (Iyari Limon), and she even gets the chance to 'redeem' her past desire to destroy the world by magically granting all potential slayers those magical powers outright in the series finale "Chosen."

Willow's connection to 'true' magic allows her to create with it a multiplicitous understanding of how power must be shared and used in wholly life-affirming endeavors (a la Nietzsche's Noble Ethics). As mentioned previously, it is rather touching to reflect on the fact that Buffy and Willow save the world from the First's army together, which implies that the make-shift family of the Scooby-gang is a rather significant force in the world because its power comes from a multiplicity of individuals who desire to engage the world in poetic and productive pursuits. The series finale of *BtVS* edifies this notion: all of the main characters' Becomings have been (up to this point) a productive rite-of-passage into an empowered adulthood.

"Yeah Buffy, What Are We Gonna Do Now?"

Joss Whedon and his team of fellow producers, writers, and directors of *BtVS* have created a rather fascinating pop culture/media phenomenon. They have taken full advantage of the multi-sensory-possibilities of the medium of network television to create a strikingly multiplicitous, inter-media art. *BtVS* is a noteworthy version of media poetry because it foregrounds the pragmatic concerns of simulated reality-productions; to read *BtVS* as media poetry edifies how appearances/meanings are never representational, which implies that the most important or significant meanings are rarely the most obvious ones. Since meaning is never purely abstract in nature, a poetic-expressionism/Becoming can challenge any and all anti-contingent-life illusions/ideals. To reinforce this insight, Alexis Denisoff, who plays Wesley Windham Price on *BtVS* and *Angel*, describes the Buffyverse (on the *Angel* season 1-dvd-featurette) in terms that would please a media poet: the creators of the Buffyverse are "constantly attempting to challenge and upset the equilibrium and, then, as a result of that, when balance is achieved, it's stronger as a result of the differences."

BtVS can therefore be interpreted as a singular model for not only how one can create media poetry that "makes one think," but how it can be entertaining and pleasurable to watch as well. There will hopefully be many more shows like *Buffy* that keep pushing the possibilities of what a social medium like prime-time television can re-mediate for the benefit of actual-world potentials.

---

1 A la *Twin Peaks*, there are too many producers, writers, and directors on *BtVS* to give adequate credit. Since Joss Whedon created the show and wrote and/or directed many of the episodes, and since he was the executive producer for all of them, the series will be referred to here as primarily his creation.

2 See Deleuze's *Preface* to *Nietzsche & Philosophy* for an account of the ways Nietzsche has been misinterpreted during the 20th century.

Coda:
The Fine Art of Convergence

> Allegra's Assistant: I don't like it here. I don't
> know what's going on. We're both stumbling
> around together in this unformed world—whose
> rules and objectives are largely unknown,
> seemingly indecipherable or possibly
> nonexistent—always on the verge of being killed
> by forces that we don't understand.
>
> Allegra Gellar: That sounds like my game alright.
>
> Allegra's assistant: It sounds like a game that's
> not gonna be easy to market.
>
> Allegra: But it's a game everyone's already
> playing.
> —from *eXistenZ*

   The above discussion occurs in David Cronenberg's *eXistenZ* (1999), a film that blurs any strict division between actual-reality and a virtual-reality-game. Cronenberg's film, therefore, reveals (like all the above media poetry) how the virtual and actual are never separate phenomenon to begin with, since one can continually transform the other in always-shifting processes of re-mediation. In fact, a la *Mulholland Drive*, *eXistenZ* implies that we viewers are *never able* to clearly differentiate between the 'real' and the simulation in the film (and thus in life as well). In such complex, actual-world situations that have no pre-determined rules or even non-existent ones—as Allegra (Jennifer Jason Leigh)'s assistant (Jude Law) describes above—one must *create* the most productive ways of dealing with such ungrounded potentialities. As stated previously, our lives may truly depend on to what extent we can author an actuality that also generates the greatest virtuality, i.e. the greatest poetic possibilities for sensory transformation.

All such un-determined states-of-affairs are ripe for the virtual significations of media poetry. Whether something is purely 'real' or 'unreal' has effectively become a pointless question, as Allegra claims above, because both artistic production and contingent-life-itself create meaning within the same "unformed" contexts. Hence, one of the best analogies to consider in mulling over such complex relations, as they exist in "the slipstream of mixed reality," is to re-visit the logic of digital convergence. Digital media make all forms of sensory phenomena (regardless of whether they are textual, audio, or visual in appearance) converge in codes of 1s and 0s, which implies that infinite possibilities for relation can be constructed between them. Therefore, multimedia/poetic "thinkers," who engage artistic productions as *problem-solving operations*, can continually transform a "global village" of new-media possibilities.

The virtual significations of media poetry are key ways to extract all appearances and signs from representation/judgment so that individuals can create free, indirect discourses, i.e. the productive conditions for new forms-of-life or Sense-events. Herein lies media poetry's socio-political import as well: singular individuals can author/re-write whatever blocks the productive possibilities of culture/contingent-life-itself and, therefore, create alternative forms of joy and pleasure as well. One then only needs the courage and conviction to act on such possibilities.

By extension, all manifestations of virtual media call into question the academic 'codification' of literary studies, which often envisions linguistic arts as a circumscribed, chronological history of styles. In virtual media, any such chronology is re-routed by the fact that its virtual space-times/databases allow any and all possibilities from the past to become simultaneously present and ready for new transformations. Inter-media art can, in effect, become a *Renaissance-discipline* that freely explores a multiplicity of styles/temporalities within the context of Sense-events. In this sense, the primary engines of simulation (which turn any history of styles or modalities into a virtual database) are modern computers, i.e. the ever-evolving multiplicities of transnational information and communication that continually re-mediate the possibilities of world cultures. However, in globally-networked, simulated environments, it's necessary to continually confront the following question: *how can aesthetic value best overcome the illusion of representation?*

One way to answer this question is to consider that media and artistic phenomena are never radically distinct to begin with. Both create contexts and perceptual processes that can give rise to multiplicitous forms of life. Since the division between producers and consumers blurs in a virtual-media environment, we either wittingly or unwittingly use media phenomena for our own processes of Becoming; therefore, we can self-consciously act on this awareness in order to co-construct the most productive social-environments possible.

Artists have, in fact, taken on networked-space itself as a viable artistic practice; one example is David Lynch, whose film *Mulholland Drive* and TV series *Twin Peaks* were explored here as key examples of media poetry; Lynch has recently launched <htttp://www.davidlynch.com>, an interactive web-site that includes internet series, animated series, short films, music videos, live-action sites, discussion boards, games, a virtual store, etc. Lynch, discussing his forthcoming film *INLAND EMPIRE*, even comments on how digital video allows for radically more avenues for new modes of inter-media art:

> I started working in DV for my Web site, and I fell in love with the medium. It's unbelievable, the freedom and the incredible different possibilities it affords, in shooting and in post-production. For me, there's no way back to film. I'm done with it. [. . .]. Film is a beautiful medium, but it's very slow and you don't get a chance to try a lot of different things. With DV, you get those chances. And in post-production, if you can think it, you can do it.   (Adam Dawtrey, "Cannes Daily," *Variety*)

For Lynch, the only limitations in a digital-media environment have become productive self-limitations. However, since globally-networked media need and use persuasion as a vital tool for privileging particular ideologies, it has become necessary for each of us to create our own, singular *critical discourse of illusions* (in order not to fall for others' illusions). Any mass-media phenomenon will become dull and boring if it does not engage the possibilities of signification as poetic processes, i.e. as productive modes of *thinking* within all socially-mediated environments. The Internet will surely become uneventful if it does not offer us pragmatic potentialities for our own creative expression/Becoming.

It is not just the Internet that might slide into a featureless inertia: both popular film and TV may as well if there are no media poets working within their milieus to keep generating productive conditions for alternative modes of signification. As *Buffy the Vampire Slayer*, *Angel*, and *Twin Peaks* are no longer airing new episodes, new shows need to step in to offer viewers something productive/transformative in prime-time TV, which would stop a dynamic social medium from sliding into a mythically-empty plain. Cable series like *Six Feet Under*, *Carnivàle*, and *Dead like Me*, as well as both Joss Whedon's *Firefly* and Bryan Fuller & Todd Holland's *Wonderfalls* that momentarily aired on *Fox*, have all shown definite, poetic promise. As corporate bottom-lines will likely threaten such artistic possibilities in both TV and popular film, media poets will have to invent ever-new ways of keeping all mass-media phenomena poetically viable. As there are media poets who have already stepped into such 'treacherous' social arenas to offer viewers/users such possibilities, there is no need for cynicism or pessimism concerning any popular media's potentialities.

Since artistic merit in virtual-media environments can be read by the conditions of possibility it creates, and not by any intellectual regime of what is a properly-formalized object, aesthetic value should only be discerned within the context of the singular instant it possesses the virtual power to transform. Aesthetic beauty, by extension, is never a transcendent or metaphysical form in such environments; it is, rather, a mode of signification or perception that is also a productive, i.e. virtual, condition of possibility. It possesses no specific end result or power outside of its own contingent context. *Perhaps the best way to conceptualize what an artist/poet is in a virtual-media environment is to envision all artistic significations as the self-conscious attempts to productively alter/transform our perceptual habits in any and all mediums of sensory expression.* Art's social value would then be commensurate with the extent to which it can *potentially* transform our ideologies/relations-to-the-contingent-world.

To re-iterate how printed poetry too can become a vital, mass-media phenomenon outright, I want to take a final look at a media poem that explores one of the most unsettling actual/media phenomena to occur in both America and the global village of a mediated world: September 11th 2001.

Poetic Convergence & Global Networks: John Kinsella's TV

The Australian poet John Kinsella offers an inclusively-global perspective on how printed poetry can generate signification like a virtual-media environment. His poetry enacts an ecstatic and high-speed interplay with the globally-networked information that saturates mass-media culture; it is also a poetry that is wholly and completely based within the context of simulation, in the sense that simulation precedes the generation of meaning and communication; it never follows afterwards. In line with Baudrillard's theory, it generates the 'real' by its simulation, which renders the categories of 'true' and 'false' obsolete. In his forthcoming book titled *TV*, Kinsella attempts to poetically capture how TV functions within McLuhan's global village. The entire book has the same inter-media form: blocks of syntax that are always disjunctive and paratactic, and which have no causal or organic links to create a strictly-linear progression. To edify the collaborative nature of *TV*, sections from Kinsella's inter-media-art poem will even come out in music-form; the Australian hip-hop/electronic outfit *The New Pollutants* have set to music sections from *TV1* and *TV Epilogue*.

For Kinsella's inter-media speaker, the "slipstream of mixed reality" creates an endless play/montage of possible as well as actual communications. 'Representation' has imploded into multiple/virtual potentialities, and any fixed position is wholly an illusion. This global vertigo of information flows allows for the infinite applications of singular interpretations and perceptions that we viewers/users also bring to such networked-environments. Information is always constructed—it's never transparently 'real'. Hence, the illusion of a representable 'real' world would edify a 'metaphysics of presence', i.e. an alienating idealism that still plagues much Western signifying-practice.

Kinsella's poem enacts multiplicities or Becomings in poetic production that are more in line with the Whitmanesque litanies of inclusion and infinitely-adaptable relations that Deleuze sees operating in Whitman's poetry (see chapter one). For example, here is a Whitmanesque section from *TV 2*:

> I am of TV, I am the room of showing,
> residence in changing districts,
> subliminal message getting under
> the fingernails, I am accused, condemned,
> and sympathetic, in the darkness
> I consume the visions. Information
> is secondary, the mudslide and earthquake,
> language of fragmentation and disaster,
> secondary, as I drink my fill.
> The powerlines in the seventeenth-
> century drama are of my making,
> I see them there, I pause on the street
> and smile when the camera roams
> in search of tableau, of scene-setting,
> incidental, I'm part of an impression.
> I am rapid-heart beat and contra-indication,
> the conscience of a UN force
> on the edge of town, adrenaline
> of "the enemy," I am documentary
> shot from both sides, I am core of the tube,
> the design sense of cabinets.
> When the sun roars through morning windows
> and blanks the TV screen, I am the picture
> happening out of sight, constant.
> I am the black nose beneath the white paw
> of the last polar bear, waiting for
> the crew to leave in despair,
> I am Sally Jesse Raphael,
> a painting, a piece of theatre.
> I am fear alone in the house,
> tacky midnight gorefest
> that'd have you laughing
> mid-morning, I am the absent
> parent, partner, soulmate.
> Connecting, I isolate.
> I see. I hear. I am light to light.

TV, for the poem's speaker, becomes an extra-personal, non-organic/virtual perceiver that can search at will all the human fears/desires that we both project onto TV as well as explore within its transmissions. TV's multi-media powers of simulation can reach infinite, poetic potentials as well. For Whitman, nature embodies such a free and infinite possibility for relation and interaction. However, Kinsella's media poem is much more ambivalent about the actual effects of media information. For Kinsella's speaker, not all information is good for you, i.e., the "fear alone in the house" can wreak havoc on one's perceptual capabilities. It may be counterintuitive to believe that mass-media significations are as necessary to life itself as the 'natural', regenerative potentialities Whitman praises in his nature poetry. However, in the virtual-media environment that saturates Kinsella's poem, information only opens one to poetic possibilities *when* it is re-created within Sense-events that can overcome alienation/isolation. The dangers inherent in both Whitman and Kinsella's conceptualisations of the world are dramatically similar, i.e., what limits the perceptual possibilities inherent in any individual's relation to the world is the lack of awareness concerning how all such fears/desires are constructs completely and absolutely. Betty/Diane, in *Mulholland Drive,* serves as a poignant and tragic example of how difficult it can be to wake up to one's own critical and creative potentials.

The apparent power of idealized media-images and information may appear absolute or reified to people who do not acknowledge the actual limitations they possess as contingent constructions. In fact, in Kinsella's poem, the usual critiques of media as derogatory cultural forces are nothing more than irrelevant jokes, since such criticisms only try to control mass-media forms from the illusory position of an 'outside to mass-media'. A section from *TV 1* appears as follows:

> Propped against the bedhead,
> a dark room, the glow of the television
> preternatural, not a source of light,
> not illumination. A crystal cabinet,
> its predictions were as the case may be,
> and ran against the conditions
> of your turpitude. Program into program,
> the power maintaining the flow.
> At three in the morning the shots
> became more revealing and language
> thickened. The same television,
> a different medium. Dozing
> and reconnecting, a confluence
> of scenes, as towards the delta
> the images inexorably flowed.
> The body clock retuned like jetlag
> and speech balloons hung in the room,

> lopsided brain relay, three-D.
> The red and the blue.
> Plasticity. A wall of TVs.
> Compound eye of internal insect.
> Ah, John Carpenter's *Vampires!*
> I know you'll have that on somewhere,
> it just has to be showing. We siphon
> personal histories, tag moments.
> Taking the set outdoors, scenarios fail
> to connect — a sea breeze arcing
> out of a vista, small commentaries
> of a local breeze. Dispersal,
> loss of focus, a dot amongst the trees,
> flooded by the pool, the white-washed fence
> unstable. Neighbours watching
> over your shoulder. Disconcerting.
> In a place without television,
> bloody TV: saps your time
> and energy, kills thinking.
> Conspiracy. Censorship.

For the speaker, such common assumptions and judgmental attitudes about popular media are completely ineffectual. What is dangerous to all media culture in the above passage is not the medium of TV. Rather, it is the lack of interactivity between the receiver and what is transmitted. *A la Wittgenstein's philosophy, it is the spirit in which one acts or receives information that determines the signification of an act or event. If one watches TV in the spirit of escapism and distracted attention, then TV itself takes on the nihilistic spirit of alienation and a lifeless inertia.*

TV's speaker implies that, in order to overcome alienation, we each must "wake up" to the infinite implication and variation of all meaning. Hence, the challenge TV extends to all viewers and participants in Kinsella's poem is equivalent to the challenge the empirical world extends, i.e., one has the choice to affirm contingent life (to enact the creative and critical potentialities within simulated perceptions) or to become anti-contingent-life (to cling to the illusory safety and stability inherent in supposedly ideal or transcendent forms). The significance of that choice becomes strikingly obvious in one of the most relevant sections in Kinsella's book, *TV—Epilogue*, which confronts the significance of 9/11 in the global village of networked media-space.

Kinsella's 9/11 poem unfolds simultaneously as news of the terrorist attacks on NYC and Washington DC rush through all mass-media sources. Here is an extensive look at the beginning section of the poem:

> The news on the email looks like a hoax
> and only television confirms
> the dreadful truth. Truth: friends

in New York, friends confirming
and denying, blanket coverage,
hype and adrenalin. A disaster film
gives way to the surreal to a film
of ash and dust and debris,
to acridity and weeping. *From my office window,*
it was like television, but so loud,
so very very loud. It is the beginning
of an ending for metaphor, and even
simile. The Age of the Image?
It's all allegory. It's loss of mobility.
It's grieving and morbidity,
it's elegy without soundtrack.
Genuine sorrow is tacky
on dance-floors and in studios,
but we wouldn't call it that.
Universities grow uneasy.
Style becomes embarrassing,
networks keep up appearances,
give us certainty. Simultaneously
electric and blunted, burning
inside and dulling the room
to clarify, the picture sharpening.
Despite replays it's all aftermaths
and body parts and pseudo-literary
articles in overseas newspapers,
playing impact backwards,
hammer of vengeance,
first war of the twentieth
century; bereft, most couldn't
mark the page, read a line
beyond the missing, and CNN
came back into its own,
as Muslims kept low,
away from the hustings.
The face of a friend on TV
brings it into the living room,
all those who lived nearby
the twin towers of capitalism,
the already dead who'd want
to take the living into darkness
with them — as if tailor-made
for the translationese of Nostradamus.
An event horizon bequeaths
signature in our growth rings:
all emails speak of the smell
the TV gloats on it as reporters
keep hair in sculptural splendour,

think prizes when all else
is vapour and emotion.
Children without parents
don't suspect them,
and they don't suspect themselves.
I have returned to the television,
I have remained stuck to the screen
for days, stomach churning
as the hawks come home to roost,
and nations like Australia
use it to dissemble,
to stimulate domestic policies
of bigotry and hatred: see
what would happen here
if we let Islamic refugees
flood in, trained from birth
to hate the infidel, dreaming
of rape and extermination.
That's what the foot soldiers
of anti-immigration politicians
spread across chat groups
and discussion lists, in the letters
pages of newspapers, in interviews
with television reporters.
If I am Australian it is only
to be ashamed of band-wagons
and closure: on weekends
they watch football, eat crepes,
shoot 'roos, and go boating.
Some of them watch *Neighbours*,
all drink America's pain
as their own, as if they owe
it to allies to watch them suffer
in slow motion, like a promotional
video. In Britain they bank
(as Barclays came out
of the slave trade) on Bush Junior's
weakness: Blair — proven Strong Man —
will lead the alliance against terrorism.
Any country harbouring will be punished
until they start attacking themselves,
imploding, the residue of commentators
and specialists and ex-diplomats
talking seriously and waspishly
among themselves. God, necessary
and appropriate force, first strike,
second strike, collapse of first tower,
collapse of second tower, full loads

of aviation fuel, steel superstructure
of towers melting as temperature
reaches 1500 degrees, back to desks,
everything is okay, fire-fighters
and police lost in the rescue attempt,
cadaver dogs, body parts,
New Yorkers stick together,
calls on cell phones, I love you,
won't be home, I'm trapped
below, the President, dizzy
from flights in Airforce One,
appears days later, to chants
of USA USA USA, I hear you,
hear you, hear you. This is ours,
on all stations of network television.
We are television. DNA,
stock-trading, overwhelming
congressional overwhelming
support, armed action, response
and reciprocation, curbing
civil liberties, patriotism smoke-screening
the extraction of rights, systems
all go, sweeping long touch war
broad sustained campaign,
and in Washington, a tour
of the monuments, and what might
have been undone. Controlled rage.

Kinsella's poem enacts not only a myriad of perspectives on such an un-representable event, but the dizzying, interconnected ramifications of that event world-wide. Such a poem is a striking example of McLuhan's global village, which continuously teems with all the conflict that interactivity and interconnection brings. 9/11 brings to the fore how each of us can re-conceptualize our perspectives on a mass-mediated global-culture in order to confront the homogenous forces/assumptions that lead to simplistic world-views (like those based solely on bigotry or hatred). For the speaker, the wrong way to approach 9/11 is through hardening one's perspective on different viewpoints and perspectives. Such fear-filled views, which support racist attitudes in places like Australia as well as the desire for violent revenge in America, only create the possibilities of further violence. For the poem's speaker, any mass-media phenomenon generates the necessity for media perceivers who can productively re-mediate hegemonic world-views/assumptions.

Kinsella's speaker also addresses many of the wrong-headed theories about how to deal with such a world-wide trauma like 9/11. The speaker echoes many of the claims made by mass-media spokespeople and ordinary citizens alike in the wake of 9/11 that we must end the 'decadent' aspects of Western culture (like irony and postmodernism): "It is the beginning / of an ending of metaphor, and even / simile. The Age of the Image? / It's all an allegory. It's loss of mobility." For the speaker, such claims only reflect a trauma that would limit or halt poetic re-mediations of mass-media forms. Kinsella's poem is completely *ironic* about such claims, since one answer to any trauma is media poetry itself, i.e. a mode of signification that can articulate alternative perspectives beyond the one-dimensional/homogenous ones many spouted to 'make quick and immediate sense' of such a horrific event. It is perhaps no coincidence that there was an explosion of poetry about 9/11 on the Internet as well as in American culture at large.

TV's speaker explores the media ramifications of 9/11, harkening to one key oversight that plagues many world-views in the "slipstream of mixed reality," i.e. the 'glossy', idealized appearances that often pass for the totalised-possibilities of reality itself. When the speaker describes such wilful ignorance, he places the responsibility squarely on all individuals: "Children without parents / don't suspect them, / and they don't suspect themselves." In this painful realization of the interconnectedness of global conflicts, each individual cannot step outside them as if such a position were tenable in a global village. Rather, a la *TV*'s speaker, one can acknowledge how all individuals are implicated, and how each person must confront the reality that "official rhetorics of domination" often speak for most individuals.

TV's speaker struggles to forge a productive perspective on all the complex issues a traumatic event like 9/11 brings to the fore in a mediated world. Kinsella's poem, as well as *TV* itself, ends as follows:

> I am what I am told I am
> on television. I am what I watch.
> I am reception. I am adverts
> gradually seeping back into the broadcast,
> I am the apogee of disaster
> where fragments increase comfort
> for at least some of us, I am the gays and the feminists
> and the abortionists and the communists
> and the Muslims and the Jews and immigrants
> accepting responsibility, conflagrating
> in my twilight of false Gods,
> a slow erosion of value values value adding.
> In the hire car a flight manual in Arabic,
> how to fly, simulation, flight schools
> in warm hot (middle-east simulacrum) Florida,
> place of elections, place of immigrants,
> you find every sort there, you'll find
> Key Largo there, you'll find
> the strains of Castro there,
> a hint of world terrorism.
> Oh my God. Replay. Impact. Fireball.

Different angles. This is amateur video tape.
Different angle. A child running
towards the camera, wanting the camera,
its nurturing, its mesmerism,
in Vietnam. Putin in Russia
gives his full support — there are terrorists
in Chechnya. A decade of war
against Afghanistan. Our expert in Slavic languages.
Last known interviewer of bin Laden.
Money out of construction. Egyptian, United Arab Emirates,
pilots with experience on Saudi Air, holy soil
tainted by troops of the Infidel.
Listen listen listen. See: impact. Pentagon.
Twin Towers. Plane down
in Pennsylvania. Today war was declared
against civilization. For the first time NATO invokes,
for the first time since the. . . the stock exchange. . .
grief is grief is I we they are grief
is, listen listen, see the grief, see it, see it,
we will not speak, we will not read,
we'll write only what we can't see or hear,
we correspond in light, the fractured
blue over the sand and parks,
exodus over the bridges
of Manhattan, out of the rubble
rebuilding: different shape,
open to all peoples,
beyond television.
May the Hudson and the East Rivers
flow unhindered, without pollution,
into the deltas of all continents,
the core of all islands,
ground zero.

The speaker ends the poem with a supplication to each and every individual to re-think/"see again" the myriad of issues surrounding 9/11. The speaker implies that hope can only effectively come from the regenerative powers inherent in a bifurcating nature/media that can continually transform itself. What is truly tragic, then, is when someone disowns the poetic potentials of media significations that can also transform perception itself. The speaker echoes the sentiment of Whitman's line in *Crossing Brooklyn Ferry*—"Flow on, river! Flow with the flood-tide, and ebb with the ebb-tide!"—which, in chapter 1, is *the* rallying-cry for poetically re-mediating *all* actual and virtual phenomena. It may appear to some that such a supplication is naïve in the face of biological and nuclear weapons, and that is a significant point. However, if individuals cannot accept the fact that they are the critical/creative agents of their own perceptual processes, the only other options are the "official rhetorics of domination" propagated by institutional and corporate bottom-lines. One does not have to be a history scholar to see how ineffectual such institutional world-views have been in solving global conflicts.

Kinsella's speaker acknowledges how individuals must courageously confront all global conflicts in a productive capacity, whether that means transforming one's own process of Becoming or social values, or both at the same time. This is the "different shape" that the speaker says is potentially "open to all peoples," and which also exists "beyond television." This shape is not a transcendent one that renders TV insignificant; rather, it is a multi-modal/virtual capacity for expression/Becoming that allows for a myriad of potential perceptions and transformations. For such "different shapes" to operate on the global stages of new media, "consumers" as well as "producers" must generate the continual re-mediations of our communal world-views for more productive outcomes. Kinsella's *TV*, therefore, is a significant example of how *aesthetic phenomena can actualize possibilities of signification for the benefits of all mass-media.* Only a "cultural"/mass-media "revolution"-that-stays-a-revolution can keep transforming digital-capitalism-societies in manners that can re-circuit/re-energize alienation (Žižek, *Organs Without Bodies* 211).

Moreover, the actual occurrences of such multiplicities might seem impossibly difficult or even a Utopian dream, but they're not radically different from the difficulties an individual can face in overcoming self-destructive cycles of idealization & disillusionment. Betty/Diane, in *Mulholland Drive,* is a poignant example of just how difficult such self-overcoming can be. The generation of poetic potentialities, which can create individual transformations, can also become the vital tools for the re-mediation of media/global conflicts— as Whitman and Kinsella's poems attest. Only then can *we all* author attitudes that truly go "some ways."

Works Cited

Altieri, Charles. "The Transformations of Objectivism: An Afterword." Pp. 301-17 in *The Objectivist Nexus*, edited by Rachel Blau DuPlessis & Peter Quartermain. Tuscaloosa: The University of Alabama Press, 1999.

Andrews, Bruce. "Poetry as Explanation, Poetry as Praxis." Pp. 668-72 in *Postmodern American Poetry: a Norton Anthology*, edited by Paul Hoover. New York: W.W. Norton and Company, 1994.

Aristotle. *Aristotle's Theory of Poetry and Fine Art*, translated by S. H. Butcher. 4th ed. New York: Dover, 1951.

Barthes, Roland. "Myth Today." Pp. 93-149 in *A Barthes Reader,* edited by Susan Sontag. New York: Hill and Wang, 1982.

————. *Mythologies*, translated by Annette Lavers. New York: Hill and Wang, 1972.

Baudrillard, Jean. "Simulacra and Simulations." Pp. 166-84 in *Selected Writings,* edited by Mark Poster. Stanford: Stanford University Press, 1988.

————. *The System of Objects*, translated by James Benedict. New York: Verso, 1996.

Benstock, Shari. *Women of the Left Bank: Paris, 1900-1940.* Austin: University of Texas Press, 1986.

Bernstein, Charles. "Blood on the Cutting Room Floor." Pp. 351-62 in *Content's Dream.* Los Angeles: Sun & Moon Press, 1986.

————. *Rough Trades*. Los Angeles: Sun & Moon Press, 1991.

————. "Words and Pictures." Pp. 114-61 in *Content's Dream.* Los Angeles: Sun & Moon Press, 1986.

Blondel, Eric. "Nietzsche: Life as Metaphor." Pp. 150-75 in *The New Nietzsche*, edited by David B. Allison. Cambridge: The MIT Press, 1985.

Breslin, Paul. *The Psycho-Political Muse: American Poetry Since the Fifties.* Chicago: The University of Chicago Press, 1987.

Bruns, Gerald L. "The Accomplishment of Inhabitation: Danto, Cavell, and the Argument of American Poetry." Pp. 133-63 in *Tragic Thought at the End of Philosophy: Language, Literature, and Ethical Theory.* Evanston Ill.: Northwestern University Press, 1999.

Cavell, Stanley. *The World Viewed: Reflections On the Ontology of Film.* Enlarged ed. Cambridge: Harvard University Press, 1979.

Clark, Mike. "*Mulholland Drive* Takes Unforgettable Twists and Turns." *USA Today.* (8 October 2001): D05.

Colebrook, Clare. *Gilles Deleuze.* New York: Routledge, 2002.

Conte, Joseph M. *UnEnding Design: The Forms of Postmodern Poetry.* Ithaca: Cornell University Press, 1991.

Davis, Lennard J. *Bending Over Backwards: Disability, Dismodernism & Other Difficult Positions.* New York: NYU Press, 2002.

Dawtrey, Adam. "Lynch Invades an *Empire*: Digital Pic Details a Mystery." *Variety.* 2005. <http://www.Lynchnet.com> (12 May 2005).

Deleuze, Gilles. *Cinema I: the Movement-Image,* translated by Hugh Tomlinson and Barbara Habberjam. Minneapolis: University of Minneapolis Press, 1986.

————. *Cinema II: the Time-Image,* translated by Hugh Tomlinson and Robert Galeta. Minneapolis: University of Minneapolis Press, 1991.

————. *Essays Critical and Clinical,* translated by Daniel W. Smith and Michael A. Greco. Minnesota: University of Minnesota Press, 1997.

————. *The Logic of Sense,* translated by Mark Lester with Charles Stivale. New York: Columbia University Press, 1990.

————. *Negotiations,* translated by Martin Joughin. New York: Columbia University Press, 1995.

————. *Nietzsche and Philosophy,* translated by Hugh Tomlinson. New York: Columbia University Press, 1983.

Deleuze, Gilles and Felix Guatarri. *A Thousand Plateaus,* translated by Brian Massumi. Minneapolis: University of Minnesota Press, 1980.

————. *Kafka: Toward a Minor Literature,* translated by Dana Polan. Minneapolis: University of Minnesota Press, 1986.

—————. *What is Philosophy?*, translated by Hugh Tomlinson and Graham Burchell. New York: Columbia University Press, 1994.

Desmet, Christy. "The Canonization of Laura Palmer." Pp. 93-108 in *Full of Secrets: Critical Approaches to Twin Peaks,* edited by David Lavery. Detroit: Wayne State University Press, 1995.

Dolan, Marc. "The Peaks and Valleys of Serial Creativity." Pp. 30-50 in *Full of Secrets: Critical Approaches to Twin Peaks,* edited by David Lavery. Detroit: Wayne State University Press, 1995.

Enzensberger, Hans Magnus. "Constituents of a Theory of the Media." 2nd Ed. Pp. 68-91 in *Media Studies,* edited by Paul Marris and Sue Thornham. New York: New York University Press, 2000.

Flaxman, Gregory. "Introduction." Pp. 1-60 in *The Brain is the Screen: Deleuze and the Philosophy of Cinema,* edited by Gregory Flaxman. Minneapolis: University of Minnesota Press, 2000.

Fletcher, John. "Introduction." Pp. 1-7 in *Abjection, Melancholia and Love: The Work of Julia Kristeva,* edited by John Fletcher and Andrew Benjamin. New York: Routledge, 1990.

Friedman, Susan Stanford. "Craving Stories: Narrative and Lyric in Contemporary Theory and Women's Long Poems." Pp. 15-42 in *Feminist Measures: Soundings in Poetry and Theory,* edited by Lynn Keller and Cristanne Miller. Ann Arbor: University of Michigan Press, 1994.

George, Diana Hume. "Lynching Women: A Feminist Reading of *Twin Peaks.* " Pp. 109-19 in *Full of Secrets: Critical Approaches to Twin Peaks,* edited by David Lavery. Detroit: Wayne State University Press, 1995.

Granier, Jean. "Nietzsche's Conception of Chaos." Pp. 135-41 in *The New Nietzsche,* edited by David B. Allison. Cambridge: The MIT Press, 1985.

Greene, Brian. *The Elegant Universe.* New York: W.W. Norton, 1999.

Hass, Robert. "Introduction." Pp. 17-27 in *The Best American Poetry 2001,* edited by David Lehman. New York: Scribner, 2001.

Hayles, N. Katherine. "The Condition of Virtuality." Pp. 68-95 in *The Digital Dialectic: New Essays on New Media,* edited by Peter Lunenfeld. Cambridge: MIT Press, 1999.

—————. *How We Became Posthuman.* Chicago: The University of Chicago Press, 1999.

Hayles, N. Katherine and Nicholas Gessler. "The Slipstream of Mixed Reality: Unstable Ontologies and Semiotic Markers in *The Thirteenth Floor, Dark City*, and *Mulholland Drive.*" *PMLA* 119, no. 3 (May 2004): 482-499.

Hayward, Susan. *Luc Besson: French Film Directors.* London: Manchester University Press, 1998.

Hejinian, Lyn. *The Language of Inquiry.* Berkeley: University of California Press, 2000.

Hibbs, Thomas. *"Buffy the Vampire Slayer* as Feminist Noir." Pp. 49-60 in *Buffy the Vampire Slayer and Philosophy*, edited by James B. South. Chicago: Open Court, 2003.

Hirsch. Edward. "Helmet of Fire: American Poetry in the 1920s." Pp. 54-83 in *A Profile of Twentieth Century Poetry,* edited by Jack Meyers & David Wojahn. Carbondale: Southern Illinois University Press, 1991.

Hollo, Anselm. "The Dream of Instant Total Representation". Pp. 288-89 in *Postmodern American Poetry: A Norton Anthology,* edited by Paul Hoover. New York: W.W. Norton and Company, 1994.

Hoover, Paul. "Introduction." Pp. xxv-xxxix in *Postmodern American Poetry: A Norton Anthology,* edited by Paul Hoover. New York: W.W. Norton and Company, 1994.

Hughes, Langston. *The Collected Poems of Langston Hughes.* ed. Arnold Rampersad. New York: Alfred A. Knopf, 1995.

Jackson, Timothy Allen. "Towards a New Media Aesthetic." Pp. 347-53 in *Reading Digital Culture,* edited by David Trend. Malden: Blackwell Publishers, 2001.

Jenkins, Phillip. *Hidden Gospels: How the Search for Jesus Lost its Way.* New York: Oxford University Press, 2001.

Keller, Lynn. *Re-making it New: Contemporary American Poetry and the Modernist Tradition.* Cambridge: Cambridge University Press, 1987.

Kinsella, John. *TV.* To be published by Arc press, 2006.

Kittler, Friedrich. *Gramophone, Film, Typewriter*, translated by Geoffrey Winthrop-Young and Michael Wutz. Stanford: Stanford University Press, 1986.

Korsmeyer, Carolyn. "Passion and Action: In and Out of Control." Pp. 160-72 in *Buffy the Vampire Slayer and Philosophy*, edited by James B. South. Chicago: Open Court, 2003.

Kristeva, Julia. "The Adolescent Novel." Pp. 8-23 in *Abjection, Melancholia and Love: The Work of Julia Kristeva*, edited by John Fletcher and Andrew Benjamin. New York: Routledge, 1990.

——. *Revolution in Poetic Language*, translated by Margaret Waller. New York: Columbia University Press, 1984.

Kwek, Dennis." Decolonializing and Re-Presenting Culture's Consequences: A Postcolonial Critique of Cross-Cultural Studies in Management." Pp. 121-48 in *Postcolonial Theory and Organizational Analysis: A Critical Engagement*. New York: Palgrave Macmillan, 2003.

Lavery, David. "The Semiotics of Cobbler: *Twin Peaks'* Interpretive Community." Pp. 1-21 in *Full of Secrets: Critical Approaches to Twin Peaks*, edited by David Lavery. Detroit: Wayne State University Press, 1995.

Lawler, James B. "Between Heaven and Hells: The Multidimensional Universe in Kant and *Buffy the Vampire Slayer.*" Pp. 103-16 in *Buffy the Vampire Slayer and Philosophy*, edited by James B. South. Chicago: Open Court, 2003.

Lechte, John. "Art, Love, and Melancholy in the Work of Julia Kristeva." Pp. 24-41 in *Abjection, Melancholia and Love: The Work of Julia Kristeva*, edited by John Fletcher and Andrew Benjamin. New York: Routledge, 1990.

Little, Tracy. "High School is Hell: Metaphor Made Literal in *Buffy the Vampire Slayer.*" Pp. 282-93 in *Buffy the Vampire Slayer and Philosophy*, edited by James B. South. Chicago: Open Court, 2003.

Lowney, John. *The American Avant-Garde Tradition: William Carlos Williams, Postmodern Poetry, and the Politics of Cultural Memory*. Lewisburg Pa.: Bucknell University Press, 1997.

Lynch, Jennifer. *The Secret Diary of Laura Palmer*. New York: Simon and Schuster, 1990.

Macaulay, Scott. "Interview with David Lynch." *Filmmaker*. 2001. <http://www.musiclog.com/m_mulholland_interview.asp> (30 Jul. 2005).

Marinucci, Mimi. "Feminism and the Ethics of Violence: Why Buffy Kicks Ass." Pp. 61-76 in *Buffy the Vampire Slayer and Philosophy*, edited by James B. South. Chicago: Open Court, 2003.

Matthews, William. *Search Party: Collected Poems*. Boston: Houghton Mifflin Company, 2004.

McLuhan, Marshall. *Understanding Media: the Extensions of Man*. 2d ed. New York: McGraw Hill, 1964.

Medina, Tony & Louis Reyes Rivera. eds. *Bum Rush the Page*. New York: Three Rivers Press, 2001.

Mevedev, P. N. and M.M. Bakhtin. *The Formal Method in Literary Scholarship: A Critical Introduction to Sociological Poetics*, translated by Albert J. Wehrle. Baltimore: The John Hopkins University Press, 1978.

Milavec, Melissa M. and Sharon M. Kaye. "Buffy in the Buff: A Slayer's Solution to Aristotle's Love Paradox." Pp. 173-84 in *Buffy the Vampire Slayer and Philosophy,* edited by James B. South. Chicago: Open Court, 2003.

Miller, Jessica Prata. "The I in Team": Buffy and Feminist Ethics." Pp. 35-48 in *Buffy the Vampire Slayer and Philosophy*. Edited by James B. South. Chicago: Open Court, 2003.

Millington, Richard H. "Hitchcock and American Character." Pp. 135-54 in *Hitchcock's America,* edited by Jonathan Freedman and Richard Millington. Oxford: Oxford University Press, 1999.

Mignolo, Walter D. *Local Histories/Global Designs: Coloniality, Subaltern Knowledge, and Border Thinking*. Princeton: Princeton University Press, 2000.

Mirzoeff, Nicholas. *An Introduction to Visual Culture*. New York: Routledge, 1999.

Nietzsche, Friedrich. *A Nietzsche Reader,* translated by R.J. Hollingdale. New York: Penguin Classics, 1977.

—————. *Beyond Good and Evil,* translated by R.J. Hollingdale. Harmondsworth: Penguin Classics, 1973.

—————. *The Gay Science,* translated by Walter Kaufmann. New York: Random House, 1974.

—————. *Thus Spoke Zarathustra,* translated by R.J. Hollingdale. New York: Penguin, 1969.

Nicholls, Peter. "Of Being Ethical: Reflections on George Oppen." Pp. 240-53 in *The Objectivist Nexus,* edited by Rachel Blau DuPlessis & Peter Quartermain. Tuscaloosa: The University of Alabama Press, 1999.

Nochimson, Martha P. "Desire Under the Douglas Firs: Entering the Body of Reality in *Twin Peaks*. Pp. 144-159 in *Full of Secrets: Critical Approaches to Twin Peaks,* edited by David Lavery. Detroit: Wayne State University Press, 1995.

—————. *The Passion of David Lynch: Wild at Heart in Hollywood*. Austin: The University of Texas Press, 1997.

Olson, Charles. "Projective Verse." Pp. 613-21 in *Postmodern American Poetry: A Norton Anthology*, edited by Paul Hoover. New York: W.W. Norton and Company, 1994.

Ong, Walter J. *Interfaces of the Word: Studies in the Evolution of Consciousness and Culture*. Ithaca: Cornell University Press, 1977.

Pasley, Jennifer L. "Old Familiar Vampires: The politics of the Buffyverse." Pp. 254-68 in *Buffy the Vampire Slayer and Philosophy*, edited by James B. South. Chicago: Open Court, 2003.

Pasolini, Pier Paolo. "The 'Cinema of Poetry'." Pp. 167-186 in *Heretical Empiricism*, edited by Louise K. Barnett. trans. Ben Lawton and Louise K. Barnett. Bloomington: Indiana University Press, 1988.

Pavlik, John V. *New Media Technology: Cultural and Commercial Perspectives*. 2d ed. Boston: Allyn and Bacon, 1998.

Perelman, Bob. "Cliff Notes." Pp. 498-99 in *Postmodern American Poetry: A Norton Anthology*, edited by Paul Hoover. New York: W.W. Norton and Company, 1994.

Perloff, Marjorie. *Radical Artifice: Writing Poetry in an Age of Media*. Chicago: The University of Chicago Press, 1991.

Poster, Mark. *The Information Subject*. The Netherlands: The Gordon and Breach Publishing Group, 2001.

Rajchman, John. *The Deleuze Connections*. Cambridge: MIT Press, 2000.

Ramos, Steve. "Boy Makes World." *City Beat*. Nov. 6, 1997. <http://www.Harmony-Korine.com> (4 Mar. 2005).

Reinfeld, Linda. *Language Poetry: Writing as Rescue*. Baton Rouge: Louisiana State University Press, 1992.

Rodman, Warren. "The Series That Will Change TV," *Connoisseur* (September 1989): 139-44.

Rodley, Chris. ed. *Lynch on Lynch*. Boston: Faber and Faber, 1997.

Rosen, Stanley. *Nihilism*. New Haven: Yale University Press, 1969.

Rosenbaum, Jonathan. "Bad Ideas: The Art and Politics of *Twin Peaks*." Pp. 22-9 in *Full of Secrets: Critical Approaches to Twin Peaks*, edited by David Lavery. Detroit: Wayne State University Press, 1995.

Ruszkiewicz, John, Daniel Anderson and Christy Friend. *Beyond Words: Reading & Writing In a Visual Age.* New York: Pearson Longman, 2006.

Salecl, Renata. *(Per)versions of Love and Hate.* London: Verso, 1998.

Schakel, Peter and Jack Ridl. eds. *250 Poems.* New York: Bedford/St. Martin's, 2003.

Schatz, Thomas. *Hollywood Genres: Formulas, Filmmaking, and The Studio System.* Philadelphia: Temple University Press, 1981.

Seid, Roberta. "Too 'Close to the Bone': The Historical Context for Women's Obsession with Slenderness." Pp. 3-16 in *Feminist Perspectives on Eating Disorders,* edited by Patricia Fallon, et al. New York: The Guilford Press, 1994.

Smith, Barbara. "Greece." Pp. 65-101 in *The Woman's Companion to Mythology,* edited by Carolyne Larrington. London: Pandora Press, 1992.

Smith, Daniel W. "Introduction." Pp. ix-lvi in *Essays Critical and Clinical,* translated by Daniel W. Smith and Michael A. Greco. Minnesota: University of Minnesota Press, 1997.

Stadler, Felix. "Digital Identities—Patterns in Information Flows." Pp. 9-17 in *Digital Identity,* edited by János Sugár. Budapest: Media Research Foundation, 2000.

Stein, Gertrude. *Tender Buttons: Objects, Food, Rooms.* New York: C. Marie, 1914.

Stevenson, Diane. "Family Romance, Family Violence, and the Fantastic in *Twin Peaks.*" Pp. 70-81 in *Full of Secrets: Critical Approaches to Twin Peaks,* edited by David Lavery. Detroit: Wayne State University Press, 1995.

Stroud, Scott R. "A Kantian Analysis of Moral Judgment in *Buffy the Vampire Slayer.*" Pp. 185-94 in *Buffy the Vampire Slayer and Philosophy,* edited by James B. South. Chicago: Open Court, 2003.

Trinidad, David. *Answer Song.* New York: High Risk Books/Serpent's Tail, 1994.

—————. *Hand Over Heart.* New York: Amethyst Press, 1991.

—————. *Plasticville.* Chappaqua: Turtle Point Press, 2000.

Vološinov, V. N. *Marxism and the Philosophy of Language,* translated by Ladislav Matejka and I.R. Titunik. New York: Seminar Press, 1973.

Wark, McKenzie. *A Hacker Manifesto.* Cambridge: Harvard University Press, 2004.
—————. "Codework," *American Book Review* 22, no. 3 (September/October 2001).

Williams, Raymond. *Problems in Materialism and Culture.* London: Verso, 1980.

Williams, William Carlos. *Kora in Hell: Improvisations,* edited by Webster Schott. New York: New Directions, 1970.

Wittgenstein, Ludwig. *Blue and Brown Books.* 2d ed. Oxford: Blackwell, 1969.

—————. *Tractatus Logico-Philosophicus,* translated by D.F. Pears and B. McGuiness. New York: Routledge & Kegan Paul, 1961.

Wojahn, David. *The Falling Hour.* Pittsburgh: The University of Pittsburgh Press, 1997.

Žižek, Slavoj. *The Art of the Ridiculous Sublime: On David Lynch's* Lost Highway. Seattle: The Walter Chapin Simpson Center for the Humanities, The University of Washington, 2000.

—————. *For the Know Not What They Do.* New York: Verso, 1991.

—————. *Organs without Bodies: On Deleuze and Consequences.* London: Routledge, 2004.

Index

About the Author

Tom O'Connor received his PhD in English literature from SUNY Binghamton in 2004. His articles have appeared in *The Journal of Film & Video, Social Semiotics, Disability Studies Quarterly*, and the essay collection *Ready Made: The Film Remake in Postmodern Times*. His poetry has been published in *Poetry Southeast, Notre Dame Review, Columbia Poetry Review, Mankato Poetry Review, Pebble Lake Review,* and *Flint Hills Review,* among other periodicals. He currently lives in Binghamton, NY.